ORMOND

BY

MARIA EDGEWORTH

MARIA EDGEWORTH

CHAPTER I.

"What! no music, no dancing at Castle Hermitage to-night; and all the ladies sitting in a formal circle, petrifying into perfect statues?" cried Sir Ulick O'Shane as he entered the drawing-room, between ten and eleven o'clock at night, accompanied by what he called his *rear-guard*, veterans of the old school of good fellows, who at those times in Ireland—times long since past—deemed it essential to health, happiness, and manly character, to swallow, and show themselves able to stand after swallowing, a certain number of bottles of claret per day or night.

"Now, then," continued Sir Ulick, "of all the figures in nature or art, the formal circle is universally the most obnoxious to conversation, and, to me, the most formidable; all my faculties are spell-bound—here I am like a bird in a circle of chalk, that dare not move so much as its head or its eyes, and can't, for the life of it, take to its legs."

A titter ran round that part of the circle where the young ladies sat—Sir Ulick was a favourite, and they rejoiced when he came among them; because, as they observed, "he always said something pleasant, or set something pleasant a-going."

"Lady O'Shane, for mercy's sake let us have no more of these permanent circle sittings at Castle Hermitage, my dear!"

"Sir Ulick, I am sure I should be very glad if it were possible," replied Lady O'Shane, "to have no more *permanent sittings* at Castle Hermitage; but when gentlemen are at their bottle, I really don't know what the ladies can do but sit in a circle."

"Can't they dance in a circle, or any way? or have not they an elegant resource in their music? There's many here who, to my knowledge, can

3

caper as well as they modulate," said Sir Ulick, "to say nothing of cards for those that like them."

"Lady Annaly does not like cards," said Lady O'Shane, "and I could not ask any of these young ladies to waste their breath and their execution, singing and playing before the gentlemen came out."

"These young ladies would not, I'm sure, do us old fellows the honour of waiting for us; and the young beaux deserted to your tea-table a long hour ago—so why you have not been dancing is a mystery beyond my comprehension."

"Tea or coffee, Sir Ulick O'Shane, for the third time of asking?" cried a sharp female voice from the remote tea-table.

"Wouldn't you swear to that being the voice of a presbyterian?" whispered Sir Ulick, over his shoulder to the curate: then aloud he replied to the lady, "Miss Black, you are three times too obliging. Neither tea nor coffee I'll take from you to-night, I thank you kindly."

"Fortunate for yourself, sir—for both are as cold as stones—and no wonder!" said Miss Black.

"No wonder!" echoed Lady O'Shane, looking at her watch, and sending forth an ostentatious sigh.

"What o'clock is it by your ladyship?" asked Miss Black. "I have a notion it's tremendously late."

"No matter—we are not pinned to hours in this house, Miss Black," said Sir Ulick, walking up to the tea-table, and giving her a look, which said as plainly as look could say, "You had better be quiet."

Lady O'Shane followed her husband, and putting her arm within his, began to say something in a fondling tone; and in a most conciliatory manner she went on talking to him for some moments. He looked absent, and replied coldly.

"I'll take a cup of coffee from you now, Miss Black," said he, drawing away his arm from his wife, who looked much mortified.

"We are too long, Lady O'Shane," added he, "standing here like lovers, talking to no one but ourselves—awkward in company."

"*Like lovers!*" The sound pleased poor Lady O'Shane's ear, and she smiled for the first time this night—Lady O'Shane was perhaps the last woman in the room whom a stranger would have guessed to be Sir Ulick's wife.

He was a fine gallant *off-hand* looking Irishman, with something of *dash* in his tone and air, which at first view might lead a common observer to pronounce him to be vulgar; but at five minutes after sight, a good judge of men and manners would have discovered in him the power of assuming whatever manner he chose, from the audacity of the callous profligate to the deference of the accomplished courtier—the capability of adapting his conversation to his company and his views, whether his object were "to set the senseless table in a roar," or to insinuate himself into the delicate female heart. Of this latter power, his age had diminished but not destroyed the influence. The fame of former conquests still operated in his favour, though he had long since passed his splendid meridian of gallantry.

While Sir Ulick is drinking his cup of cold coffee, we may look back a little into his family history. To go no farther than his legitimate loves, he had successively won three wives, who had each, in her turn, been desperately enamoured: the first he loved, and married imprudently for love, at seventeen; the second he admired, and married prudently, for ambition, at thirty; the third he hated, but married, from necessity, for money, at five-and-forty. The first wife, Miss Annaly, after ten years' martyrdom of the heart, sank, childless,—a victim, it was said, to love and jealousy. The second wife, Lady Theodosia, struggled stoutly for power, backed by strong and high connexions; having, moreover, the advantage of being a mother, and mother of an only son and heir, the representative of a father in whom ambition had, by this time, become the ruling passion: the Lady Theodosia stood her ground, wrangling and wrestling through a fourteen years' wedlock, till at last, to Sir Ulick's great relief, not to say joy, her ladyship was carried off by a bad fever, or a worse apothecary. His present lady, formerly Mrs. Scraggs, a London widow of very large fortune, happened to see Sir Ulick when he went to present some address, or settle some point between the English and Irish government:—he was in deep mourning at the time, and the widow pitied him very much. But she was not the sort of woman he would ever have suspected could like him—she was a strict pattern lady, severe on the times, and, not unfrequently, lecturing young men gratis. Now Sir Ulick O'Shane was a sinner; how then could he please a saint? He did, however—but the saint did not please him—though she set to work for the good of his soul, and in her own person relaxed, to please his taste, even to the wearing of rouge and pearl-powder, and false hair, and false eyebrows, and all the falsifications which the *setters-up* could furnish. But after she had purchased all of youth which age can purchase for money, it would not do. The Widow Scraggs might, with her "lack lustre" eyes, have speculated for ever in vain upon Sir Ulick, but that, fortunately for her passion, at one and the same time, the Irish ministry were turned out, and an Irish canal burst. Sir Ulick losing his place by the change of ministry, and one half of his fortune by the canal, in which it had been sunk; and having spent in unsubstantial schemes and splendid living more than the other half; now, in desperate misery, laid hold of the Widow Scraggs. After a nine days' courtship she became a bride, and she and her plum in the stocks—but not her messuage, house, and lands, in Kent—became the property of Sir Ulick O'Shane. "Love was then lord of all" with her, and she was now to accompany Sir Ulick to Ireland. Late in life she was carried to a new country, and set down among a people whom she had all her previous days been taught to hold in contempt or aversion: she dreaded Irish disturbances much, and Irish dirt more; she was persuaded that nothing could be right, good, or genteel, that was not English. Her habits and tastes were immutably fixed. Her experience had been confined to a London life, and in proportion as her sphere of observation had been contracted, her disposition was intolerant. She made no allowance for the difference of opinion, customs, and situation, much less for the faults or foibles of people who were to her strangers and foreigners—her ladyship was therefore little likely to please or be pleased in her new situation. Her husband was the only individual, the only thing, animate or inanimate, that she liked in Ireland —and while she was desperately in love with an Irishman, she disliked Ireland and the Irish: even the Irish talents and virtues, their wit, humour, generosity of character, and freedom of manner, were lost upon her—her country neighbours were repelled by her air of taciturn self-sufficiency— and she, for her part, declared she would have been satisfied to have lived alone at Castle Hermitage with Sir Ulick. But Sir Ulick had no notion of living alone with her, or for any body. His habits were all social and convivial—he loved show and company: he had been all his life in the habit of entertaining all ranks of people at Castle Hermitage, from his excellency the Lord-Lieutenant and the commander-in-chief for the time being, to Tim the gauger, and honest Tom Kelly, the *stalko*.

He talked of the necessity of keeping up a neighbourhood, and maintaining his interest in the county, as the first duties of man. Ostensibly Sir Ulick had no motive in all this, but the hospitable wish of seeing Castle Hermitage one continued scene of festivity; but under this good fellowship and apparent thoughtlessness and profusion, there was an eye to his own interest, and a keen view to the improvement of his fortune and the advancement of his family. With these habits and views, it was little likely that he should yield to the romantic, jealous, or economic tastes of his new lady—a bride ten years older than himself! Lady O'Shane was, soon after her arrival in Ireland, compelled to see her house as full of company as it could possibly hold; and her ladyship was condemned eternally, to do the honours to successive troops of *friends*, of whom she knew nothing, and of whom she disliked all she saw or heard. Her dear Sir Ulick was, or seemed, so engrossed by the business of pleasure, so taken up with his guests, that but a few minutes in the day could she ever obtain of his company. She saw herself surrounded by the young, the fair, and the gay, to whom Sir Ulick devoted his assiduous and gallant attentions; and though his age, and his being a married man, seemed to preclude, in the opinion of the cool or indifferent spectator, all idea of any real cause for jealousy, yet it was not so with poor Lady O'Shane's magnifying imagination. The demon of jealousy tortured her; and to enhance her sufferings, she was obliged to conceal them, lest they should become subjects of private mockery or public derision. It is the peculiar misfortune or punishment of misplaced, and yet more of unseasonable, passions, that in their distresses they obtain no sympathy; and while the passion is in all its consequence tragic to the sufferer, in all its exhibitions it is—ludicrous to the spectator. Lady O'Shane could not be young, and would not be old: so without the charms of youth, or the dignity of age, she could neither inspire love, nor command respect; nor could she find fit occupation or amusement, or solace or refuge, in any combination of company or class of society. Unluckily, as her judgment, never discriminating, was now blinded by jealousy, the two persons of all his family connexions upon whom she pitched as the peculiar objects of her fear and hatred were precisely those who were most disposed to pity and befriend her—to serve her in private with Sir Ulick, and to treat her with deference in public: these two persons were Lady Annaly and her daughter. Lady Annaly was a distant relation of Sir Ulick's first wife, during whose life some circumstances had occurred which had excited her ladyship's indignation against him. For many years all commerce between them had ceased. Lady Annaly was a woman of generous indignation, strong principles, and warm affections. Her rank, her high connexions, her high character, her having, from the time she was left a young and beautiful widow, devoted herself to the education and the interests of her children; her having persevered in her lofty course, superior to all the numerous temptations of love, vanity, or ambition, by which she was assailed; her long and able administration of a large property, during the minority of her son; her subsequent graceful resignation of power; his affection, gratitude, and deference for his mother, which now continued to prolong her influence, and exemplify her precepts in every act of his own; altogether placed this lady high in public consideration—high as any individual could stand in a country, where national enthusiastic attachment is ever excited by certain noble qualities congenial with the Irish nature. Sir Ulick O'Shane, sensible of the disadvantage of having estranged such a family connexion, and fully capable of appreciating the value of her friendship, had of late years taken infinite pains to redeem himself in Lady Annaly's opinion. His consummate address, aided and abetted and concealed as it was by his off-hand manner, would scarcely have succeeded, had it not been supported also by some substantial good qualities, especially by the natural candour and generosity of his disposition. In favour of the originally strong, and, through all his errors, wonderfully surviving taste for virtue, some of his manifold transgressions might be forgiven: there was much hope and promise of amendment; and besides, to state things just as they were, he had propitiated the mother, irresistibly, by his enthusiastic admiration of the daughter—so that Lady Annaly had at last consented to revisit Castle Hermitage. Her ladyship and her daughter were now on this reconciliation visit; Sir Ulick was extremely anxious to make it agreeable. Besides the credit of her friendship, he had other reasons for wishing to conciliate her: his son Marcus was just twenty—two years older than Miss Annaly—in course of time, Sir Ulick thought it might be a match—his son could not possibly make a better—beauty, fortune, family connexions, every thing that the hearts of young and old desire. Besides (for in Sir Ulick's calculations *besides* was a word frequently occurring), besides, Miss Annaly's brother was not as strong in body as in mind—in two illnesses his life had been despaired of—a third might carry him off—the estate would probably come to Miss Annaly. *Besides*, be this hereafter as it might, there was at this present time a considerable debt due by Sir Ulick to these Annalys, with accumulated interest, since the time of his first marriage; and this debt would be merged in Miss Annaly's portion, should she become his son's wife. All this was well calculated; but to say nothing of the character or affections of the son, Sir Ulick had omitted to consider Lady O'Shane, or he had taken it for granted that her love for him would induce her at once to enter into and second his views. It did not so happen. On the contrary, the dislike which Lady O'Shane took at sight to both the mother and daughter—to the daughter instinctively, at sight of her youth and beauty; to the mother reflectively, on account of her matronly dress and dignified deportment, in too striking contrast to her own frippery appearance—increased every day, and every hour, when she saw the attentions, the adoration, that Sir Ulick paid to Miss Annaly, and the deference and respect he showed to Lady Annaly, all for qualities and accomplishments in which Lady O'Shane was conscious that she was irremediably deficient. Sir Ulick thought to extinguish her jealousy, by opening to her his views on Miss Annaly for his son; but the jealousy, taking only a new direction, strengthened in its course. Lady O'Shane did not like her stepson—had indeed no great reason to like him; Marcus disliked her, and was at no pains to conceal his dislike. She dreaded the accession of domestic power and influence he would gain by such a marriage. She could not bear the thoughts of having a daughter-in-law brought into the house—placed in eternal comparison with her. Sir Ulick O'Shane was conscious that his marriage exposed him to some share of ridicule; but hitherto, except when his taste for raillery, and the diversion of exciting her causeless jealousy, interfered with his purpose, he had always treated her ladyship as he conceived that Lady O'Shane ought to be treated. Naturally good-natured, and habitually attentive to the sex, he had indeed kept up appearances better than could have been expected, from a man of his former habits, to a woman of her ladyship's present age; but if she now crossed his favourite scheme, it would be all over with her—her submission to his will had hitherto been a sufficient and a convenient proof, and the only proof he desired, of her love. Her ladyship's evil genius, in the shape of Miss Black, her humble companion, was now busily instigating her to be refractory. Miss Black had frequently whispered, that if Lady O'Shane would show more spirit, she would do better with Sir Ulick; that his late wife, Lady Theodosia, had ruled him, by showing proper spirit; that in particular, she should make a stand against the encroachments of Sir Ulick's son Marcus, and of his friend and companion, young Ormond. In consequence of these suggestions, Lady O'Shane had most judiciously thwarted both these young men in trifles, till she had become their aversion: this aversion Marcus felt more than he expressed, and Ormond expressed more strongly than he felt. To Sir Ulick, his son and heir was his first great object in life; yet, though in all things he preferred the interest of Marcus, he was not as fond of Marcus as he was of young Ormond. Young Ormond was the son of the friend of Sir Ulick O'Shane's youthful and warm-hearted days—the son of an officer who had served in the same regiment with him in his first campaign. Captain Ormond afterwards made an unfortunate marriage— that is, a marriage without a fortune—his friends would not see him or his wife—he was soon in debt, and in great distress. He was obliged to leave his wife and go to India. She had then one child at nurse in an Irish cabin. She died soon afterwards. Sir Ulick O'Shane took the child, that had been left at nurse, into his own house. From the time it was four years old, little Harry Ormond became his darling and grew up his favourite. Sir Ulick's fondness, however, had not extended to any care of his education—quite the contrary; he had done all he could to spoil him by the most injudicious indulgence, and by neglect of all instruction or discipline. Marcus had been sent to school and college; but Harry Ormond, meantime, had been let to run wild at home: the gamekeeper, the huntsman, and a cousin of Sir Ulick, who called himself the King of the Black Islands, had had the principal share in his education. Captain Ormond, his father, was not heard of for many years; and Sir Ulick always argued, that there was no use in giving Harry Ormond the education of an estated gentleman, when he was not likely to have an estate. Moreover, he prophesied that Harry would turn out the cleverest man of the two; and in the progress of the two boys towards manhood Sir Ulick had shown a strange sort of double and inconsistent vanity in his son's acquirements, and in the orphan Harry's natural genius. Harry's extremely warm, generous, grateful temper, delighted Sir Ulick; but he gloried in the superior polish of his own son. Harry Ormond grew up with all the faults that were incident to his natural violence of passions, and that might necessarily be expected from his neglected and deficient education. His devoted gratitude and attachment to his guardian father, as he called Sir Ulick, made him amenable in an instant, even in the height and tempest of his passions, to whatever Sir Ulick desired; but he was ungovernable by most other people, and rude even to insolence, where he felt tyranny or suspected meanness. Miss Black and he were always at open war; to Lady O'Shane he submitted, though with an ill grace; yet he did submit, for his guardian's sake, where he himself only was concerned; but most imprudently and fiercely he contended upon every occasion where Marcus, when aggrieved, had declined contending with his mother-in-law.

Upon the present occasion the two youths had been long engaged to dine with, and keep the birthday of, Mr. Cornelius O'Shane, the King of the Black Islands—next to Sir Ulick the being upon earth to whom Harry Ormond thought himself most obliged, and to whom he felt himself most attached. This he had represented to Lady O'Shane, and had earnestly requested that, as the day for the intended dance was a matter of indifference to her, it might not be fixed on this day; but her ladyship had purposely made it a trial of strength, and had insisted upon their returning at a certain hour. She knew that Sir Ulick would be much vexed by their want of punctuality on this occasion, where the Annalys were concerned, though, in general, punctuality was a virtue for which he had no regard.

Sir Ulick had finished his cup of coffee. "Miss Black, send away the tea-things—send away all these things," cried he. "Young ladies, better late than never, you know—let's have dancing now; clear the decks for action."

The young ladies started from their seats immediately. All was now in happy motion. The servants answered promptly—the tea-things retired in haste—tables rolled away—chairs swung into the back-ground—the folding-doors of the dancing-room were thrown open—the pyramids of wax-candles in the chandeliers (for this was ere argands were on earth) started into light—the musicians tuning, screwing, scraping, sounded, discordant as they were, joyful notes of preparation.

"But where's my son—where's Marcus?" said Sir Ulick, drawing Lady O'Shane aside. "I don't see him any where."

"No," said Lady O'Shane; "you know that he would go to dine to-day with that strange cousin of yours, and neither he nor his companion have thought proper to return yet."

"I wish you had given me a hint," said Sir Ulick, "and I would have waited; for Marcus ought to lead off with Miss Annaly."

"*Ought*—to be sure." said Lady O'Shane; "but that is no rule for young gentlemen's conduct. I told both the young gentlemen that we were to have a dance to-night. I mentioned the hour, and begged them to be punctual."

"Young men are never punctual," said Sir Ulick; "but Marcus is inexcusable to-night on account of the Annalys."

Sir Ulick pondered for a moment with an air of vexation, then turning to the musicians, who were behind him, "You four-and-twenty fiddlers all in a row, you gentlemen musicians, scrape and tune on a little longer, if you please. Remember *you are not ready* till I draw on my gloves. Break a string or two, if necessary."

"We will—we shall—plase your honour."

"I wish, Lady O'Shane," continued Sir Ulick in a lower tone, "I wish you had given me a hint of this."

"Truth to tell, Sir Ulick, I did, I own, conceive from your walk and way, that you were not in a condition to take any hint I could give."

"Pshaw, my dear, after having known me, I won't say loved me, a calendar year, how can you be so deceived by outward appearances? Don't you know that I hate drinking? But when I have these county electioneering friends, the worthy red noses, to entertain, I suit myself to the company, by acting spirits instead of swallowing them, for I should scorn to appear to flinch!"

This was true. Sir Ulick could, and often did, to the utmost perfection, counterfeit every degree of intoxication. He could act the rise, decline, and fall of the drunken man, marking the whole progress, from the first incipient hesitation of reason to the glorious confusion of ideas in the highest state of *elevation*, thence through all the declining cases of stultified paralytic ineptitude, down to the horizontal condition of preterpluperfect ebriety.

"Really, Sir Ulick, you are so good an actor that I don't pretend to judge —I can seldom find out the truth from you."

"So much the better for you, my dear, if you knew but all," said Sir Ulick, laughing.

"If I knew but all!" repeated her ladyship, with an alarmed look.

"But that's not the matter in hand at present, my dear."

Sir Ulick protracted the interval before the opening of the ball as long as he possibly could—but in vain—the young gentlemen did not appear. Sir

Ulick drew on his gloves. The broken strings of the violins were immediately found to be mended. Sir Ulick opened the ball himself with Miss Annaly, after making as handsome an apology for his son as the case would admit—an apology which was received by the young lady with the most graceful good-nature. She declined dancing more than one dance, and Sir Ulick sat down between her and Lady Annaly, exerting all his powers of humour to divert them, at the expense of his cousin, the King of the Black Islands, whose tedious ferry, or whose claret, or more likely whose whiskey-punch, he was sure, had been the cause of Marcus's misdemeanour. It was now near twelve o'clock. Lady O'Shane, who had made many aggravating reflections upon the disrespectful conduct of the young gentlemen, grew restless on another *count*. The gates were left open for them—the gates ought to be locked! There were disturbances in the country. "Pshaw!" Sir Ulick said. Opposite directions were given at opposite doors to two servants.

"Dempsey, tell them they need not lock the gates till the young gentlemen come home, or at least till one o'clock," said Sir Ulick.

"Stone," said Lady O'Shane to her own man in a very low voice, "go down directly, and see that the gates are locked, and bring me the keys."

Dempsey, an Irishman, who was half drunk, forgot to see or say any thing about it. Stone, an Englishman, went directly to obey his lady's commands, and the gates were locked, and the keys brought to her ladyship, who put them immediately into her work-table.

Half an hour afterwards, as Lady O'Shane was sitting with her back to the glass-door of the green house, which opened into the ball-room, she was startled by a peremptory tap on the glass behind her; she turned, and saw young Ormond, pale as death, and stained with blood.

"The keys of the gate instantly," cried he, "for mercy's sake!"

CHAPTER II.

Lady O'Shane, extremely terrified, had scarcely power to rise. She opened the drawer of the table, and thrust her trembling hand down to the bottom of the silk bag, into which the keys had fallen. Impatient of delay, Ormond pushed open the door, snatched the keys, and disappeared. The whole passed in a few seconds. The music drowned the noise of the opening door, and of the two chairs, which Ormond had thrown down: those who sat near, thought a servant had pushed in and gone out; but, however rapid the movement, the full view of the figure had been seen by Miss Annaly, who was sitting on the opposite side of the room; Sir Ulick was sitting beside her, talking earnestly. Lady Annaly had just retired. "For Heaven's sake, what's the matter?" cried he, stopping in the middle of a sentence, on seeing Miss Annaly grow suddenly pale as death. Her eyes were fixed on the door of the green-house; his followed that direction. "Yes," said he, "we can get out into the air that way—lean on me." She did so—he pushed his way through the crowd at the bottom of the country dance; and, as he passed, was met by Lady O'Shane and Miss Black, both with faces of horror.

"Sir Ulick, did you see," pointing to the door, "did you see Mr. Ormond? —There's blood!"

"There's mischief, certainly," said Miss Black. "A quarrel—Mr. Marcus, perhaps."

"Nonsense! No such thing, you'll find," said Sir Ulick, pushing on, and purposely jostling the arm of a servant who was holding a salver of ices, overturning them all; and whilst the surrounding company were fully occupied about their clothes, and their fears, and apologies, he made his way onwards to the green-house—Lady O'Shane clinging to one arm— Miss Annaly supported by the other—Miss Black following, repeating, "Mischief! mischief! you'll see, sir."

"Miss Black, open the door, and not another word."

He edged Miss Annaly on, the moment the door opened, dragged Lady O'Shane after him, pushed Miss Black back as she attempted to follow: but, recollecting that she might spread the report of mischief, if he left her behind, drew her into the green-house, locked the door, and led Miss Annaly out into the air.

"Bring salts! water! something, Miss Black—follow me, Lady O'Shane."

"When I'm hardly able—your wife! Sir Ulick, you might," said Lady O'Shane, as she tottered on, "you might, I should have *thought*—"

"No time for such thoughts, my dear," interrupted he. "Sit down on the steps—there, she is better now—now what is all this?"

"I am not to speak," said Miss Black.

Lady O'Shane began to say how Mr. Ormond had burst in, covered with blood, and seized the keys of the gates.

"The keys!" But he had no time for *that* thought. "Which way did he go?"

"I don't know; I gave him the keys of both gates."

The two entrances were a mile asunder. Sir Ulick looked for footsteps on the grass. It was a fine moonlight night. He saw footsteps on the path leading to the gardener's house. "Stay here, ladies, and I will bring you intelligence as soon as possible."

"This way, Sir Ulick—they are coming," said Miss Annaly, who had now recovered her presence of mind.

Several persons appeared from a turn in the shrubbery, carrying some one on a hand-barrow—a gentleman on horseback, with a servant and many persons walking. Sir Ulick hastened towards them; the gentleman on horseback spurred his horse and met him.

"Marcus!—is it you?—thank God! But Ormond—where is he, and what has happened?"

The first sound of Marcus's voice, when he attempted to answer, showed that he was not in a condition to give a rational account of any thing. His servant followed, also much intoxicated. While Sir Ulick had been stopped by their ineffectual attempts to explain, the people who were carrying the man on the hand-barrow came up. Ormond appeared from the midst of them. "Carry him on to the gardener's house," cried he, pointing the way, and coming forward to Sir Ulick. "If he dies, I am a murderer!" cried he.

"Who is he?" said Sir Ulick.

"Moriarty Carroll, please your honour," answered several voices at once.

"And how happened it?" said Sir Ulick.

"The long and the short of it, sir," said Marcus, as well as he could articulate, "the fellow was insolent, and we cut him down—and if it were to do again, I'd do it again with pleasure."

"No, no! you won't say so, Marcus, when you are yourself," said Ormond. "Oh! how dreadful to come to one's senses all at once, as I did —the moment after I had fired that fatal shot—the moment I saw the poor fellow stagger and fall—"

"It was you, then, that fired at him," interrupted Sir Ulick.

"Yes, oh! yes!" said he, striking his forehead: "I did it in the fury of passion."

Then Ormond, taking all the blame upon himself, and stating what had passed in the strongest light against himself, gave this account of the matter. After having drunk too much at Mr. Cornelius O'Shane's, they were returning from the Black Islands, and afraid of being late, they were galloping hard, when at a narrow part of the road they were stopped by some cars. Impatient of the delay, they abused the men who were driving them, insisting upon their getting out of the way faster than they could. Moriarty Carroll made some answer, which Marcus said was insolent; and inquiring the man's name, and hearing it was Carroll, said all the Carrolls were bad people—rebels. Moriarty defied him to prove *that*— and added some expressions about tyranny, which enraged Ormond. This part of the provocation Ormond did not state, but merely said he was thrown into a passion by some observation of Moriarty's; and first he lifted his whip to give the fellow a horsewhipping. Moriarty seized hold of the whip, and struggled to wrest it from his hand; Ormond then snatched a pistol from his holster, telling Moriarty he would shoot him, if he did not let the whip go. Moriarty, who was in a passion himself, struggled, still holding the whip. Ormond cocked the pistol, and before he was aware he had done so, the pistol accidentally went off—the ball entered Moriarty's breast. This happened within a quarter of a mile of Castle Hermitage. The poor fellow bled profusely; and, in assisting to lift him upon the hand-barrow, Ormond was covered with blood, as has been already described.

"Have you sent for a surgeon?" said Sir Ulick, coolly.

"Certainly—sent off a fellow on my own horse directly. Sir, will you come on to the gardener's house; I want you to see him, to know what you'll think. If he die, I am a murderer," repeated Ormond.

This horrible idea so possessed his imagination, that he could not answer or hear any of the farther questions that were asked by Lady O'Shane and Miss Black; but after gazing upon them with unmeaning eyes for a moment in silence, walked rapidly on: as he was passing by the steps of the green-house, he stopped short at the sight of Miss Annaly, who was still sitting there. "What's the matter?" said he, in a tone of great compassion, going close up to her. Then, recollecting himself, he hurried forward again.

"As I can be of no use—unless I can be of any use," said Miss Annaly, "I will, now that I am well enough, return—my mother will wonder what has become of me."

"Sir Ulick, give me the key of the conservatory, to let Miss Annaly into the ball-room."

"Miss Annaly does not wish to dance any more to-night, I believe," said Sir Ulick.

"Dance—oh! no."

"Then, without exciting observation, you can all get in better at the back door of the house, and Miss Annaly can go up the back stairs to Lady Annaly's room, without meeting any one; and you, Lady O'Shane," added he, in a low voice, "order up supper, and say nothing of what has passed. Miss Black, you hear what I desire—no gossiping."

To get to the back door they had to walk round the house, and in their way they passed the gardener's. The surgeon had just arrived.

"Go on, ladies, pray," said Sir Ulick; "what stops you?"

"'Tis I stop the way, Sir Ulick," said Lady O'Shane, "to speak a word to the surgeon. If you find the man in any dangerous way, for pity's sake don't let him die at our gardener's—indeed, the bringing him here at all I think a very strange step and encroachment of Mr. Ormond's. It will make the whole thing so public—and the people hereabouts are so revengeful—if any thing should happen to him, it will be revenged on our whole family—on Sir Ulick in particular."

"No danger—nonsense, my dear."

But now this idea had seized Lady O'Shane, it appeared to her a sufficient reason for desiring to remove the man even this night. She asked why he could not be taken to his own home and his own people; she repeated, that it was very strange of Mr. Ormond to take such liberties, as if every thing about Castle Hermitage was quite at his disposal. One of the men who had carried the hand-barrow, and who was now standing at the gardener's door, observed, that Moriarty's *people* lived five miles off. Ormond, who had gone into the house to the wounded man, being told what Lady O'Shane was saying, came out; she repeated her words as he re-appeared. Naturally of sudden violent temper, and being now in the highest state of suspense and irritation, he broke out, forgetful of all proper respect. Miss Black, who was saying something in corroboration of Lady O'Shane's opinion, he first attacked, pronouncing her to be an unfeeling, *canting* hypocrite: then, turning to Lady O'Shane, he said that she might send the dying man away, if she pleased; but that if she did, he would go too, and that never while he existed would he enter her ladyship's doors again.

Ormond made this threat with the air of a superior to an inferior, totally forgetting his own dependent situation, and the dreadful circumstances in which he now stood.

"You are drunk, young man! My dear Ormond, you don't know what you are saying," interposed Sir Ulick.

At his voice, and the kindness of his tone, Ormond recollected himself. "Forgive me," said he, in a very gentle tone. "My head certainly is not— Oh! may you never feel what I have felt this last hour! If this man die— Oh! consider."

"He will not die—he will not die, I hope—at any rate, don't talk so loud within hearing of these people. My dear Lady O'Shane, this foolish boy —this Harry Ormond is, I grant, a sad scapegrace, but you must bear with him for my sake. Let this poor wounded fellow remain here—I won't have him stirred to-night—we shall see what ought to be done in the morning. Ormond, you forgot yourself strangely towards Lady O'Shane—as to this fellow, don't make such a rout about the business; I dare say he will do very well: we shall hear what the surgeon says. At first I was horribly frightened—I thought you and Marcus had been quarrelling. Miss Annaly, are not you afraid of staying out? Lady O'Shane, why do you keep Miss Annaly? Let supper go up directly."

"Supper! ay, every thing goes on as usual," said Ormond, "and I—"

"I must follow them in, and see how things *are* going on, and prevent gossiping, for your sake, my boy," resumed Sir Ulick, after a moment's pause. "You have got into an ugly scrape. I pity you from my soul—I'm rash myself. Send the surgeon to me when he has seen the fellow. Depend upon me, if the worst come to the worst, there's nothing in the world I would not do to serve you," said Sir Ulick: "so keep up your spirits, my boy—we'll contrive to bring you through—at the worst, it will only be manslaughter."

Ormond wrung Sir Ulick's hand—thanked him for his kindness; but repeated, "it will be murder—it will be murder—my own conscience tells me so! If he die, give me up to justice."

"You'll think better of it before morning," said Sir Ulick, as he left Ormond.

The surgeon gave Ormond little comfort. After extracting the bullet, and examining the wound, he shook his head—he had but a bad opinion of the case; and when Ormond took him aside, and questioned him more closely, he confessed that he thought the man would not live—he should not be surprised if he died before morning. The surgeon was obliged to leave him to attend another patient; and Ormond, turning all the other people out of the room, declared he would sit up with Moriarty himself. A terrible night it was to him. To his alarmed and inexperienced eyes the danger seemed even greater than it really was, and several times he thought his patient expiring, when he was faint from loss of blood. The moments in which Ormond was occupied in assisting him were the least painful. It was when he had nothing left to do, when he had leisure to think, that he was most miserable; then the agony of suspense, and the horror of remorse, were felt, till feeling was exhausted; and he would sit motionless and stupified, till he was wakened again from this suspension of thought and feeling by some moan of the poor man, or some delirious startings. Toward morning the wounded man lay easier; and as Ormond was stooping over his bed to see whether he was asleep, Moriarty opened his eyes, and fixing them on Ormond, said, in broken sentences, but so as very distinctly to be understood, "Don't be in such trouble about the likes of me—I'll do very well, you'll see—and even suppose I wouldn't—not a friend I have shall ever prosecute—I'll charge 'em not—so be easy—for you're a good heart—and the pistol went off unknownst to you—I'm sure there was no malice—let that be your comfort. It might happen to any man, let alone gentleman—don't *take on*so. Only think of young Mr. Harry sitting up the night with me!—Oh! if you'd go now and settle yourself yonder on t'other bed, sir—I'd be a grate dale asier, and I don't doubt but I'd get a taste of sleep myself—while now wid you standing over or *forenent* me, I can't close an eye for thinking of you, Mr. Harry."

Ormond immediately threw himself upon the other bed, that he might relieve Moriarty's feelings. The good nature and generosity of this poor fellow increased Ormond's keen sense of remorse. As to sleeping, for him it was impossible; whenever his ideas began to fall into that sort of confusion which precedes sleep, suddenly he felt as if his heart were struck or twinged, and he started with the recollection that some dreadful thing had happened, and wakened to the sense of guilt and all its horrors. Moriarty now lying perfectly quiet and motionless, and Ormond not hearing him breathe, he was struck with the dread that he had breathed his last. A cold tremor came over Ormond—he rose in his bed, listening in acute agony, when to his relief he at last distinctly heard Moriarty breathing strongly, and soon afterwards (no music was ever so delightful to Ormond's ear) heard him begin to breathe loudly, as if asleep. The morning light dawned soon afterwards, and the crowing of a cock was heard, which Ormond feared might waken him; but the poor man slept soundly through all these usual noises: the heaving of the bed-clothes over his breast went on with uninterrupted regularity. The gardener and his wife softly opened the door of the room, to inquire how things were going on; Ormond pointed to the bed, and they nodded, and smiled, and beckoned to him to come out, whispering that a *taste* of the morning air would do him good. He suffered them to lead him out, for he was afraid of debating the point in the room with the sleeping patient. The good people of the house, who had known Harry Ormond from a child, and who were exceedingly fond of him, as all the poor people in the neighbourhood were, said every thing they could think of upon this occasion to comfort him, and reiterated about a hundred times their prophecies, that Moriarty would be as sound and *good* a man as ever in a fortnight's time.

"Sure, when he'd take the soft sleep he couldn't but do well."

Then perceiving that Ormond listened to them only with faint attention, the wife whispered to her husband, "Come off to our work, Johnny—he'd like to be alone—he's not equal to listen to our talk yet—it's the surgeon must give him hope—and he'll soon be here, I trust."

They went to their work, and left Ormond standing in the porch. It was a fine morning—the birds were singing, and the smell of the honeysuckle with which the porch was covered, wafted by the fresh morning air, struck Ormond's senses, but struck him with melancholy.

"Every thing in nature is cheerful except myself! Every thing in this world going on just the same as it was yesterday—but all changed for me!—within a few short hours—by my own folly, my own madness! Every animal," thought he, as his attention was caught by the house dog, who was licking his hand, and as his eye fell upon the hen and chickens, who were feeding before the door, "every animal is happy—and innocent! But *if this man die—I shall be a murderer*."

This thought, perpetually recurring, so oppressed him, that he stood motionless, till he was roused by the voice of Sir Ulick O'Shane.

"Well, Harry Ormond, how is it with you, my boy?—The fellow's alive, I hope?"

"Alive—Thank Heaven!—yes; and asleep."

"Give ye joy—it would have been an ugly thing—not but what we could have brought you through: I'd go through thick and thin, you know, for you, as if it were for my own son. But Lady O'Shane," said Sir Ulick, changing his tone, and with a face of great concern, "I must talk to you about her—I may as well speak now, since it must be said."

"I am afraid," said Ormond, "that I spoke too hastily last night: I beg your pardon."

"Nay, nay, put *me* out of the question: you may do what you please with me—always could, from the time you were four years old; but, you know, the more I love any body, the more Lady O'Shane hates them. The fact is," continued Sir Ulick, rubbing his eyes, "that I have had a weary night of it—Lady O'Shane has been crying and whining in my ears. She says I encourage you in being insolent, and so forth: in short, she cannot endure you in the house any longer. I suspect that sour one" (Sir Ulick, among his intimates, always designated Miss Black in this manner) "*puts her up to it*. But I will not give up my own boy—I will take it with a high hand. Separations are foolish things, as foolish as marriages; but I'd sooner part with Lady O'Shane at once than let Harry Ormond think I'd forsake him, especially in awkward circumstances."

"That, Sir Ulick, is what Harry Ormond can never think of you. He would be the basest, the most suspicious, the most ungrateful—But I must not speak so loud," continued he, lowering his voice, "lest it should waken Moriarty." Sir Ulick drew him away from the door, for Ormond was cool enough at this moment to have common sense.

"My dear guardian-father, allow me still to call you by that name," continued Ormond, "believe me, your kindness is too fully— innumerable instances of your affection now press upon me, so that—I can't express myself; but depend upon it, suspicion of your friendship is the last that could enter my mind: I trust, therefore, you will do me the same sort of justice, and never suppose me capable of ingratitude— though the time is come when we must *part*."

Ormond could hardly pronounce the word.

"Part!" repeated Sir Ulick: "no, by all the saints, and all the devils in female form!"

"I am resolved," said Ormond, "firmly resolved on one point—never to be a cause of unhappiness to one who has been the source of so much happiness to me: I will no more be an object of contention between you and Lady O'Shane. Give her up rather than me—Heaven forbid! I the cause of separation!—never—never! I am determined, let what will become of me, I will no more be an inmate of Castle Hermitage."

Tears started into Ormond's eyes; Sir Ulick appeared much affected, and in a state of great embarrassment and indecision.

He could not bear to think of it—he swore it must not be: then he gradually sunk to hoping it was not necessary, and proposing palliatives and half measures. Moriarty must be moved to-day—sent to his own friends. That point he had, for peace sake, conceded to her ladyship, he said; but he should expect, on her part, that after a proper, a decent apology from Ormond, things might still be accommodated and go on smoothly, if that meddling Miss Black would allow them.

In short he managed so, that whilst he confirmed the young man in his resolution to quit Castle Hermitage, he threw all the blame on Lady O'Shane; Ormond never doubting the steadiness of Sir Ulick's affection, nor suspecting that he had any secret motive for wishing to get rid of him.

"But where can you go, my dear boy?—What will you do with yourself? —What will become of you?"

"Never mind—never mind what becomes of me, my dear sir: I'll find means—I have the use of head and hands."

"My cousin, Cornelius O'Shane, he is as fond of you almost as I am, and he is not cursed with a wife, and is blessed with a daughter," said Sir Ulick, with a sly smile.

"Oh! yes," continued he, "I see it all now: you have ways and means—I no longer object—I'll write—no, you'd write better yourself to King Corny, for you are a greater favourite with his majesty than I am. Fare ye well—Heaven bless you! my boy," said Sir Ulick, with warm emphasis. "Remember, whenever you want supplies, Castle Hermitage is your bank —you know I have a bank at my back (Sir Ulick was joined in a banking-house)'—Castle Hermitage is your bank, and here's your quarter's allowance to begin with."

Sir Ulick put a purse into Ormond's hand, and left him.

CHAPTER III.

But is it natural, is it possible, that this Sir Ulick O'Shane could so easily part with Harry Ormond, and thus "whistle him down the wind to prey at fortune?" For Harry Ormond, surely, if for any creature living, Sir Ulick O'Shane's affection had shown itself disinterested and steady. When left a helpless infant, its mother dead, its father in India, he had taken the child from the nurse, who was too poor even to feed or clothe it as her own; and he had brought little Harry up at his castle with his own son—as his own son. He had been his darling—literally his spoiled child; nor had this fondness passed away with the prattling, playful graces of the child's first years—it had grown with its growth. Harry became Sir Ulick's favourite companion—hunting, shooting, carousing, as he had been his plaything during infancy. On no one occasion had Harry, violent and difficult to manage as he was to others, ever crossed Sir Ulick's will, or in any way incurred his displeasure. And now, suddenly, without any cause, except the aversion of a wife, whose aversions seldom troubled him in any great degree, is it natural that he should give up Harry Ormond, and suffer him to sacrifice himself in vain for the preservation of a conjugal peace, which Sir Ulick ought to have known could not by such a sacrifice be preserved? Is it possible that Sir Ulick should do this? Is it in human nature?

Yes, in the nature of Sir Ulick O'Shane. Long use had brought him to this; though his affections, perhaps, were naturally warm, he had on many occasions in his life sacrificed them to his scheming imaginations. Necessity—the necessity of his affairs, the consequences of his extravagance—had brought him to this: the first sacrifices had not been made without painful struggles; but by degrees his mind had hardened, and his warmth of heart had cooled. When he said or *swore* in the most cordial manner that he "would do any thing in the world to serve a friend," there was always a mental reservation of "any thing that does not hurt my own interest, or cross my schemes."

And how could Harry Ormond hurt his interest, or cross his schemes? or how had Sir Ulick discovered this so suddenly? Miss Annaly's turning pale was the first cause of Sir Ulick's change of sentiments towards his young favourite. Afterwards, during the whole that passed, Sir Ulick had watched the impression made upon her—he had observed that it was not for Marcus O'Shane's safety that she was anxious; and he thought she had betrayed a secret attachment, the commencement of an attachment he thought it, of which she was perhaps herself unconscious. Were such an attachment to be confirmed, it would disappoint Sir Ulick's schemes: therefore, with the cool decision of a practised *schemer*, he determined directly to get rid of Ormond. He had no intention of parting with him for ever, but merely while the Annalys were at Castle Hermitage: till his scheme was brought to bear, he would leave Harry at the Black Islands, and he could, he thought, recal him from banishment, and force a reconciliation with Lady O'Shane, and reinstate him in favour, at pleasure.

But is it possible that Miss Annaly, such an amiable and elegant young lady as she is described to be, should feel any attachment, any predilection for such a young man as Ormond; ill-educated, unpolished, with a violent temper, which had brought him early into life into the dreadful situation in which he now stands? And at the moment when, covered with the blood of an innocent man, he stood before her, an object of disgust and horror; could any sentiment like love exist or arise in a well-principled mind?

Certainly not. Sir Ulick's acquaintance with unprincipled women misled him completely in this instance, and deprived him of his usual power of discriminating character. Harry Ormond was uncommonly handsome; and though so young, had a finely-formed, manly, graceful figure; and his manner, whenever he spoke to women, was peculiarly prepossessing. These personal accomplishments, Sir Ulick thought, were quite sufficient to win any lady's heart—but Florence Annaly was not to be won by such means: no feeling of love for Mr. Ormond had ever touched her heart, nor even crossed her imagination; none under such circumstances could have arisen in her innocent and well-regulated mind. Sudden terror, and confused apprehension of evil, made her grow very pale at the sight of his bloody apparition at the window of the ball-room. Bodily weakness, for she was not at this time in strong health, must be her apology, if she need any, for the faintness and loss of presence of mind, which Sir Ulick construed into proofs of tender anxiety for the personal fate of this young man. In the scene that followed, horror of his crime, pity for the agony of his remorse, was what she felt—what she strongly expressed to her mother, the moment she reached her apartment that night: nor did her mother, who knew her thoroughly, ever for an instant suspect that in her emotion, there was a mixture of any sentiments but those which she expressed. Both mother and daughter were extremely shocked. They were also struck with regret at the idea, that a young man, in whom they had seen many instances of a generous, good disposition, of natural qualities and talents, which might have made him a useful, amiable, and admirable member of society, should be, thus early, a victim to his own undisciplined passion. During the preceding winter they had occasionally seen something of Ormond in Dublin. In the midst of the dissipated life which he led, upon one or two occasions, of which we cannot now stop to give an account, he had shown that he was capable of being a very different character from that which he had been made by bad education, bad example, and profligate indulgence, or shameful neglect on the part of his guardian.

Immediately after Sir Ulick had left Ormond, the surgeon appeared, and a new train of emotions arose. He had no time to reflect on Sir Ulick's conduct. He felt hurried on rapidly, like one in a terrible dream. He returned with the surgeon to the wounded man.

Moriarty had wakened, much refreshed from his sleep, and the surgeon confessed that his patient was infinitely better than he had expected to find him. Moriarty evidently exerted himself as much as he possibly could to appear better, that he might calm Ormond's anxiety, who stood waiting, with looks that showed his implicit faith in the oracle, and feeling that his own fate depended upon the next words that should be uttered. Let no one scoff at his easy faith: at this time Ormond was very young, not yet nineteen, and had no experience, either of the probability, or of the fallacy of medical predictions. After looking very grave and very wise, and questioning and cross-questioning a proper time, the surgeon said it was impossible for him to pronounce any thing decidedly, till the patient should have passed another night; but that if the next night proved favourable, he might then venture to declare him out of immediate danger, and might then begin to hope that, with time and care, he would do well. With this opinion, guarded and dubious as it was, Ormond was delighted—his heart felt relieved of part of the heavy load by which it had been oppressed, and the surgeon was well feed from the purse which Sir Ulick had put into Ormond's hands. Ormond's next business was to send a *gossoon* with a letter to his friend the King of the Black Islands, to tell him all that had passed, and to request an asylum in his dominions. By the time he had finished and despatched his letter, it was eight o'clock in the morning; and he was afraid that before he could receive an answer, it might be too late in the day to carry a wounded man as far as the Black Islands: he therefore accepted the hospitable offer of the village school-mistress, to give him and his patient a lodging for that night. There was indeed no one in the place who would not have done as much for Master Harry. All were in astonishment and sorrow when they heard that he was going to leave the castle; and their hatred to Lady O'Shane would have known no bounds, had they learned that she was the cause of his *banishment*: but this he generously concealed, and forbade those of his followers or partisans, who had known any thing of what had passed, to repeat what they had heard. It was late in the day before Marcus rose; for he had to sleep off the effects of his last night's intemperance. He was in great astonishment when he learned that Ormond was really going away; and "could scarcely believe," as he said repeatedly, "that Harry was so mad, or such a fool. As to Moriarty, a few guineas would have settled the business, if no rout had been made about it. Sitting up all night with such a fellow, and being in such agonies about him—how absurd! What more could he have done, if he had shot a gentleman, or his best friend? But Harry Ormond was always in extremes."

Marcus, though he had not a very clear recollection of the events of the preceding night, was conscious, however, that he had been much more to blame than Ormond had stated; he had a remembrance of having been very violent, and of having urged Ormond to chastise Moriarty. It was not the first time that Ormond had screened him from blame, by taking the whole upon himself. For this Marcus was grateful to a certain degree: he thought he was fond of Harry Ormond; but he had not for him the solid friendship that would stand the test of adversity, still less would it be capable of standing against any difference of party opinion. Marcus, though he appeared a mild, indolent youth, was violent where his prejudices were concerned. Instead of being governed by justice in his conduct towards his inferiors, he took strong dislikes, either upon false informations, or without sufficient examination of the facts: cringing and flattery easily won his favour; and, on the other hand, he resented any spirit of independence, or even the least contradiction, from an inferior. These defects in his temper appeared more and more in him every year. As he ceased to be a boy, and was called upon to act as a man, the consequences of his actions became of greater importance; but in acquiring more power, he did not acquire more reason, or greater command over himself. He was now provoked with Ormond for being so anxious about Moriarty Carroll, because he disliked the Carrolls, and especially Moriarty, for some slight cause not worth recording. He went to Ormond, and argued the matter with him, but in vain. Marcus resented this sturdiness, and they parted, displeased with each other. Though Marcus expressed in words much regret at his companion's adhering to the resolution of quitting his father's house, yet it might be doubted whether, at the end of the conference, these professions were entirely sincere, whatever they might have been at the beginning: he had not a large mind, and perhaps he was not sorry to get rid of a companion who had often rivalled him in his father's favour, and who might rival him where it was still more his ambition to please. The coldness of Marcus's manner at parting, and the little difficulty which he felt in the separation, gave exquisite pain to poor Ormond, who, though he was resolved to go, did wish to be regretted, especially by the companion, the friend of his childhood. The warmth of his guardian's manner had happily deceived him; and to the recollection of this he recurred for comfort at this moment, when his heart ached, and he was almost exhausted with the succession of the painful, violently painful, feelings of the last four-and-twenty hours.

The gossoon who had been sent with the despatch to the King of the Black Islands did not return this day—disappointment upon disappointment. Moriarty, who had exerted himself too much, that he might appear better than he really was, suffered proportionably this night; and so did Ormond, who, never before having been with any person delirious from fever, was excessively alarmed. What he endured cannot be described: it was, however, happy for him that he was forced to bear it all—nothing less could have made a sufficient impression on his mind—nothing less could have been a sufficient warning to set a guard upon the violence of his temper.

In the morning the fever abated: about eight o'clock the patient sunk into a sound sleep; and Ormond, kneeling by his bedside, ardent in devotion as in all his sentiments, gave thanks to Heaven, prayed for Moriarty's perfect recovery, and vowed with the strongest adjurations that if he might be spared for this offence, if he might be saved from the horror of being a murderer, no passion, no provocation should ever, during the whole future course of his life, tempt him to lift his hand against a fellow-creature.

As he rose from his knees, after making this prayer and this vow, he was surprised to see standing beside him Lady Annaly—she had made a sign to the sick man not to interrupt Ormond's devotion by any exclamation at her entrance.

"Be not disturbed—let me not feel that I embarrass you, Mr. Ormond," said she: "I came here not to intrude upon your privacy. Be not ashamed, young gentleman," continued she, "that I should have witnessed feelings that do you honour, and that interest me in your future fate."

"Interest Lady Annaly in my future fate!—Is it possible!" exclaimed Ormond: "Is it possible that one of whom I stood so much in awe—one whom I thought so much too good, ever to bestow a thought on—such a one as I am—as I was, even before this fatal—" (his voice failed).

"Not fatal, I hope—I trust," said Lady Annaly: "this poor man's looks at this moment assure me that he is likely to do well."

"True for ye, my lady," said Moriarty, "I'll do my best, surely: I'd live through all, if possible, for his sake, let alone my mudther's, or shister's, or my own—'twould be too bad, after; all the trouble he got these two nights, to be dying at last, I and *hanting* him, may be, whether I would or no—for as to prosecuting, that would never be any way, if I died twenty times over. I sint off that word to my mudthier and shister, with my curse if they'd do *other*—and only that they were at the fair, and did not get the word, or the news of my little accident, they'd have been here long ago; and the minute they come, I'll swear 'em not to prosecute, or harbour a thought of revenge again' him, who had no malice again' me, no more than a child. And at another's bidding, more than his own, he drew the trigger, and the pistol went off unknownst, in a passion: so there's the case for you, my lady."

Lady Annaly, who was pleased with the poor fellow's simplicity and generosity in this tragi-comic statement of the case, inquired if she could in any way afford him assistance.

"I thank your ladyship, but Mr. Harry lets me want for nothing."

"Nor ever will, while I have a farthing I can call my own," cried Ormond.

"But I hope, Mr. Ormond," said Lady Annaly, smiling, "that when Moriarty—is not that his name?—regains his strength, to which he seems well inclined, you do not mean to make him miserable and good for nothing, by supporting him in idleness?"

"No, he sha'n't, my lady—I would not let him be wasting his little substance on me. And did ye hear, my lady, how he is going to lave Castle Hermitage? Well, of all the surprises ever I got! It come upon me like a shot—*my shot* was nothing to it!"

It was necessary to insist upon Moriarty's submitting to be silent and quiet; for not having the fear of the surgeon before his eyes, and having got over his first awe of the lady, he was becoming too full of oratory and action. Lady Annaly took Ormond out with her, that she might speak to him of his own affairs.

"You will not, I hope, Mr. Ormond, ascribe it to idle curiosity, but to a wish to be of service, if I inquire what your future plans in life may be?"

Ormond had never formed any, distinctly. "He was not fit for any profession, except, perhaps, the army—he was too old for the navy—he was at present going, he believed, to the house of an old friend, a relation of Sir Ulick, Mr. Cornelius O'Shane."

"My son, Sir Herbert Annaly, has an estate in this neighbourhood, at which he has never yet resided, but we are going there when we leave Castle Hermitage. I shall hope to see you at Annaly, when you have determined on your plans; perhaps you may show us how we can assist in forwarding them."

"Is it possible," repeated Ormond, in unfeigned astonishment, "that your ladyship can be so very good, so condescending, to one who so little deserves it? But I *will* deserve it in future. If I get over this—interested in *my* future fate—Lady Annaly!"

"I knew your father many years ago," said Lady Annaly; "and as his son, I might feel some interest for you; but I will tell you sincerely, that, on some occasions, when we met in Dublin, I perceived traits of goodness in you, which, on your own account, Mr. Ormond, have interested me in your fate. But fate is an unmeaning commonplace—worse than commonplace—word: it is a word that leads us to imagine that we are *fated* or doomed to certain fortunes or misfortunes in life. I have had a great deal of experience, and from all I have observed, it appears to me, that far the greatest part of our happiness or misery in life depends upon ourselves."

Ormond stopped short, and listened with the eagerness of one of quick feeling and quick capacity, who seizes an idea that is new to him, and the truth and value of which he at once appreciates. For the first time in his life he heard good sense from the voice of benevolence—he anxiously desired that she should go on speaking, and stood in such an attitude of attentive deference as fully marked that wish.

But at this moment Lady O'Shane's footman came up with a message from his lady; her ladyship sent to let Lady Annaly know that breakfast was ready. Repeating her good wishes to Ormond she bade him adieu, while he was too much overpowered with his sense of gratitude to return her thanks.

"Since there exists a being, and such a being, interested for me, I must be worth something—and I will make myself worth something more: I will begin from this moment, I am resolved, to improve; and who knows but in the end I may become every thing that is good? I don't want to be great."

Though this resolution was not steadily adhered to, though it was for a time counteracted by circumstances, it was never afterwards entirely forgotten. From this period, in consequence of the great and painful impression which had been suddenly made on his mind, and from a few words of sense and kindness spoken to him at a time when his heart was happily prepared to receive them, we may date the commencement of our hero's reformation and improvement—hero, we say; but certainly never man had more faults than Ormond had to correct, or to be corrected, before he could come up to the received idea of any description of hero. Most heroes are born perfect—so at least their biographers, or rather their panegyrists, would have us believe. Our hero is far from this happy lot; the readers of his story are in no danger of being wearied, at first setting out, with the list of his merits and accomplishments; nor will they be awed or discouraged by the exhibition of virtue above the common standard of humanity—beyond the hope of imitation. On the contrary, most people will comfort and bless themselves with the reflection, that they never were quite so foolish, nor quite so bad, as Harry Ormond.

For the advantage of those who may wish to institute the comparison, his biographer, in writing the life of Ormond, deems it a point of honour to extenuate nothing; but to trace, with an impartial hand, not only every improvement and advance, but every deviation or retrograde movement.

CHAPTER IV.

Full of sudden zeal for his own improvement, Ormond sat down at the foot of a tree, determined to make a list of all his faults, and of all his good resolutions for the future. He took out his pencil, and began on the back of a letter the following resolutions, in a sad scrawling hand and incorrect style.

HARRY OSMOND'S GOOD RESOLUTIONS.

Resolved 1st.—That I will never drink more than (*blank number* of) glasses.

Resolved 2ndly.—That I will cure myself of being passionate.

Resolved 3rdly.—That I will never keep low company.

Resolved.—That I am too fond of flattery—women's, especially, I like most. To cure myself of that.

Ormond. Here he was interrupted by the sight of a little gossoon, with a short stick tucked under his arm, who came pattering on bare-foot in a kind of pace indescribable to those who have never seen it—it was something as like walking or running as chanting is to speaking or singing.

"The answer I am from the Black Islands, Master Harry; and would have been back wid you afore nightfall yesterday, only *he*—King Corny—was at the fair of Frisky—could not write till this morning any way—but has his service to ye, Master Harry, will be in it for ye by half after two with a bed and blanket for Moriarty, he bid me say on account he forgot to put it in the note. In the Sally Cove the boat will be there *abow* in the big lough, forenent the spot where the fir dale was cut last seraph by them rogues."

The despatch from the King of the Black Islands was then produced from the messenger's bosom, and it ran as follows:

"Dear Harry. What the mischief has come over Cousin Ulick to be banishing you from Castle Hermitage? But since he *conformed*, he was never the same man, especially since his last mis-marriage. But no use moralizing—he was always too much of a courtier for me. Come you to me, my dear boy, who is no courtier, and you'll be received and embraced with open arms—was I Briareus, the same way—Bring Moriarty Carroll (if that's his name), the boy you shot, which has given you so much concern—for which I like you the better—and honour that boy, who, living or dying, forbade to prosecute. Don't be surprised to see the roof the way it is:—since Tuesday I wedged it up bodily without stirring a stick:—you'll see it from the boat, standing three foot high above the walls, waiting while I'm building up to it—to get attics— which I shall for next to nothing—by my own contrivance. Meantime, good dry lodging, as usual, for all friends at the palace. *He* shall be well tended for you by Sheelah Dunshaughlin, the mother of Betty, worth a hundred of her! and we'll soon set him up again with the help of such a nurse, as well as ever, I'll engage; for I'm a bit of a doctor, you know, as well as every thing else. But don't let any other doctor, surgeon, or apothecary, be coming after him for your life—for none ever gets a permit to land, to my knowledge, on the Black Islands—to which I attribute, under Providence, to say nothing of my own skill in practice, the wonderful preservation of my people in health—that, and woodsorrell, and another secret or two not to be committed to paper in a hurry—all which I would not have written to you, but am in the gout since four this morning, held by the foot fast—else I'd not be writing, but would have gone every inch of the way for you myself in style, in lieu of sending, which is all I can now do, my six-oared boat, streamers flying, and piper playing like mad—for I would not have you be coming like a banished man, but in all glory, to Cornelius O'Shane, commonly called King *Corny*—but no *king* to you, only your hearty old friend."

"Heaven bless Cornelius O'Shane!" said Harry Ormond to himself, as he finished this letter. "King or no king, the most warm-hearted man on earth, let the other be who he will."

Then pressing this letter to his heart, he put it up carefully, and rising in haste, he dropped the list of his faults. That train of associations was completely broken, and for the present completely forgotten; nor was it likely to be soon renewed at the Black Islands, especially in the palace, where he was now going to take up his residence. Moriarty was laid on a bed; and was transported, with Ormond, in the six-oared boat, streamers flying, and piper playing, across the lake to the islands. Moriarty's head ached terribly, but he nevertheless enjoyed the playing of the pipes in his ear, because of the air of triumph it gave Master Harry, to go away in this grandeur, in the face of the country. King Corny ordered the discharge of twelve guns on his landing, which popped one after another gloriously— the *hospitable echoes*, as Moriarty called them, repeating the sound. A horse, decked with ribands, waited on the shore, with King Corny's compliments for *Prince* Harry, as the boy, who held the stirrup for Ormond to mount, said he was instructed to call him, and to proclaim him "*Prince Harry*" throughout the island, which he did by sound of horn, the whole way they proceeded to the palace—very much to the annoyance of the horse, but all for the greater glory of the prince, who managed his steed to the admiration of the shouting ragged multitude, and of his majesty, who sat in state in his gouty chair at the palace door. He had had himself rolled out to welcome the coming guest.

"By all that's princely," cried he, "then, that young Harry Ormond was intended for a prince, he sits ahorse so like myself; and that horse requires a master hand to manage him."

Ormond alighted.

The gracious, cordial, fatherly welcome, with which he was received, delighted his heart.

"Welcome, prince, my adopted son, welcome to Corny *castle—palace*, I would have said, only for the constituted authorities of the post-office, that might take exceptions, and not be sending me my letters right. As I am neither bishop nor arch, I have, in their blind eyes or conceptions, no right—Lord help them!—to a temporal palace. Be that as it may, come you in with me, here into the big room—and see! there's the bed in the corner for your first object, my boy—your wounded chap; and I'll visit his wound, and fix it and him the first thing for ye, the minute he comes up."

His majesty pointed to a bed in the corner of a large apartment, whose beautiful painted ceiling and cornice, and fine chimney-piece with caryatides of white marble, ill accorded with the heaps of oats and corn, the thrashing cloth and flail, which lay on the floor.

"It is intended for a drawing-room, understand," said King Corny; "but till it is finished, I use it for a granary or a barn, when it would not be a barrack-room or hospital, which last is most useful at present."

To this hospital Moriarty was carefully conveyed. Here, notwithstanding his gout, which affected only his feet, King Corny dressed Moriarty's wound with exquisite tenderness and skill; for he had actually acquired knowledge and address in many arts, with which none could have suspected him to have been in the least acquainted.

Dinner was soon announced, which was served up with such a strange mixture of profusion and carelessness, as showed that the attendants, who were numerous and ill-caparisoned, were not much used to gala-days. The crowd, who had accompanied Moriarty into the house, were admitted into the dining-room, where they stood round the king, prince, and Father Jos the priest, as the courtiers, during the king's supper at Versailles, surrounded the King of France. But these poor people were treated with more hospitality than were the courtiers of the French king; for as soon as the dishes were removed, their contents were generously distributed among the attendant multitude. The people blest both king and prince, "wishing them health and happiness long to reign over them;" and bowing suitably to his majesty the king, and to his reverence the priest, without standing upon the order of their going, departed.

"And now, Father Jos," said the king to the priest, "say grace, and draw close, and let me see you do justice to my claret, or the whiskey punch if you prefer; and you, Prince Harry, we will set to it regally as long as you please."

"Till tea-time," thought young Harry. "Till supper-time," thought Father Jos. "Till bed-time," thought King Corny.

At tea-time young Harry, in pursuance of his *resolution* the first, rose, but he was seized instantly, and held down to his chair. The royal command was laid upon him "to sit still and be a good fellow." Moreover the door was locked—so that there was no escape or retreat.

The next morning when he wakened with an aching head, he recollected with disgust the figure of Father Jos, and all the noisy mirth of the preceding night. Not without some self-contempt, he asked himself what had become of his resolution.

"The wounded boy was axing for you, Master Harry," said the girl, who came in to open the shutters.

"How is he?" cried Harry, starting up.

"He is *but soberly*; [Footnote: But soberly—not very well, or in good spirits.] he got the night but middling; he concaits he could not sleep becaase he did not get a sight of your honour afore he'd settle—I tell him 'tis the change of beds, which always hinders a body to sleep the first night."

The sense of having totally forgotten the poor fellow—the contrast between this forgetfulness and the anxiety and contrition of the two preceding nights, actually surprised Ormond: he could hardly believe that he was one and the same person. Then came excuses to himself: "Gratitude—common civility—the peremptoriness of King Corny—his passionate temper, when opposed on this tender point—the locked door —and two to one: in short, there was an impossibility in the circumstances of doing otherwise than what he had done. But then the same impossibility—the same circumstances—might recur the next night, and the next, and so on: the peremptory temper of King Corny was not likely to alter, and the moral obligation of gratitude would continue the same; so that at nineteen was he to become, from complaisance, what his soul and body abhorred—an habitual drunkard? And what would become of Lady Annaly's interest in his fate or his improvement?"

The two questions were not of equal importance, but our hero was at this time far from having any just proportion in his reasoning: it was well he reasoned at all. The argument as to the obligation of gratitude—the view he had taken of the never-ending nature of the evil, which must be the consequence of beginning with weak complaisance—above all, the *feeling* that he had so lost his reason as not only to forget Moriarty, but to have been again incapable of commanding his passions, if any thing had occurred to cross his temper, determined Ormond to make a firm resistance on the next occasion that should occur: it did occur the very next night. After a dinner given to his chief tenants and the *genteel*people of the islands—a dinner in honour and in introduction of his *adopted son*, King Corny gave a toast "to the Prince presumptive," as he now styled him—a bumper toast. Soon afterwards he detected *daylight* in Harry's glass, and cursing it properly, he insisted on flowing bowls and full glasses. "What! are you Prince *presumptuous?*" cried he, with a half angry and astonished look. "Would you resist and contradict your father and king at his own table after dinner? Down with the glass!"

Farther and steady resistance changed the jesting tone and half angry look of King Corny into sullen silence, and a black portentous brow of serious displeasure. After a decent time of sitting, the bottle passing him without farther importunity, Ormond rose—it was a hard struggle; for in the face of his benefactor he saw reproach and rage bursting from every feature: still he moved on towards the door. He heard the words "sneaking off sober!—let him sneak!"

Ormond had his hand on the lock of the door—it was a bad lock, and opened with difficulty.

"There's gratitude for you! No heart, after all—I mistook him."

Ormond turned back, and firmly standing and firmly speaking, he said, "You did not mistake me formerly, sir; but you mistake me now!—Sneaking!—Is there any man here, sober or drunk," continued be, impetuously approaching the table, and looking round full in every face, —"is there any man here dares to say so but yourself?—You, *you*, my benefactor, my friend; you have said it—think it you did not—you could not, but say it you may—*You* may say what you will to Harry Ormond, bound to you as he is—bound hand and foot and heart I—Trample on him as you will—*you* may. *No heart*! Oblige me, gentlemen, some of you," cried he, his anger rising and his eyes kindling as he spoke, "some of you gentlemen, if any of you think so, oblige me by saying so. No gratitude, sir!" turning from them, and addressing himself to the old man, who held an untasted glass of claret as he listened—"No gratitude! Have not I?—Try me, try me to the death—you have tried me to the quick of the heart, and I have borne it."

He could bear it no longer: he threw himself into the vacant chair, flung out his arms on the table, and laying his face down upon them, wept aloud. Cornelius O'Shane pushed the wine away. "I've wronged the boy grievously," said he; and forgetting the gout, he rose from his chair, hobbled to him, and leaning over him, "Harry, 'tis I—look up, my own boy, and say you forgive me, or I'll never forgive myself. That's well," continued he, as Harry looked up and gave him his hand; "that's well!— you've taken the twinge out of my heart worse than the gout: not a drop of gall or malice in your nature, nor ever was, more than in the child unborn. But see, I'll tell you what you'll do now, Harry, to settle all things—and lest the fit should take me ever to be mad with you on this score again. You don't choose to drink more than's becoming?—Well, you'se right, and I'm wrong. 'Twould be a burning shame of me to make of you what I have made of myself. We must do only as well as we can. But I will ensure you against the future; and before we take another glass —there's the priest—and you, Tom Ferrally there, step you for my swearing book. Harry Ormond, you shall take an oath against drinking more glasses than you please evermore, and then you're safe from me. But stay—you are a heretic. Phoo! what am I saying? 'twas seeing the priest put that word *heretic* in my head—you're not a catholic, I mean. But an oath's an oath, taken before priest or parson—an oath, taken how you will, will operate. But stay, to make all easy, 'tis I'll take it."

"Against drinking, you! King Corny!" said Father Jos, stopping his hand, "and in case of the gout in your stomach?"

"Against drinking! do you think I'd perjure myself? No! But against pressing *him* to it—I'll take my oath I'll never ask him to drink another glass more than he likes."

The oath was taken, and King Corny concluded the ceremony by observing that, after all, there was no character he despised more than that of a sot. But every gentleman knew that there was a wide and material difference betwixt a gentleman who was fond of his bottle, and that unfortunate being, an habitual drunkard. For his own part, it was his established rule never to go to bed without a proper quantity of liquor under his belt; but he defied the universe to say he was ever known to be drunk.

At a court where such ingenious casuistry prevailed, it was happy for our hero that an unqualifying oath now protected his resolution.

CHAPTER V.

In the middle of the night our hero was wakened by a loud bellowing. It was only King Corny in a paroxysm of the gout. His majesty was naturally of a very impatient temper, and his maxims of philosophy encouraged him to the most unrestrained expression of his feelings—the maxims of his philosophy—for he had read, though in most desultory manner, and he had thought often deeply, and not seldom justly. The turns of his mind, and the questions he asked, were sometimes utterly unexpected. "Pray, now," said he to Harry, who stood beside his bed, "now that I've a moment's ease—did you ever hear of the Stoics that the bookmen talk of? and can you tell me what good any one of them ever got by making it a point to make no noise, when they'd be *punished* and racked with pains of body or mind? Why, I will tell you all they got—all they got was no pity: who would give them pity that did not require it? I could bleed to death in a bath, as well as the best of them, if I chose it; or chew a bullet if I set my teeth to it, with any man in a regiment—but where's the use? nature knows best, and she says *roar!*" And he roared—for another twinge seized him.

Nature said *sleep!* several times this night to Harry, and to every body in the palace; but they did not sleep, they could not, while the roaring continued: so all had reason to rejoice, and Moriarty in particular, when his majesty's paroxysm was past. Harry was in a sound sleep at twelve o'clock the next day, when he was summoned into the royal presence. He found King Corny sitting at ease in his bed, and that bed strewed over with a variety of roots and leaves, weeds and plants. An old woman was hovering over the fire, stirring something in a black kettle. "Simples these—of wonderful unknown power," said King Corny to Harry, as he approached the bed; "and I'll engage you don't know the name even of the half of them."

Harry confessed his ignorance.

"No shame for you—was you as wise as King Solomon himself, you might not know them, for he did not, nor couldn't, he that had never set his foot a grousing on an Irish bog. Sheelah, come you over, and say what's this?"

The old woman now came to assist at this bed of botany, and with spectacles slipping off, and pushed on her nose continually, peered over each green thing, and named in Irish "every herb that sips the dew."

Sheelah was deeper in Irish lore than King Corny could pretend to be: but then he humbled her with the "black hellebore of the ancients," and he had, in an unaccountable manner, affected her imagination by talking of "that famous howl of narcotic poisons, which that great man Socrates drank off." Sheelah would interrupt herself in the middle of a sentence, and curtsy if she heard him pronounce the name of Socrates—and at the mention of the bowl, she would regularly sigh, and exclaim, "Lord save us!—But that was a wicked bowl."

Then after a cast of her eyes up to heaven, and crossing herself on the forehead, she would take up her discourse at the word where she had left off.

King Corny set to work compounding plasters and embrocations, preparing all sorts of decoctions of roots and leaves, famous *through the country*. And while he directed and gesticulated from his bed, the old woman worked over the fire in obedience to his commands; sometimes, however, not with that "prompt and mute obedience," which the great require.

It was fortunate for Moriarty that King Corny, not having the use of his nether limbs, could not attend even in his gouty chair to administer the medicines he had made, and to see them fairly swallowed. Sheelah, whose conscience was easy on this point, contented herself with giving him a strict charge to "take every bottle to the last drop." All she insisted upon for her own part was, that she must tie the charm round his neck and arm. She would fain have removed the dressings of the wound to substitute plasters of her own, over which she had pronounced certain prayers or incantations; but Moriarty, who had seized and held fast one good principle of surgery, that the air must never be let into the wound, held mainly to this maxim, and all Sheelah could obtain was permission to clap on her charmed plaster over the dressing.

In due time, or, as King Corny triumphantly observed, in "a wonderful short period," Moriarty got quite well, long before the king's gout was cured, even with the assistance of the black hellebore of the ancients. King Corny was so well pleased with his patient for doing such credit to his medical skill, that he gave him and his family a cabin, and spot of land, in the islands—a cabin near the palace; and at Harry's request made him his wood-ranger and his gamekeeper—the one a lucrative place, the other a sinecure.

Master Harry—Prince Harry—was now looked up to as a person all-powerful with *the master*; and petitions and requests to speak for them, to speak just one word, came pouring from all sides: but however enviable his situation as favourite and prince presumptive might appear to others, it was not in all respects comfortable to himself.

Formerly, when a boy, in his visits to the Black Islands, he used to have a little companion of whom he was fond—Dora—Corny's daughter. Missing her much, he inquired from her father where she was gone, and when she was likely to return.

"She is gone off to the *continent*—to the continent of Ireland, that is; but not banished for any misdemeanour. You know," said King Corny, "'tis generally considered as a punishment in the Black Islands to be banished to Ireland. A threat of that kind, I find sufficient to bring the most refractory and ill-disposed of my subjects, if I had any of that description, to rason in the last resort; but to that ultimate law I have not recourse, except in extreme cases; I understand my business of king too well, to wear out either shame or fear; but you are no legislator yet, Prince Harry. So what was you asking me about Dora? She is only gone a trip to the continent, to her aunt's, by the mother's side, Miss O'Faley, that you never saw, to get the advantage of a dancing-master, which myself don't think she wants—a natural carriage, with native graces, being, in my unsophisticated opinion, worth all the dancing-master's positions, contortions, or drillings; but her aunt's of a contrary opinion, and the women say it is essential. So let 'em put Dora in the stocks, and punish her as they will, she'll be the gladder to get free, and fly back from their continent to her own Black Islands, and to you and me—that is, to me—I ax your pardon, Harry Ormond; for you know, or I should tell you in time, she is engaged already to White Connal, of Glynn—from her birth. That engagement I made with the father over a bowl of punch—I promised—I'm afraid it was a foolish business—I promised if ever he, Old Connal, should have a son, and I should have a daughter, his son should marry my daughter. I promised, I say—I took my oath: and then Mrs. Connal that was, had, shortly after, not one son, but two—and twins they were: and I had—unluckily—ten years after, the daughter, which is Dora—and then as she could not marry both, the one twin was to be fixed on for her, and that was him they call White Connal—so there it was. Well, it was altogether a rash act! So you'll consider her as a married woman, though she is but a child—it was a rash act, between you and I—for Connal's not grown up a likely lad for the girl to fancy; but that's neither here nor there: no, my word is passed—when half drunk, may be—but no matter—it must be kept sober—drunk or sober, a gentleman must keep his word—*à fortiori* a king—*à fortiori* King Corny. See! was there this minute no such thing as parchment, deed, stamp, signature, or seal in the wide world, when once Corny has squeezed a friend's hand on a bargain, or a promise, 'tis fast, was it ever so much against me—'tis as strong to me as if I had squeezed all the lawyers' wax in the creation upon it."

Ormond admired the honourable sentiment; but was sorry there was any occasion for it—and he sighed; but it was a sigh of pity for Dora: not that he had ever seen White Connal, or known any thing of him—but *White Connal* did not sound well; and her father's avowal, that it had been a rash engagement, did not seem to promise happiness to Dora in this marriage.

From the time he had been a boy, Harry Ormond had been in the habit of ferrying over to the Black Islands whenever Sir Ulick could spare him. The hunting and shooting, and the life of lawless freedom he led on the Islands, had been delightful. King Corny, who had the command not only of boats, and of guns, and of fishing-tackle, and of men, but of carpenters' tools, and of smiths' tools, and of a lathe, and of brass and ivory, and of all the things that the heart of boy could desire, had appeared to Harry, when he was a boy, the richest, the greatest, the happiest of men—the cleverest, too—the most ingenious: for King Corny had with his own hands made a violin and a rat-trap; and had made the best coat, and the best pair of shoes, and the best pair of boots, and the best hat; and had knit the best pair of stockings, and had made the best dunghill in his dominions; and had made a quarter of a yard of fine lace, and had painted a panorama. No wonder that King Corny had been looked up to, by the imagination of childhood, as "a personage high as human veneration could look."

But now, although our hero was still but a boy in many respects, yet in consequence of his slight commerce with the world, he had formed some comparisons, and made some reflections. He had heard, accidentally, the conversation of a few people of common sense, besides the sly, witty, and satirical remarks of Sir Ulick, upon *cousin Cornelius*; and it had occurred to Harry to question the utility and real grandeur of some of those things, which had struck his childish imagination. For example, he began to doubt whether it were worthy of a king or a gentleman to be his own shoemaker, hatter, and tailor; whether it were not better managed in society, where these things are performed by different tradesmen: still the things were wonderful, considering who made them, and under what disadvantages they were made: but Harry having now seen and compared Corny's violin with other violins, and having discovered that so much better could be had for money, with so much less trouble, his admiration had a little decreased. There were other points relative to external appearance, on which his eyes had been opened. In his boyish days, King Corny, going out to hunt with hounds and horn, followed with shouts by all who could ride, and all who could run, King Corny hallooing the dogs, and cheering the crowd, appeared to him the greatest, the happiest of mankind.

But he had since seen hunts in a very different style, and he could no longer admire the rabble rout.

Human creatures, especially young human creatures, are apt to swing suddenly from one extreme to the other, and utterly to despise that which they had extravagantly admired. From this propensity Ormond was in the present instance guarded by affection and gratitude. Through all the folly of his kingship, he saw that Cornelius O'Shane was not a person to be despised. He was indeed a man of great natural powers, both of body and mind—of inventive genius, energy, and perseverance, which might have attained the greatest objects; though from insufficient knowledge, and self-sufficient perversity, they had wasted themselves on absurd or trivial purposes.

There was a strong contrast between the characters of Sir Ulick and his cousin Cornelius O'Shane. They disliked and despised each other: differing as far in natural disposition as the subtle and the bold, their whole course through life, and the habits contracted during their progress, had widened the original difference.

The one living in the world, and mixing continually with men of all ranks and character, had, by bending easily, and being all things to all men, won his courtier-way onwards and upwards to the possession of a seat in parliament, and the prospect of a peerage.

The other, inhabiting a remote island, secluded from all men but those over whom he *reigned*, caring for no earthly consideration, and for no human opinion but his own, had *for*himself and *by* himself, hewed out his way to his own objects, and then rested, satisfied—

"Lord of himself, and all his (*little*) world his own."

CHAPTER VI.

One morning, when Harry Ormond was out shooting, and King Corny, who had recovered tolerably from the gout, was reinstated in his arm-chair in the parlour, listening to Father Jos reading "The Dublin Evening Post," a gossoon, one of the runners of the castle, opened the door, and putting in his curly red head and bare feet, announced, *in all haste*, that *he "just seen* Sir Ulick O'Shane in the boat, crossing the lake for the Black Islands."

"Well, breathless blockhead! and what of that?" said King Corny—"did you never see a man in a boat before?"

"I did, plase your honour."

"Then what is there extraordinary?"

"Nothing at all, plase your honour, only—thought your honour might like to know."

"Then you thought wrong, for I neither like it, nor mislike it. I don't care a rush about the matter—so take yourself down stairs."

"'Tis a long time," said the priest, as the gossoon closed the door after him, "'tis a longer time than he ought, since Sir Ulick O'Shane paid his respects here, even in the shape of a morning visit."

"Morning visit!" repeated Mrs. Betty Dunshaughlin, the housekeeper, who entered the room, for she was a privileged person, and had *les grandes et les petites entrées in this palace*"—Morning visit!—are you sure, Father Jos—are you clear he isn't come intending to stay dinner?"

"What, in the devil's name, Betty, does it signify?" said the king.

"About the dinner!"

"What about it?" said Corny, proudly: "whether he comes, stays, or goes, I'll not have a scrap, or an iota of it changed," added he in a despotic tone.

"*Wheugh.*" said Betty, "one would not like to have a dinner of scraps—for there's nothing else to-day for him."

"Then if there *is* nothing else, there *can* be nothing else," said the priest, very philosophically.

"But when strangers come to dine, one would make a bit of an exertion, if one could," said Betty.

"It's his own fault to be a stranger," said Father Jos, watching his majesty's clouding countenance; then whispering to Betty, "that was a faulty string you touched upon, Mrs. Betty; and can't you make out your dinner without saying any thing?"

"A person may speak in this house, I suppose, besides the clergy, Father Jos," said Mrs. Betty, under her breath.

Then looking out of the window, she added, "He's half-way over the lake, and he'll make his own apologies good, I'll engage, when he comes in; for he knows how to speak for himself as well as any gentleman—and I don't doubt but he'll get my Micky made an exciseman, as he promised to; and sure he has a good right—Isn't he a cousin of King Corny's? wherefore I'd wish to have all things proper. So I'll step out and kill a couple of chickens—won't I?"

"Kill what you please," said King Corny; "but without my warrant, nothing killed or unkilled shall come up to my table this day—and that's enough. No more reasoning—quit the subject and the room, Betty."

Betty quitted the room; but every stair, as she descended to the kitchen, could bear witness that she did not quit the subject; and for an hour afterwards, she reasoned against the obstinacy and folly of man, and the chorus in the kitchen moralized, in conformity and commiseration—in vain.

Meantime Father Jos, though he regretted the exertions which Mrs. Betty might discreetly have made in favour of a good dinner, was by no means, as he declared, a friend or *fauterer* of Sir Ulick O'Shane—how could he, when Sir Ulick had recanted?—The priest looked with horror upon the apostasy—the King with contempt upon the desertion of his party. "Was he sincere any way, I'd honour him," said Cornelius, "or forgive him; but, not to be ripping up old grievances when there's no occasion, can't forgive the way he is at this present double-dealing with poor Harry Ormond—cajoling the grateful heart, and shirking the orphan boy that he took upon him to patronise. Why there I thought nobly of him, and forgave him all his sins, for the generous protection he afforded the son of his friend."

"Had Captain Ormond, the father, no fortune?" asked the priest.

"Only a trifle of three hundred a year, and no provision for the education or maintenance of the boy. Ulick's fondness for him, more than all, showed him capable of the disinterested *touch*; but then to belie his own heart—to abandon him he bred a favourite, just when the boy wants him most—Oh! how could he? And all for what? To please the wife he hates: that can't be—that's only the ostensible—but what the raal rason is I can't guess. No matter—he'll soon tell us."

"Tell us! Oh! no," said the priest, "he'll keep his own secret."

"He'll let it out, I'll engage, trying to hide it," said Corny: "like all cunning people, he *woodcocks*—hides his head, and forgets his body can be seen. But hark! he is coming up. Tommy!" said he, turning to a little boy of five years old, Sheelah's grandchild, who was playing about in the room, "hand, me that whistle you're whistling with, till I see what's the matter with it for you."

King Corny seemed lost in examination of the whistle when Sir Ulick entered the room; and after receiving and seating him with proud courtesy, he again returned to the charge, blowing through the whistle, earnestly dividing his observation between Sir Ulick and little Tommy, and asking questions, by turns, about the whistle, and about all at Castle Hermitage.

"Where's my boy? Where's Harry Ormond?" was the first leading question Sir Ulick asked.

"Harry Ormond's out shooting, I believe, somewhere or somehow, taking his pleasure, as I hope he will long, and always as long as he likes it, at the Black Islands; at least as long as I live."

Sir Ulick branched off into hopes of his cousin Cornelius's living long, very long; and in general terms, that were intended to avoid committing himself, or pinning himself to any thing, he protested that he must not be robbed of his boy, that he had always, with good reason, been jealous of Harry's affection for King Corny, and that he could not consent to let his term of stay at the Black Islands be either as long as Harry himself should like, or during what he hoped would be the life of his cousin, Cornelius O'Shane.

"There's something wrong, still, in this whistle. Why, if you loved him so, did you let him go when you had him?" said Corny.

"He thought it necessary, for domestic reasons," replied Sir Ulick.

"*Continental policy*, that is; what I never understood, nor never shall," said Corny. "But I don't inquire any farther. If you are satisfied with yourself, we are all satisfied, I believe."

"Pardon me, I cannot be satisfied without seeing Harry this morning, for I've a little business with him—will you have the goodness to send for him?"

Father Jos, who, from the window, saw Harry's dog snuffing along the path to the wood, thought he could not be far from the house, and went to make inquiries; and now when Sir Ulick and King Corny were left alone together, a dialogue—a sort of single combat, without any object but to try each other's powers and temper—ensued between them; in which the one on the offensive came on with a tomahawk, and the other stood on the defensive parrying with a polished blade of Damascus; and sometimes, when the adversary was off his guard, making a sly cut at an exposed part.

"What are you so busy about?" said Sir Ulick.

"Mending the child's toy," said Cornelius. "A man must be doing something in this world."

"But a man of your ingenuity! 'tis a pity it should be wasted, as I have often said, upon mere toys."

"Toys of one sort or other we are all taken up with through life, from the cradle to the grave. By-the-bye, I give you joy of your baronetage. I hope they did not make you pay, now, too much in conscience for that poor tag of nobility."

"These things are not always matters of bargain and sale—mine was quite an unsolicited honour, a mark of approbation and acceptance of my poor services, and as such, gratifying;—as to the rest, believe me, it was not, if I must use so coarse an expression, *paid* for."

"Not paid for—what, then, it's owing for? To be paid for still? Well, that's too hard, after all you've done for them. But some men have no manner of conscience. At least, I hope you paid the fees."

"The fees, of course—but we shall never understand one another," said Sir Ulick.

"Now what will be the next title or string you look forward to, Ulysses, may I ask? Is it to be Baron Castle Hermitage, or to get a riband, or a garter, or a thistle, or what?—A thistle! What asses some men are!"

What savages some men are, thought Sir Ulick: he walked to the window, and looking out, hoped that Harry Ormond would soon make his appearance. "You are doing, or undoing, a great deal here, cousin Cornelius, I see, as usual."

"Yes, but what I am doing, stand or fall, will never be my undoing—I am no speculator. How do your silver mines go on, Sir Ulick? I hear all the silver mines in Ireland turn out to be lead."

"I wish they did," said Sir Ulick, "for then we could turn all our lead to gold. Those silver mines certainly did not pay—I've a notion you found the same with your reclaimed bog here, cousin Cornelius—I understand that after a short time it relapses, and is worse than ever, like most things pretending to be reclaimed."

"Speak for yourself, there, Sir Ulick," said Cornelius; "you ought to know, certainly, for some thirty years ago, I think you pretended to be a reclaimed rake."

"I don't remember it," said Sir Ulick.

"I do, and so would poor Emmy Annaly, if she was alive, which it's fortunate for her she is not (broken-hearted angel, if ever there was one, by wedlock! and the only one of the Annalys I ever liked)," said

Cornelius to himself, in a low leisurely voice of soliloquy. Then resuming his conversation tone, and continuing his speech to Sir Ulick, "I say you pretended thirty years ago, I remember, to be a reformed rake, and looked mighty smooth and plausible—and promised fair that the improvement was solid, and was to last for ever and a day. But six months after marriage comes a relapse, and the reclaimed rake's worse than ever. Well, to be sure, that's in favour of your opinion against all things pretending to be reclaimed. But see, my poor bog, without promising so well, performs better; for it's six years, instead of six months, that I've seen no tendency to relapse. See, the *cattle* upon it speak for themselves; an honest calf won't lie for any man."

"I give you joy of the success of your improvements. I admire, too, your ploughing team and ploughing tackle," said Sir Ulick, with an ironical smile. "You don't go into any indiscreet expense for farming implements or prize cattle."

"No," said Cornelius, "I don't prize the prize cattle; the best prize a man can get, and the only one worth having, is that which he must give himself, or not get, and of which he is the best judge at all sasons."

"What prize, may I ask?"

"You may ask, and I'll answer—the prize of *success*; and, success to myself, I have, it."

"And succeeding in all your ends by such noble means must be doubly gratifying—and is doubly commendable and surprising," said Sir Ulick.

"May I ask—for it's my turn now to play ignoramus—may I ask, what noble means excites this gratuitous commendation and surprise?"

"I commend, in the first place, the economy of your ploughing tackle—hay ropes, hay traces, and hay halters—doubly useful and convenient for harness and food."

Corny replied, "Some people I know, think the most expensive harness and tackle, and the most expensive ways of doing every thing, the best;

but I don't know if that is the way for the poor to grow rich—it may be the way for the rich to grow poor: we are all poor people in the Black Islands, and I can't afford, or think it good policy, to give the example of extravagant new ways of doing old things."

"'Tis a pity you don't continue the old Irish style of ploughing by the tail," said Sir Ulick.

"That is against humanity to brute *bastes*, which, without any sickening palaver of sentiment, I practise. Also, it's against an act of parliament, which I regard sometimes—that is, when I understand them; which, the way you parliament gentlemen draw them up, is not always particularly intelligible to plain common sense; and I have no lawyers here, thank Heaven! to consult: I am forced to be legislator, and lawyer, and ploughman, and all, you see, the best I can for myself."

He opened the window, and called to give some orders to the man, or, as he called him, the boy—a boy of sixty—who was ploughing.

"Your team, I see, is worthy of your tackle," pursued Sir Ulick—"A mule, a bull, and two lean horses. I pity the foremost poor devil of a horse, who must starve in the midst of plenty, while the horse, bull, and even mule, in a string behind him, are all plucking and *munging* away at their hay ropes."

Cornelius joined in Sir Ulick's laugh, which shortened its duration.

"'Tis comical ploughing, I grant," said he, "but still, to my fancy, any thing's better and more profitable *nor* the tragi-comic ploughing you practise every sason in Dublin."

"I?" said Sir Ulick.

"Ay, you and all your courtiers, ploughing the half acre [Footnote: Ploughing the half acre. The English reader will please to inquire the meaning of this phrase from any Irish courtier.] continually, pacing up and down that Castle-yard, while you're waiting in attendance there. Every one to his taste, but—

'If there's a man on earth I hate,
Attendance and dependence be his fate.'"

"After all, I have very good prospects in life," said Sir Ulick.

"Ay, you've been always living on prospects; for my part, I'd rather have a mole-hill in possession than a mountain in prospect."

"Cornelius, what are you doing here to the roof of your house?" said Sir Ulick, striking off to another subject. "What a vast deal of work you do contrive to cut out for yourself."

"I'd rather cut it out for myself than have any body to cut it out for me," said Cornelius.

"Upon my word, this will require all your extraordinary ingenuity, cousin."

"Oh, I'll engage I'll make a good job of it, in my sense of the word, though not in yours; for I know, in your vocabulary, that's only a good job where you pocket money and do nothing; now my good jobs never bring me in a farthing, and give me a great deal to do into the bargain."

"I don't envy you such jobs, indeed," said Sir Ulick; "and are you sure that at last you make them good jobs in any acceptation of the term?"

"Sure! a man's never sure of any thing in this world, but of being abused. But one comfort, my own conscience, for which I've a trifling respect, can't reproach me; since my jobs, good or bad, have cost my poor country nothing."

On this point Sir Ulick was particularly sore, for he had the character of being one of the greatest *jobbers* in Ireland. With a face of much political prudery, which he well knew how to assume, he began to exculpate himself. He confessed that much public money had passed through his hands; but he protested that none of it had stayed with him. No man, who had done so much for different administrations, had been so ill paid.

"Why the deuce do you work for them, then? You won't tell me it's for love—Have you got any character by it?—if you haven't profit, what have you? I would not let them make me a dupe, or may be something worse, if I was you," said Cornelius, looking him full in the face.

"Savage!" said Sir Ulick again to himself. The tomahawk was too much for him—Sir Ulick felt that it was fearful odds to stand fencing according to rule with one who would not scruple to gouge or scalp, if provoked. Sir Ulick now stood silent, smiling forced smiles, and looking on while Cornelius played quite at his ease with little Tommy, blew shrill blasts through the whistle, and boasted that he had made a good job of that whistle any way.

Harry Ormond, to Sir Ulick's great relief, now appeared. Sir Ulick advanced to meet him with an air of cordial friendship, which brought the honest flush of pleasure and gratitude into the young man's face, who darted a quick look at Cornelius, as much as to say, "You see you were wrong—he is glad to see me—he is come to see me."

Cornelius said nothing, but stroked the child's head, and seemed taken up entirely with him; Sir Ulick spoke of Lady O'Shane, and of his hopes that prepossessions were wearing off. "If Miss Black were out of the way, things would all go right; but she is one of the mighty good—too good ladies, who are always meddling with other people's business, and making mischief."

Harry, who hated her, that is, as much as he could hate any body, railed at her vehemently, saying more against her than he thought, and concluded by joining in Sir Ulick's wish for her departure from Castle Hermitage, but not with any view to his own return thither: on that point he was quite resolute and steady. He would never, he said, be the cause of mischief. Lady O'Shane did not like him—why, he did not know, and had no right to inquire—and was too proud to inquire, if he had a right. It was enough that her ladyship had proved to him her dislike, and refused him protection at his utmost need: he should never again sue for her hospitality. He declared that Sir Ulick should no more be disquieted by his being an inmate at Castle Hermitage.

Sir Ulick became more warm and eloquent in dissuading him from this resolution, the more he perceived that Ormond was positively fixed in his determination.

The cool looker-on all the time remarked this, and Cornelius was convinced that he had from the first been right in his own opinion, that Sir Ulick was "*shirking the boy.*"

"And where's Marcus, sir? would not he come with you to see us?" said Ormond.

"Marcus is gone off to England. He bid me give you his kindest love: he was hurried, and regretted he could not come to take leave of you; but he was obliged to go off with the Annalys, to escort her ladyship to England, where he will remain this year, I dare say. I am much concerned to say, that poor Lady Annaly and Miss Annaly—" Sir Ulick cleared his throat, and gave a suspicious look at Ormond.

This glance at Harry, the moment Sir Ulick pronounced the words *Miss Annaly*, first directed aright the attention of Cornelius.

"Lady Annaly and Miss Annaly! are they ill? What's the matter, for Heaven's sake!" exclaimed Harry with great anxiety; but pronouncing both the ladies' names precisely in the same tone, and with the same freedom of expression.

Sir Ulick took breath. "Neither of the ladies are ill—absolutely ill; but they have both been greatly shocked by accounts of young Annaly's sudden illness. It is feared an inflammation upon his lungs, brought on by violent cold—his mother and sister left us this morning—set off for England to him immediately. Lady Annaly thought of you, Harry, my boy—you must be a prodigious favourite—in the midst of all her affliction, and the hurry of this sudden departure, this morning: she gave me a letter for you, which I determined to deliver with my own hands."

While he spoke, Sir Ulick, affecting to search for the letter among many in his pocket, studied with careless intermitting glances our young hero's countenance, and Cornelius O'Shane studied Sir Ulick's: Harry tore open the letter eagerly, and coloured a good deal when he saw the inside.

"I have no business here reading that boy's secrets in his face," cried Cornelius O'Shane, raising himself on his crutches—"I'll step out and look at my roof. Will you come, Sir Ulick, and see how the job goes on?" His crutch slipped as he stepped across the hearth—Harry ran to him: "Oh, sir, what are you doing? You are not able to walk yet without me— why are you going? Secrets did you say?" (The words recurred to his ear.) "I have no secrets—there's no secrets in this letter—it's only—the reason I looked foolish was that here's a list of my own faults, which I made like a fool, and dropped like a fool—but they could not have fallen into better or kinder hands than Lady Annaly's."

He offered the letter and its enclosure to Cornelius and Sir Ulick. Cornelius drew back. "I don't want to see the list of your faults, man," said he: "do you think I haven't them all by heart already? and as to the lady's letter, while you live never show a lady's letter."

Sir Ulick, without ceremony, took the letter, and in a moment satisfying his curiosity that it was merely a friendly note, returned it and the list of his faults to Harry, saying. "If it had been a young lady's letter, I am sure you would not have shown it to me, Harry, nor, of course, would I have looked at it. But I presumed that a letter from old Lady Annaly could only be, what I see it is, very edifying."

"Old Lady Annaly, is it?" cried Cornelius: "oh! then there's no indiscretion, young man, in the case. You might as well scruple about your mother's letter, if you had one; or your mother's-in-law, which, to be sure, you'll have, I hope, in due course of nature."

At the sound of the words mother-in-law, a cloud passed over Sir Ulick's brow, not unnoticed by the shrewd Cornelius; but the cloud passed away quickly, after Sir Ulick had darted another reconnoitring glance on Harry's open unconscious countenance.

"All's safe," said Sir Ulick to himself, as he took leave.

"*Woodcocked*! that he has—as I foresaw he would," cried King Corny, the moment his guest had departed. "*Woodcocked*! if ever man did, by all that's cunning!"

CHAPTER VII.

King Corny sat for some minutes after Sir Ulick's departure perfectly still and silent, leaning both hands and his chin on his crutch. Then, looking up at Harry, he exclaimed, "What a dupe you are! but I like you the better for it."

"I am glad you like me the better, at all events," said Harry; "but I don't think I am a dupe."

"No—if you *did*, you would not be one: so you don't see that it was and *is* Sir Ulick, and not her ladyship, that wanted and wants to get rid of you?"

No, Harry did not see this, and would not be persuaded of it. He defended his guardian most warmly; he was certain of Sir Ulick's affection; he was sure Sir Ulick was incapable of acting with such duplicity.

His majesty repeated, at every pause, "You are a dupe; but I like you the better for it. And," added he, "you don't—blind buzzard! as your want of conceit makes you, for which I like you the better, too—you don't see the reason why he banished you from Castle Hermitage—you don't see that he is jealous of your rivalling that puppy, Marcus, his son."

"Rivalling Marcus in what, or how?"

"*With* whom? boy, is the question you should ask; and in that case the answer is—Dunce, can't you guess now?—Miss Annaly."

"Miss Annaly!" repeated Harry with genuine surprise, and with a quick sense of inferiority and humiliation. "Oh, sir, you would not be so ill-natured as to make a jest of me!—I know how ignorant, how uninformed, what a raw boy I am. Marcus has been educated like a gentleman."

"More shame for his father that couldn't do the same by you when he was about it."

"But Marcus, sir—there ought to be a difference—Marcus is heir to a large fortune—I have nothing. Marcus may hope to marry whoever he pleases."

"Ay, whoever he *pleases*; and who will that be, if women are of my mind?" muttered Corny. "I'll engage, if you had a mind to rival him—"

"Rival him! the thought of rivalling my friend never entered my head."

"But is he your friend?" said Cornelius.

"As to that, I don't know: he was my friend, and I loved him sincerely—warmly—he has cast me off—I shall never complain—never blame him directly or indirectly; but don't let me be accused or suspected unjustly—I never for one instant had the treachery, presumption, folly, or madness, to think of Miss Annaly."

"Nor she of you, I suppose, you'll swear?"

"Nor she of me! assuredly not, sir," said Harry, with surprise at the idea. "Do you consider what I am—and what she is?"

"Well, I am glad they are gone to England out of the way!" said Cornelius.

"I am very sorry for that," said Harry; "for I have lost a kind friend in Lady Annaly—one who at least I might have hoped would have become my friend, if I had deserved it."

"*Might have hoped!—would have become!*—That's a friend in the air, who may never be found on earth. *If you deserved it!*—Murder!—who knows how that might turn out—*if*—I don't like that kind of subjunctive mood tenure of a friend. Give me the good imperative mood, which I understand—be my friend—at once—or not at all—that's my mood. None of your *if* friends for me, setting out with a proviso and an excuse to be off; and may be when you'd call upon 'em at your utmost need, 'Oh! I said if you deserve it—Lie there like a dog.' Now, what kind of a friend is that? If Lady Annaly is that sort, no need to regret her. My compliments to her, and a good journey to England—Ireland well rid of her! and so are you, too, my boy!"

"But, dear sir, how you have worked yourself up into a passion against Lady Annaly for nothing."

"It's not for nothing—I've good rason to dislike the woman. What business had she, because she's an old woman and you a young man, to set up preaching to you about your faults? I hate prachers, feminine gender, especially."

"She is no preacher, I assure you, sir."

"How dare you tell me that—was not her letter very *edifying?* Sir Ulick said."

"No, sir; it was very kind—will you read it?"

"No, sir, I won't; I never read an edifying letter in my life with my eyes open, nor never will—quite enough for me that impertinent list of your faults she enclosed you."

"That list was my own, not hers, sir: I dropped it under a tree."

"Well, drop it into the fire now, and no more about it. Pray, after all, Harry, for curiosity's sake, what faults have you?"

"Dear sir, I thought you told me you knew them by heart."

"I always forget what I learn by heart; put me in mind, and may be I'll recollect as you go on."

"Well, sir, in the first place, I am terribly passionate."

"Passionate! true; that is Moriarty you are thinking of; and I grant you, that had like to have been a sad job—you had a squeak for your life there, and I pitied you as if it had been myself; for I know what it is after one of them blind rages is over, and one opens one's eyes on the wrong one has done—and then such a cursed feel to be penitent in vain—for that sets no bones. You were blind drunk that night, and that was my fault; but my late vow has prevented the future, and Moriarty's better in the world than ever he was."

"Thanks to your goodness, sir." "Oh! I wasn't thinking of my goodness —little enough that same; but to ease your conscience, it was certainly the luckiest turn ever happened him the shot he got, and so he says himself. Never think of that more in the way of penitence."

"In the way of reformation though, I hope, I shall all my life," said Harry. "One comfort—I have never been in a passion since."

"But, then, a rasonable passion's allowable: I wouldn't give a farthing for a man that couldn't be in a passion on a proper occasion. I'm passionate myself, rasonably passionate, and I like myself the better for it."

"I thought you said just now you often repented."

"Oh! never mind what I said *just now*—mind what I'm saying now. Isn't a red heat that you can see, and that warms you, better than a white heat that blinds you? I'd rather a man would knock me down than stand smiling at me, as cousin Ulick did just now, when I know he could have kilt me; he is not passionate—he has the command of himself—every feature under the courtier's regimen of hypocrisy. Harry Ormond, don't set about to cure yourself of your natural passions—why, this is rank methodism, all!"

"Methodism, sir?"

"*Methodism*, sir!—don't contradict or repeat me—methodism, that the woman has brought you to the brink of, and I warn you from it! I did not know till now that your Lady Annaly was such a methodist—no methodist shall ever darken my doors, or lighten them either, with their *new* lights. New lights! new nonsense!—for man, woman, or beast. But enough of this, and too much, Harry. Prince Harry, pull that bell a dozen times for me this minute, till they bring out my old horse."

Before it was possible that any one could have come up stairs, the impatient monarch, pointing with his crutch, added, "Run to the head of the stairs, Prince Harry dear, and call and screech to them to make no delay; and I want you out with me; so get your horse, Harry."

"But, sir—is it possible—are you able?"

"I am able, sir, possible or not," cried King Corny, starting up on his crutches. "Don't stand talking to me of possibilities, when 'tis a friend I am going to serve, and that friend as dear as yourself. Aren't you at the head of the stairs yet? Must I go and fall down them myself?"

To prevent this catastrophe, our young hero ran immediately and ordered the horses: his majesty mounted, or rather was mounted, and they proceeded to one of the prettiest farms in the Black Islands. As they rode to it, he seemed pleased by Harry's admiring, as he could, with perfect truth, the beauty of the situation.

"And the land—which you are no judge of yet, but you will—is as good as it is pretty," said King Corny, "which I am glad of for your sake, Prince Harry; I won't have you, like that *donny* English prince or king, they nicknamed *Lackland*.—No: you sha'n't lack land while I have it to let or give. I called you prince—Prince of the Black Islands—and here's your principality. Call out my prime minister, Pat Moore. I sent him across the bog to meet us at Moriarty's. Here he is, and Moriarty along with him to welcome you. Patrick, give Prince Harry possession—with sod and twig. Here's the kay from my own hand, and I give you joy. Nay, don't deny me the pleasure—I've a right to it. No wrong to my daughter, if that's what you are thinking of—a clear improvement of my own,—and she will have enough without it. Besides, her betrothed White Connal is a fat grazier, who will make her as rich as a Jew; and any way she is as generous as a princess herself. But if it pains you so, and weighs you down, as I see it does, to be under any obligation—you shall be under none in life. You shall pay me rent for it, and you shall give it up whenever you please. Well! we'll settle that between ourselves," continued his majesty; "only take possession, that's all I ask. But I hope," added he, "before we've lived a year, or whatever time it is till you arrive at years of discretion, you'll know me well enough, and love me well enough, not to be so stiff about a trifle, that's nothing between friend and friend—let alone the joke of king and prince, dear Harry."

The gift of this *principality* proved a most pernicious, nearly a fatal, gift to the young prince. The generosity, the delicacy, with which it was made, a delicacy worthy of the most polished, and little to have been expected from the barbarian mock-monarch, so touched our young hero's heart, so subjected his grateful spirit to his benefactor, that he thenceforth not only felt bound to King Corny for life, but prone to deem every thing he did or thought, wisest, fittest, best.

When he was invested with his petty principality, it was expected of him to give a dinner and a dance to the island: so he gave a dinner and a dance, and every body said he was a fine fellow, and had the spirit of a prince. "King Corny, God bless him! couldn't go astray in his choice of a favourite—long life to him and Prince Harry! and no doubt there'd be fine hunting, and shooting, and coursing continually. Well, was not it a happy thing for the islands, when Harry Ormond first set foot on them? From a boy 'twas *a*sy to see what a man he'd be. Long may he live to *reign* over us!"

The taste for vulgar praise grew by what it fed upon. Harry was in great danger of forgetting that he was too fond of flattery, and too fond of company—not the best. He excused himself to himself, by saying that companions of some kind or other he must have, and he was in a situation where good company was not to be had. Then Moriarty Carroll was gamekeeper, and Moriarty Carroll was always out hunting or shooting with him, and he was led by kind and good feelings to be more familiar and *free* with this man than he would have been with any other in the same rank of life. The poor fellow was ardently attached to him, and repeated, with delight, all the praises he heard of Master Harry, through *the Islands*. The love of popularity seized him—popularity on the lowest scale! To be popular among the unknown, unheard-of inhabitants of the Black Islands,—could this be an object to any man of common sense, any one who had lived in civilized society, and who had had any thing like the education of a gentleman? The fact, argue about it as you will—the fact was as is here stated; and let those who hear it with a disdainful smile recollect that whether in Paris, London, or the Black Islands, the mob are, in all essential points, pretty nearly the same.

It happened about this time that Betty Dunshaughlin was rummaging in her young lady's work-basket for some riband, "which she knew she might take," to dress a cap that was to be hung upon a pole as a prize, to be danced for at the *pattern*, [Footnote: *Patron*, probably—an entertainment held in honour of the *patron* saint. A festive meeting, similar to a wake in England.] to be given next Monday at Ormond Vale, by Prince Harry. Prince Harry was now standing by, giving some instructions about the ordering of the entertainment; Betty, in the mean time, pursued her own object of the riband, and as she emptied the basket in haste, threw out a book, which Harry, though not much at this time addicted to reading, snatched impatiently, eager to know what book it was: it was one he had often heard of—often intended to read some time or other, but somehow or other he had never had time: and now he was in the greatest possible hurry, for the hounds were out. But when once he had opened the book, he could not shut it: he turned over page after page, peeped at the end, the beginning, and the middle, then back to the beginning; was diverted by the humour—every Irishman loves humour; delighted with the wit—what Irishman is not? And his curiosity was so much raised by the story, his interest and sympathy so excited for the hero, that he read on, standing for a quarter of an hour, fixed in the same position, while Betty held forth unheard, about cap, supper, and *pattern*. At last he carried off the book to his own room, that he might finish it in peace; nor did he ever stop till he came to the end of the volume. The story not finishing there, and breaking off in a most interesting part, he went in search of the next volume, but that was not to be found. His impatience was ravenous.

"Mercy, Master Harry," cried Mrs. Betty, "don't eat one up! I know nothing at-all-at-all about the book, and I'm very sorry I tumbled it out of the basket. That's all there is of it to be had high or low—so don't be tormenting me any more out of my life for nothing."

But having seized upon her, he refused to let her go, and protested that he would continue to be the torment of her life, till she should find the other volume. Betty, when her memory was thus racked, put her hand to her forehead, and recollected that in *the apple-room* there was a heap of old books. Harry possessed himself of the key of the apple-room, tossed over the heap of tattered mouldy books, and at last found the precious volume. He devoured it eagerly—nor was it forgotten as soon as finished. As the chief part of the entertainment depended on the characters, it did not fade from his imagination. He believed the story to be true, for it was constructed with unparalleled ingenuity, and developed with consummate art. The character which particularly interested him was that of the hero, the more peculiarly, because he saw, or fancied that he saw, a resemblance to his own; with some differences, to be sure—but young readers readily assimilate and identify themselves with any character, the leading points of which resemble their own, and in whose general feelings they sympathize. In some instances, Harry, as he read on, said to himself, "I would not—I could not have done so and so." But upon the whole, he was charmed by the character—that of a warm-hearted, generous, imprudent young man, with little education, no literature, governed more by feeling than by principle, never upon any occasion reasoning, but keeping right by happy moral instincts; or when going wrong, very wrong, forgiven easily by the reader and by his mistress, and rewarded at the last with all that love and fortune can bestow, in consideration of his being "a very fine fellow."

Closing the book, Harry Ormond resolved to be what he admired—and, if possible, to shine forth an Irish Tom Jones. For this purpose he was not at all bound to be a moral gentleman, nor, as he conceived, to be a *gentleman* at all—not, at least, in the commencement of his career: he might become accomplished at any convenient period of his life, and become moral at the end of it, but he might begin by being an accomplished—blackguard. Blackguard is a harsh word; but what other will express the idea? Unluckily, the easiest points to be imitated in any character are not always the best; and where any latitude is given to conscience, or any precedents are allowed to the grosser passions for their justification, those are the points which are afterwards remembered and applied in practice, when the moral salvo sentences are forgotten, or are at best but of feeble countervailing effect.

At six o'clock on Monday evening the cap—the prize cap, flaming with red ribands from the top of the pole, streamed to the summer air, and delighted the upturned eyes of assembled crowds upon the green below. The dance began, and our popular hero, the delight of all the nymphs, and the envy of all the swains, danced away with one of the prettiest, "smartest," "most likely-looking" "lasses," that ever appeared at any former patron. She was a degree more refined in manner, and polished in appearance, than the fair of the Black Islands, for she came from the continent of Ireland—she had the advantage of having been sometimes at the big house at Castle Hermitage—she was the gardener's daughter— Peggy Sheridan—distinguished among her fellows by a nosegay, such as no other could have procured—distinguished more by her figure and her face than by her nosegay, and more by her air and motions, than even by her figure or her face: she stepped well, and stepped out—she danced an Irish jig to admiration, and she was not averse from admiration; village prudes, perhaps, might call her a village coquette; but let not this suggest a thought derogatory to the reputation of the lively Peggy. She was a well-behaved, well-meaning, innocent, industrious girl—a good daughter, a good sister, and more than one in the neighbourhood thought she would make a good wife. She had not only admirers, but suitors in abundance. Harry Ormond could not think of her as a wife, but he was evidently—more evidently this day than ever before—one of Peggy's admirers. His heart or his fancy was always warmly susceptible to the charms of beauty; and, never well guarded by prudence, he was now, with his head full of Tom Jones, prone to run into danger himself, and rashly ready to hurry on an innocent girl to her destruction. He was not without hopes of pleasing—what young man of nineteen or twenty is? He was not without chance of *success*, as it is called, with Peggy—what woman can be pronounced safe, who ventures to extend to a young lover the encouragement of coquettish smiles? Peggy said, "innocent smiles sure," "meaning nothing;" but they were interpreted to mean something: less would in his present dispositions have excited the hero who imitated Tom Jones to enterprise. Report says that, about this time, Harry Ormond was seen disguised in a slouched hat and *trusty* [Footnote: Great coat.], wandering about the grounds at Castle Hermitage. Some swear they saw him pretending to dig in the garden; and even under the gardener's windows, seeming to be nailing up jessamine. Some would not swear, but if they might trust their own eyes, they might verily believe, and *could*, only that they would not, take their oath to having seen him once cross the lake alone by moonlight. But without believing above half what the world says, candour obliges us to acknowledge, that there was some truth in these scandalous reports. He certainly pursued, most imprudently "pursued the chase of youth and beauty;" nor would he, we fear, have dropped the chase till Peggy was his prey, but that *fortunately*, in the full headlong career of passion, he was suddenly startled and stopped by coming in view of an obstacle that he could not overleap—a greater wrong than he had foreseen, at least a different wrong, and in a form that made his heart tremble. He reined in his passion, and stood appalled.

In the first hurry of that passion he had seen nothing, heard nothing, understood nothing, but that Peggy was pretty, and that he was in love. It happened one evening that he, with a rose yet unfaded in his hand—a rose which he had snatched from Peggy Sheridan—took the path towards Moriarty Carroll's cottage. Moriarty, seeing him from afar, came out to meet him; but when he came within sight of the rose, Moriarty's pace slackened, and turning aside, he stepped out of the path, as if to let Mr. Ormond pass.

"How now, Moriarty?" said Harry. But looking in his face, he saw the poor fellow pale as death.

"What ails you, Moriarty?"

"A pain I just took about my heart," said Moriarty, pressing both hands to his heart.

"My poor fellow!—Wait!—you'll be better just now, I hope," said Ormond, laying his hand on Moriarty's shoulder.

"I'll never be better of it, I fear," said Moriarty, withdrawing his shoulder; and giving a jealous glance at the rose, he turned his head away again.

"I'll thank your honour to go on, and leave me—I'll be better by myself. It is not to your honour, above all, that I can open my heart."

A suspicion of the truth now flashed across Ormond's mind—he was determined to know whether it was the truth or not.

"I'll not leave you, till I know what's the matter," said he.

"Then none will know that till I die," said Moriarty; adding, after a little pause, "there's no knowing what's wrong withinside of a man till he is opened."

"But alive, Moriarty, if the heart is in the case only," said Ormond, "a man can open himself to a friend."

"Ay, if he had a friend," said Moriarty. "I'll beg your honour to let me pass—I am able for it now—I am quite stout again."

"Then if you are quite stout again, I shall want you to row me across the lake."

"I am not able for that, sir," replied Moriarty, pushing past him.

"But," said Ormond, catching hold of his arm, "aren't you able or willing to carry a note for me?" As he spoke, Ormond produced the note, and let him see the direction—to Peggy Sheridan.

"Sooner stab me to the heart *again*," cried Moriarty, breaking from him.

"Sooner stab myself to the heart then," cried Ormond, tearing the note to bits. "Look, Moriarty: upon my honour, till this instant, I did not know you loved the girl—from this instant I'll think of her no more—never more will I see her, hear of her, till she be your wife."

"Wife!" repeated Moriarty, joy illuminating, but fear as instantly darkening his countenance. "How will that be now?"

"It *will* be—it shall be—as happily as honourably. Listen to me, Moriarty —as honourably now as ever. Can you think me so wicked, so base, as to say, *wife*, if—no, passion might hurry me to a rash, but of a base action I'm incapable. Upon my soul, upon the sacred honour of a gentleman—"

Moriarty sighed.

"Look!" continued Ormond, taking the rose from his breast; "this is the utmost that ever passed between us, and that was my fault: I snatched it, and thus—thus," cried he, tearing the rose to pieces, "I scatter it to the winds of heaven; and thus may all trace of past fancy and folly be blown from remembrance!"

"Amen!" said Moriarty, watching the rose-leaves for an instant, as they flew and were scattered out of sight; then, as Ormond broke the stalk to pieces, and flung it from him, he asked, with a smile, "Is the pain about your heart gone now, Moriarty?"

"No, plase your honour, not gone; but a quite different—better—but worse. So strange with me—I can't speak rightly—for the pleasure has seized me stronger than the pain."

"Lean against me, poor fellow. Oh, if I had broken such a heart!"

"Then how wrong I was when I said that word I did!" said Moriarty. "I ask your honour, your dear honour's pardon on my knees."

"For what?—For what?—You have done no wrong."

"No:—but I said wrong—very wrong—when I said stab me to the heart *again*. Oh, that word *again*—it was very ungenerous."

"Noble fellow!" said Ormond.

"Good night to your honour, kindly," said Moriarty.

"How happy I am now!" said our young hero to himself, as he walked home, "which I never should have been if I had done this wrong."

A fortunate escape!—yes: but when the escape is owing to good fortune, not to prudence—to good feeling, not to principle—there is no security for the future.

Ormond was steady to his promise toward Moriarty: to do him justice, he was more than this—he was generous, actively, perseveringly generous, in his conduct to him. With open heart, open purse, public overture, and private negotiation with the parents of Peggy Sheridan, he at last succeeded in accomplishing Moriarty's marriage.

Ormond's biographer may well be allowed to make the most of his persevering generosity on this occasion, because no other scrap of good can be found, of which to make any thing in his favour, for several months to come. Whether Tom Jones was still too much, and Lady Annaly too little, in his head—whether it was that King Corny's example and precepts were not always edifying—whether this young man had been prepared by previous errors of example and education—or whether he fell into mischief because he had nothing else to do in these Black Islands; certain it is, that from the operation of some or all of these causes conjointly, he deteriorated sadly. He took to "vagrant courses," in which the muse forbears to follow him.

CHAPTER VIII.

It is said that the Turks have a very convenient recording angel, who, without dropping a tear to blot out that which might be wished unsaid or undone, fairly shuts his eyes, and forbears to record whatever is said or done by man in three circumstances: when he is drunk, when he is in a passion, and while he is *under age*. What the *under age*, or what the years of discretion of a Turk may be, we do not at this moment recollect. We only know that our own hero is not yet twenty. Without being quite as accommodating as the Mahometan angel, we should wish to obliterate from our record some months of Ormond's existence. He felt and was ashamed of his own degradation; but, after having lost, or worse than lost, a winter of his life, it was in vain to lament; or rather, it was not enough to weep over the loss—how to repair it was the question.

Whenever Ormond returned to his better self, whenever he thought of improving, he remembered Lady Annaly; and he now recollected with shame, that he had never had the grace to answer or to thank her for her letter. He had often thought of writing, but he had put it off from day to day, and now months had passed; he wrote a sad scrawling hand, and he had always been ashamed that Lady Annaly should see it; but now the larger shame got the better of the lesser, and he determined he would write. He looked for her letter, to read it over again before he answered it —the letter was very safe, for he considered it as his greatest treasure.

On recurring to the letter, he found that she had mentioned a present of books which she intended for him: a set of books which belonged to her son, Sir Herbert Annaly, and of which she found they had duplicates in their library. She had ordered the box containing them to be sent to Annaly, and had desired her agent there to forward it; but in case any delay should occur, she begged Mr. Ormond would take the trouble to inquire for them himself. This whole affair about the books had escaped Ormond's memory: he felt himself blush all over when he read the letter again; and sent off a messenger immediately to the agent at Annaly, who had kept the box till it was inquired for. It was too heavy for the boy to carry, and he returned, saying that two men would not carry it, nor four —a slight exaggeration! A car was sent for it, and at last Harry obtained possession of the books. It was an excellent collection of what may be called the English and French classics: the French books were, at this time, quite useless to him, for he could not read French. Lady Annaly, however, sent these books on purpose to induce him to learn a language, which, if he should go into the army, as he seemed inclined to do, would be particularly useful to him. Lady Annaly observed that Mr. Ormond, wherever he might be in Ireland, would probably find even the priest of the parish a person who could assist him sufficiently in learning French; as most of the Irish parish priests were, at that time, educated at St. Omer's or Louvain.

Father Jos had been at St. Omer's, and Harry resolved to attack him with a French grammar and dictionary; but the French that Father Jos had learnt at St. Omer's was merely from ear—he could not bear the sight of a French grammar. Harry was obliged to work on by himself. He again put off writing to thank Lady Annaly, till he could tell her that he had obeyed her commands; and that he could read at least a page of Gil Blas. Before this was accomplished, he learnt from the agent that Lady Annaly was in great affliction about her son, who had broken a blood-vessel. He could not think of intruding upon her at such a time—and, in short, he put it off till it seemed too late to write at all.

Among the English books was one in many volumes, which did not seize his attention forcibly, like Tom Jones, at once, but which won upon him by degrees, drew him on against his will, and against his taste. He hated moralizing and reflections; and there was here an abundance both of reflections and morality; these he skipped over, however, and went on. The hero and the heroine too were of a stiff fashion, which did not suit his taste; yet still there was something in the book that, in spite of the terrible array of *good people*, captivated his attention. The heroine's perpetual egotism disgusted him—she was always too good and too full of herself—and she wrote dreadfully long letters. The hero's dress and manner were too splendid, too formal, for every day use: at first he detested Sir Charles Grandison, who was so different from the friends he loved in real life, or the heroes he had admired in books; just as in old portraits, we are at first struck with the costume, but soon, if the picture be really by a master hand, our attention is fixed on the expression of the features and the life of the figure.

Sensible as Ormond was of the power of humour and ridicule, he was still more susceptible, as all noble natures are, of sympathy with elevated sentiments and with generous character. The character of Sir Charles Grandison, in spite of his ceremonious bowing on the hand, touched the nobler feelings of our young hero's mind, inspired him with virtuous emulation, and made him ambitious to be a *gentleman* in the best and highest sense of the word: in short, it completely counteracted in his mind the effects of his late study. All the generous feelings which were so congenial to his own nature, and which he had seen combined in Tom Jones, as if necessarily, with the habits of an adventurer, a spendthrift, and a rake, he now saw united with high moral and religious principles, in the character of a man of virtue, as well as a man of honour; a man of cultivated understanding, and accomplished manners. In Sir Charles Grandison's history, he read that of a gentleman, who, fulfilling every duty of his station in society, eminently *useful*, respected and beloved, as brother, friend, master of a family, guardian, and head of a large estate, was admired by his own sex, and, what struck Ormond far more forcibly, was loved, passionately loved, by women—not by the low and profligate, but by the highest and most accomplished of the sex. Indeed, to him it appeared no fiction, while he was reading it; his imagination was so full of Clementina, and the whole Porretta family, that he saw them in his sleeping and waking dreams. The deep pathos so affected him, that he could scarcely recall his mind to the low concerns of life. Once, when King Corny called him to go out shooting—he found him with red eyes. Harry was ashamed to tell him the cause, lest he should laugh at him. But Corny was susceptible of the same kind of enthusiasm himself; and though he had, as he said, never been regularly what is called a *reading man*, yet the books he had read left ineffaceable traces in his memory. Fictions, if they touched him at all, struck him with all the force of reality; and he never spoke of the characters as in a book, but as if they had lived and acted. Harry was glad to find that here again, as in most things, they sympathized, and suited each other.

But Corny, if ready to give sympathy, was likewise imperious in requiring it; and Harry was often obliged to make sudden transitions from his own thoughts and employments, to those of his friend. These transitions, however difficult and provoking at the time, were useful discipline to his mind, giving him that versatility, in which persons of powerful imagination, accustomed to live in retirement, and to command their own time and occupations, are often most deficient. At this period, when our young hero was suddenly seized with a voracious appetite for books, it was trying to his patience to be frequently interrupted.

"Come, come—Harry Bookworm you are growing!—no good!—come out!" cried King Corny. "Lay down whatever you have in your hand, and come off this minute, till I show you a badger at bay, with half-a-dozen dogs."

"Yes, sir—this minute—be kind enough to wait one minute."

"It has been hiding and skulking this week from me—we have got it out of its snug hole at last. I bid them keep the dogs off till you came. Don't be waiting any longer. Come off, Harry, come! Phoo! phoo! That book will keep cold, and what is it? Oh! the last volume of Sir Charles—not worth troubling your eyes with. The badger is worth a hundred of it—not a pin's worth in that volume but worked stools and chairs, and China jugs and mugs. Oh! throw it from you. Come away."

Another time, at the very death of Clarissa, King Corny would have Harry out to see a Solan goose.

"Oh! let Clarissa die another time; come now, you that never saw a Solan goose—it looks for all the world as if it wore spectacles; Moriarty says so."

Harry was carried off to see the goose in spectacles, and was pressed into the service of King Corny for many hours afterwards, to assist in searching for its eggs. One of the Black Islands was a bare, high, pointed, desert rock, in which the sea-fowl built; and here, in the highest point of rock, this Solan goose had deposited some of her eggs, instead of leaving them in nests on the ground, as she usually does. The more dangerous it was to obtain the eggs, which the bird had hidden in this pinnacle of the rock, the more eager Corny was to have them; and he, and Ormond, and Moriarty, were at this perilous work for hours. King Corny directing and bawling, and Moriarty and Ormond with pole, net, and polehook, swinging and leaping from one ledge of rock to another, clambering, clinging, sliding, pushing, and pulling each other alternately, from hold to hold, with frightful precipices beneath them. As soon as Ormond had warmed to the business, he was delighted with the dangerous pursuit; but suddenly, just as he had laid his hand on the egg, and that King Corny shouted in triumph, Harry, leaping back across the cleft in the rock, missed his footing and fell, and must have been dashed to pieces, but for a sort of projecting landing-place, on which he was caught, where he lay for some minutes stunned. The terror of poor Corny was such that he could neither move nor look up, till Moriarty called out to him, that Master Harry was safe all to a sprained ankle. The fall, and the sprain, would not have been deemed worthy of a place in these memoirs of our hero but from their consequences—the consequences not on his body but on his mind. He could not for some weeks afterwards stir out, or take any bodily exercise; confined to the house, and forced to sit still, he was glad to read, during these long hours, to amuse himself. When he had read all the novels in the collection, which were very few, he went on to other books. Even those, which were not mere works of amusement, he found more entertaining than netting, fishing-nets, or playing backgammon with Father Jos, who was always cross when he did not win. Kind-hearted King Corny, considering always that Harry's sprain was incurred in his service, would have sat with him all day long; but this Harry would not suffer, for he knew that it was the greatest *punishment* to Corny to stay within doors a whole day. When Corny in the evening returned from his various out-of-doors occupations and amusements, Harry was glad to talk to him of what he had been reading, and to hear his odd summary reflections.

"Well, Harry, my boy, now I've told you how it has been with me all day, let's hear how you have been getting on with your bookmen:—has it been a good day with you to-day?—were you with Shakspeare—worth all the rest—all the world in him?"

Corny was no respecter of authorities in hooks; a great name went for nothing with him—it did not awe his understanding in the slightest degree.

If it were poetry, "did it touch the heart, or inflame the imagination?" If it were history, "was it true?" If it were philosophy, "was it sound reasoning?" These were the questions he asked. "No cramming any thing down his throat," he said. This daring temper of mind, though it sometimes led him wrong, was advantageous to his young friend. It wakened Ormond's powers, and prevented his taking upon trust the assertions, or the reputations, even of great writers.

The spring was now returning, and Dora was to return with spring. He looked forward to her return as to a new era in his existence: then he should live in better company, he should see something better than he had seen of late—be something better. His chief, his best occupations during this winter, had been riding, leaping, and breaking in horses: he had broken in a beautiful mare for Dora. Dora, when a child, was very fond of riding, and constantly rode out with her father. At the time when Harry Ormond's head was full of Tom Jones, Dora had always been his idea of Sophy Western, though nothing else that he could recollect in her person, mind, or manner, bore any resemblance to Sophia: and now that Tom Jones had been driven out of his head by Sir Charles Grandison; now that his taste for women was a little raised by the pictures which Richardson had left in his imagination, Dora, with equal facility, turned into his new idea of a heroine—not *his* heroine, for she was engaged to White Connal—merely a heroine in the abstract. Ormond had been warned that he was to consider Dora as a married woman—well, so he would, of course. She was to be Mrs. Connal—so much the better:—he should be quite at ease with her, and she should teach him French, and drawing, and dancing, and improve his manners. He was conscious that his manners had, since his coming to the Black Islands, rusticated sadly, and lost the little polish they had acquired at Castle Hermitage, and during one *famous* winter in Dublin. His language and dialect, he was afraid, had become somewhat vulgar; but Dora, who had been refined by her residence with her aunt, and by her dancing-master, would polish him, and set all to rights, in the most agreeable manner possible. In the course of these his speculations on his rapid improvements, and his reflections on the perfectibility of man's nature under the tuition of woman, some idea of its fallibility did cross his imagination or his memory; but then he blamed, most unjustly, his imagination for the suggestion. The danger would prove, as he would have it, to be imaginary. What danger could there be, when he knew, as he began and ended by saying to himself, that he was to consider Dora as a married woman—Mrs. Connal?

Dora's aunt, an aunt by the mother's side, a maiden aunt, who had never before been at the Black Islands, and whom Ormond had never seen, was to accompany Dora on her return to Corny Castle: our young hero had settled it in his head that this aunt must be something like Aunt Ellenor in Sir Charles Grandison; a stiff-backed, prim, precise, old-fashioned looking aunt. Never was man's astonishment more visible in his countenance than was that of Harry Ormond on the first sight of Dora's aunt. His surprise was so great as to preclude the sight of Dora herself.

There was nothing surprising in the lady, but there was, indeed, an extraordinary difference between our hero's preconceived notion, and the real person whom he now beheld. *Mademoiselle*—as Miss O'Faley was called, in honour of her French parentage and education, and in commemoration of her having at different periods spent above half her life in France, looking for an estate that could never be found— Mademoiselle was dressed in all the peculiarities of the French dress of that day; she was of that indefinable age, which the French describe by the happy phrase of "une femme *d'un certain age,*" and which Miss O'Faley happily translated, "a woman of *no particular age.*" Yet though of no particular age in the eye of politeness, to the vulgar eye she looked like what people, who knew no better, might call an elderly woman; but she was as alert and lively as a girl of fifteen: a little wrinkled, but withal in fine preservation. She wore abundance of rouge, obviously—still more obviously took superabundance of snuff—and without any obvious motive, continued to play unremittingly a pair of large black French eyes, in a manner impracticable to a mere Englishwoman, and which almost tempted the spectator to beg she would let them rest. Mademoiselle, or Miss O'Faley, was in fact half French and half Irish—born in France, she was the daughter of an officer of the Irish brigade, and of a French lady of good family. In her gestures, tones, and language, there was a striking mixture or rapid succession of French and Irish. When she spoke French, which she spoke well, and with a true Parisian accent, her voice, gestures, air, and ideas, were all French; and she looked and moved a well-born, well-bred woman: the moment she attempted to speak English, which she spoke with an inveterate brogue, her ideas, manner, air, voice, and gestures were Irish; she looked and moved a vulgar Irishwoman.

"What do you see so wonderful in Aunt O'Faley?" said Dora.

"Nothing—only—"

The sentence was never finished, and the young lady was satisfied; for she perceived that the course of his thoughts was interrupted, and all idea of her aunt effaced, the moment he turned his eyes upon herself. Dora, no longer a child and his playfellow, but grown and formed, was, and looked as if she expected to be treated as, a woman. She was exceedingly pretty, not regularly handsome, but with most brilliant eyes—there was besides a childishness in her face, and in her slight figure, which disarmed all criticism on her beauty, and which contrasted strikingly, yet as our hero thought agreeably, with her womanish airs and manner. Nothing but her external appearance could be seen this first evening—she was tired and went to bed early.

Ormond longed to see more of her, on whom so much of his happiness was to depend.

CHAPTER IX.

This was the first time Mdlle. O'Faley had ever been at Corny Castle. Hospitality, as well as gratitude, determined the King of the Black Islands to pay her honour due.

"Now Harry Ormond," said he, "I have made one capital good resolution. Here is my sister-in-law, Mdlle. O'Faley, coming to reside with me here, and has conquered her antipathy to solitude, and the Black Islands, and all from natural love and affection for my daughter Dora; for which I have a respect for her, notwithstanding all her eternal jabbering about *politesse*, and all her manifold absurdities, and infinite female vanities, of which she has a double proportion, being half French. But so was my wife, that I loved to distraction—for a wise man may do a foolish thing. Well, on all those accounts, I shall never contradict or gainsay this Mademoiselle—in all things, I shall make it my principle to give her her swing and her fling. But now observe me, Harry, I have no eye to her money—let her leave that to Dora or the cats, whichever pleases her—I am not looking to, nor squinting at, her succession. I am a great hunter, but not legacy-hunter—that is a kind of hunting I despise— and I wish every hunter of that kind may be thrown out, or thrown off, and may never be in at the death!"

Corny's tirade against legacy-hunters was highly approved of by Ormond, but as to the rest, he knew nothing about Miss O'Faley's fortune. He was now to learn that a rich relation of hers, a merchant in Dublin, whom living she had despised, because he was "neither *noble*, nor *comme il faut*," dying had lately left her a considerable sum of money: so that after having been many years in straitened circumstances, she was now quite at her ease. She had a carriage, and horses, and servants; she could indulge her taste for dress, and make a figure in a country place.

The Black Islands were, to be sure, of all places, the most unpromising for her purpose, and the first sight of Corny Castle was enough to throw her into despair.

As soon as breakfast was over, she begged her brother-in-law would show her the whole of the chateau from the top to the bottom.

With all the pleasure in life, he said, he would attend her from the attics to the cellar, and show her all the additions, improvements, and contrivances, he had made, and all he intended to make, if Heaven should lend him life to complete every thing, or any thing—there was nothing *finished*.

"Nor ever will be," said Dora, looking from her father to her aunt with a sort of ironical smile.

"Why, what has he been doing all this life?" said mademoiselle.

"Making a *shift*," said Dora: "I will show you dozens of them as we go over this house. He calls them substitutes—*I* call them make-shifts."

Ormond followed as they went over the house; and though he was sometimes amused by the smart remarks which Dora made behind backs as they went on, yet he thought she laughed too scornfully at her father's *oddities*, and he was often in pain for his good friend Corny.

His majesty was both proud and ashamed of his palace: proud of the various instances it exhibited of his taste, originality, and *daring*; ashamed of the deficiencies and want of comfort and finish.

His ready wit had excuses, reasons, or remedies, for all Mademoiselle's objections. Every alteration she proposed, he promised to get executed, and he promised impossibilities with the best faith imaginable.

"As the Frenchman answered to the Queen of France," said Corny, "if it is possible, it *shall* be done; and if it is impossible, it *must* be done."

Mademoiselle, who had expected to find her brother-in-law, as she owned, a little more difficult to manage, a little savage, and a little restive, was quite delighted with his politeness; but presuming on his complaisance, she went too far. In the course of a week, she made so many innovations, that Corny, seeing the labour and ingenuity of his life in danger of being at once destroyed, made a sudden stand.

"This is Corny Castle, Mademoiselle," said he, "and you are making it Castle Topsy-Turvy, which must not be. Stop this work; for I'll have no more architectural innovations done here—but by my own orders. Paper and paint, and furnish and finish, you may, if you will—I give you a carte-blanche; but I won't have another wall touched, or chimney pulled down: so far shalt thou go, but no farther, Mdlle. O'Faley." Mademoiselle was forced to submit, and to confine her brilliant imagination to papering, painting, and glazing.

Even in the course of these operations, King Corny became so impatient, that she was forced to get them finished surreptitiously, while he was out of the way in the mornings.

She made out who resided at every place within possible reach of morning or dinner visit: every house on the opposite banks of the lake was soon known to her, and she was current in every house. The boat was constantly rowing backwards and forwards over the lake; cars waiting or driving on the banks: in short, this summer all was gaiety at the Black Islands. Miss O'Faley was said to be a great acquisition in the neighbourhood: she was so gay, so sociable, so communicative; and she certainly, above all, knew so much of the world; she was continually receiving letters, and news, and patterns, from Dublin, and the Black Rock, and Paris. Each of which places, and all standing nearly upon the same level, made a great figure in her conversation, and in the imagination of the half or quarter gentry, with whom she consorted in this remote place. Every thing is great or small by comparison, and she was a great person in this little world. It had been the report of the country, that her niece was promised to the eldest son of Mr. Connal of Glynn; but the aunt seemed so averse to the match, and expressed this so openly, that some people began to think it would be broken off; others, who knew Cornelius O'Shane's steadiness to his *word of honour*, were convinced that Miss O'Faley would never shake King Corny, and that Dora would assuredly be Mrs. Connal. All agreed that it was a foolish promise—that he might do better for his daughter. Miss O'Shane, with her father's fortune and her aunt's, would be a great prize; besides, she was thought quite a beauty, and *remarkable elegant*.

Dora was just the thing to be the belle and coquette of the Black Islands; the alternate scorn and familiarity with which she treated her admirers, and the interest and curiosity she excited, by sometimes taking delightful pains to attract, and then capriciously repelling, *succeeded*, as Miss O'Faley observed, admirably. Harry Ormond accompanied her and her aunt on all their parties of pleasure: Miss O'Faley would never venture in the boat or across the lake without him. He was absolutely essential to their parties: he was useful in the boat; he was useful to drive the car— Miss O'Faley would not trust any body else to drive her; he was an ornament to the ball—Miss O'Faley dubbed him her beau: she undertook to polish him, and to teach him to speak French—she was astonished by the quickness with which he acquired the language, and caught the true Parisian pronunciation. She often reiterated to her niece, and to others, who repeated it to Ormond, "that it was the greatest of pities he had but three hundred a year upon earth; but that, even with that pittance, she would prefer him for a nephew to another with his thousands. Mr. Ormond was well-born, and he had some *politesse*; and a winter at Paris would make him quite another person, quite a charming young man. He would have great *success*, she could answer for it, in certain *circles* and *salons* that she could name, only it might turn his head too much." So far she said, and more she thought.

It was a million of pities that such a woman as herself, and such a girl as Dora, and such a young man as Mr. Ormond might be made, should be buried all their days in the Black Islands. Mdlle. O'Faley's heart still turned to Paris: in Paris she was determined to live—there was no *living*, what you call *living*, any where else—elsewhere people only vegetate, as somebody said. Miss O'Faley, nevertheless, was excessively fond of her niece; and how to make the love for her niece and the love for Paris coincide, was the question. She long had formed a scheme of carrying her dear niece to Paris, and marrying her there to some M. le Baron or M. le Marquis; but Dora's father would not hear of her living any where but in Ireland, or marrying any one but an Irishman. Miss O'Faley had lived long enough in Ireland to know that the usual method, in all disputes, is to split the difference: therefore she decided that her niece should marry some Irishman who would take her to Paris, and reside with her there, at least a great part of his time—the latter part of the bargain to be kept a secret from the father till the marriage should be accomplished. Harry Ormond appeared to be the very man for this purpose: he seemed to hang loosely upon the world—no family connexions seemed to have any rights over him; he had no profession—but a very small fortune. Miss O'Faley's fortune might be very convenient, and Dora's person very agreeable to him; and it was scarcely to be doubted that he would easily be persuaded to quit the Black Islands, and the British Islands, for Dora's sake. The petit menage was already quite arranged in Mdlle. O'Faley's head—even the wedding-dresses had floated in her fancy. "As to the promise given to White Connal," as she said to herself, "it would be a mercy to save her niece from such a man; for she had seen him lately, when he had called upon her in Dublin, and he was a vulgar person: his hair looked as if it had not been cut these hundred years, and he wore—any thing but what he should wear; therefore it would be a favour to her brother-in-law, for whom she had in reality a serious regard,—it would be doing him the greatest imaginable benefit, to save him from the shame of either keeping or breaking his ridiculous and savage promise." Her plan was therefore to prevent the possibility of his keeping it, by marrying her niece privately to Ormond before White Connal should return in October. When the thing was done, and could not be undone, Cornelius O'Shane, she was persuaded, would be very glad of it, for Harry Ormond was his particular favourite: he had called him his son—son-in-law was almost the same thing. Thus arguing with happy female casuistry, Mademoiselle went on with the prosecution of her plan. To the French spirit of intrigue and gallantry she joined Irish acuteness, and Irish varieties of odd resource, with the art of laying suspicion asleep by the appearance of an imprudent, blundering good nature; add to all this a degree of *confidence*, that could not have been acquired by any means but one. Thus accomplished, "rarely did she manage matters." By the very boldness and openness of her railing against the intended bridegroom, she convinced her brother-in-law that she meant nothing more than *talk*. Besides, through all her changing varieties of objections, there was one point on which she never varied—she never objected to going to Dublin, in September, to buy the wedding-clothes for Dora. This seemed to Cornelius O'Shane perfect proof, that she had no serious intention to break off or defer the match. As to the rest, he was glad to see his own Harry such a favourite: he deserved to be a favourite with every body, Cornelius thought. The young people were continually together. "So much the better," he would say: "all was above-board, and there could be no harm going forward, and no danger in life." All was above-board on Harry Ormond's part; he knew nothing of Miss O'Faley's designs, nor did he as yet feel that there was for him much *danger*. He was not thinking as a lover of Dora in particular, but he felt a new and extraordinary desire to please in general. On every fair occasion, he liked to show how well he could ride; how well he could dance; how gallant and agreeable he could be: his whole attention was now turned to the cultivation of his personal accomplishments. He succeeded: he danced, he rode to admiration—his glories of horsemanship, and sportsmanship, the birds that he shot, and the fish that he caught, and the leaps that he took, are to this hour recorded in the tradition of the inhabitants of the Black Islands. At that time, his feats of personal activity and address made him the theme of every tongue, the delight of every eye, the admiration of every woman, and the envy of every man: not only with the damsels of Peggy Sheridan's class was he *the* favourite, but with all the young ladies, the belles of the half gentry, who filled the ball-rooms; and who made the most distinguished figure in the riding, boating, walking, tea-drinking parties. To all, or any of these belles, he devoted his attention rather than to Dora, for he was upon honour; and very honourable he was, and very prudent, moreover, he thought himself. He was, at present, quite content with general admiration: there was, or there seemed, at this time, more danger for his head than his heart—more danger that his head should be turned with the foolish attentions paid him by many silly girls, than that he should be a dupe to a passion for any one of them: there was imminent danger of his becoming a mere dancing, driving, country coxcomb.

CHAPTER X.

One day when Harry Ormond was out shooting with Moriarty Carroll, Moriarty abruptly began with, "Why then, 'tis what I am thinking, Master Harry, that King Corny don't know as much of that White Connal as I do." "What do *you* know of Mr. Connal?" said Harry, loading his piece. "I didn't know you had ever seen him." "Oh! but I did, and no great sight to see. Unlike the father, old Connal, of Glynn, who is the gentleman to the last, every inch, even with the coat dropping off his back; and the son, with the best coat in Christendom, has not the look of a gentleman at-all—at-all—nor hasn't it in him, inside no more than outside." "You may be mistaken there, as you have never been withinside of him, Moriarty," said Ormond. "Oh! faith, and if I have not been withinside of him, I have heard enough from them that seen him turned inside out, hot and cold. Sure I went down there last summer, to his country, to see a shister of my own that's married in it; and lives just by Connal's Town, as the man calls that sheep farm of his." "Well, let the gentleman call his own place what he will—" "Oh! he may call it what he plases for me—I know what the country calls him; and lest your honour should not ax me, I'll tell you: they call him White Connal the negre!—Think of him that would stand browbating the butcher an hour, to bate down the farthing a pound in the price of the worst bits of the mate, which he'd bespake always for the servants; or stand, he would— I've seen him with my own eyes—higgling with the poor child with the apron round the neck, that was sent to sell him the eggs—" "Hush! Moriarty," said Ormond, who did not wish to hear any farther particulars of Mr. Connal's domestic economy: and he silenced Moriarty, by pointing to a bird. But the bird flew away, and Moriarty returned to his point. "I wouldn't be telling the like of any jantleman, but to show the nature of him. The minute after he had screwed the halfpenny out of the child, he'd throw down, may be, fifty guineas in gould, for the horse he'd fancy for his own riding: not that he rides better than the sack going to the mill, nor so well; but that he might have it to show, and say he was better mounted than any man at the fair: and the same he'd throw away more guineas than I could tell, at the head of a short-horned bull, or a long-horned bull, or some kind of a bull from England, may be, just becaase he'd think nobody else had one of the breed in all Ireland but himself." "A very good thing, at least, for the country, to improve the breed of cattle." "The country!—'Tis little the man thinks of the country that never thought of any thing but himself, since his mother sucked him." "Suckled him, you mean," said Harry. "No matter—I'm no spaker —but I know that man's character nevertheless: he is rich; but a very bad character the poor gives him up and down." "Perhaps, because he is rich." "Not at all; the poor loves the rich that helps with the kind heart. Don't we all love King Corny to the blacking of his shoes?—Oh! there's the difference!—who could like the man that's always talking of the *craturs*, and yet, to save the life of the poorest cratur that's forced to live under him, wouldn't forbear to drive, and pound, and process, for the little *con* acre, the potatoe ridge, the cow's grass, or the trifle for the woman's peck of flax, was she dying, and sell the woman's last blanket? —White Connal is a hard man, and takes all to the uttermost farthing the law allows." "Well, even so, I suppose the law does not allow him more than his due," said Ormond. "Oh! begging your pardon, Master Harry," said Moriarty, "that's becaase you are not a lawyer." "And are you?" said Harry.

"Only as we all are through the country. And now I'll only just tell you, Master Harry, how this White Connal sarved my shister's husband, who was an under-tenant to him:—see, the case was this—" "Oh! don't tell me a long case, for pity's sake. I am no lawyer—I shall not understand a word of it." "But then, sir, through the whole consarning White Connal, what I'm thinking of, Master Harry," said Moriarty, "is, I'm grieving that a daughter of our dear King Corny, and such a pretty likely girl as Miss Dora—" "Say no more, Moriarty, for there's a partridge." "Oh! is it so with you?" thought Moriarty—"that's just what I wanted to know—and I'll keep your secret: I don't forget Peggy Sheridan—and his goodness."

Moriarty said not a word more about White Connal, or Miss Dora; and he and Harry shot a great many birds this day.

It is astonishing how quickly, and how justly, the lower class of people in Ireland discover and appreciate the characters of their superiors, especially of the class just above them in rank.

Ormond hoped that Moriarty had been prejudiced in his account of White Connal, and that private feelings had induced him to exaggerate. Harry was persuaded of this, because Cornelius O'Shane had spoken to him of Connal, and had never represented him to be a *hard* man. In fact, O'Shane did not know him. White Connal had a property in a distant county, where he resided, and only came from time to time to see his father. O'Shane had then wondered to see the son grown so unlike the father; and he attributed the difference to White Connal's having turned grazier. The having derogated from the dignity of an idle gentleman, and having turned grazier was his chief fault in King Corny's eyes: so that the only point in Connal's character and conduct, for which he deserved esteem, was that for which his intended father-in-law despised him. Connal had early been taught by his father's example, who was an idle, decayed, good gentleman, of the old Irish stock, that genealogies and old maps of estates in other people's possessions, do not gain quite so much respect in this world as solid wealth. The son was determined, therefore, to get money; but in his horror of his father's indolence and poverty, he ran into a contrary extreme—he became not only industrious, but rapacious.

In going lately to Dublin to settle with a sales master, he had called on Dora at her aunt's in Dublin, and he had been "greatly struck," as he said, "with Miss O'Shane; she was as fine a girl as any in Ireland—turn out who they could against her; all her *points* good. But, better than beauty, she would be no contemptible fortune: with her aunt's assistance, she would cut up well; she was certain of all her father's Black Islands— fine improvable land, if well managed."

These considerations had their full effect. Connal, knowing that the young lady was his destined bride, had begun by taking the matter coolly, and resolving to wait for the properest time to wed; yet the sight of Dora's charms had so wrought upon him, that he was now impatient to conclude the marriage immediately. Directly after seeing Dora in Dublin, he had gone home and "put things in order and in train to bear his absence," while he should pay a visit to the Black Islands. Business, which must always be considered before pleasure, had detained him at home longer than he had foreseen: but now certain rumours he heard of gay doings in the Black Islands, and a letter from his father, advising him not to delay longer paying his respects at Corny Castle, determined him to set out. He wrote to Mr. O'Shane to announce his intention, and begged to have the answer directed to his father's at Glynn.

One morning as Miss O'Faley, Mr. O'Shane, and Ormond, were at breakfast, Dora, who was usually late, not having yet appeared, Miss O'Faley saw a little boy running across the fields towards the house. "That boy runs as if he was bringing news," said she.

"So he has a right to do," said Corny: "if I don't mistake that's the post; that is, it is not the post, but a little *special* of my own—a messenger I sent off to *catch post*."

"To do what?" said Mademoiselle.

"Why, to catch post," said Corny. "I bid him gallop off for the life and *put across (lake* understood) to the next post town, which is Ballynaslugger, and to put in the letters that were too late here at that office there; and to bring back whatever he found, with no delay—but gallop off for the bare life."

This was an operation which the boy performed, whenever requisite, at the imminent hazard of his neck every time, to say nothing of his chance of drowning.

"Well, Catch-post, my little rascal," said King Corny, "what have you for us the day?"

"I got nothing at all, only a wetting for myself, plase your honour, and one bit of a note for your honour, which I have here for you as dry as the bone in my breast."

He produced the bit of a note, which, King Corny's hands being at that time too full of the eggs and the kettle to receive graciously, was laid down on the corner of the table, from which it fell, and Miss O'Faley picking it up, and holding it by one corner, exclaimed, "Is this what you call dry as a bone, in this country? And mighty clean, too—faugh! When will this entire nation leave off chewing tobacco, I wonder! This is what you style clean, too, in this country?"

"Why, then," said the boy, looking close at the letter, "I thought it was clane enough when I got it—and give it—but 'tis not so clane now, sure enough; this corner—whatever come over it—would it be the snuff, my lady?"

The mark of Miss O'Faley's thumb was so visible, and the snuff so palpable, and the effort to brush it from the wet paper so disastrous, that Miss O'Faley let the matter rest where it was. King Corny put silver into the boy's hand, bidding him not be too much of a rogue; the boy, smiling furtively, twitched the hair on his forehead, bobbed his head in sign of thanks, and drawing, not shutting, the door after him, disappeared.

"As sure as I'm Cornelius O'Shane, this is White Connal *in propria persona*," said he, opening the note.

"Mon Dieu! Bon Dieu! Ah, Dieu!" cried Mdlle. O'Faley.

"Hush! Whisht!" cried the father—"here's Dora coming." Dora came in. "Any letter for me?" "Ay, darling, one for *you*."

"Oh, give it me! I'm always in a desperate hurry for my letters: where is it?"

"No—you need not hold out your pretty hand; the letter is *for you*, but not to you," said King Corny; "and now you know—ay, now you guess—my quick little blusher, who 'tis from."

"I guess? not I, indeed—not worth my guessing," cried Dora, throwing herself sideways into a chair. "My tea, if you please, aunt." Then, taking the cup, without adverting to Harry, who handed it to her, she began stirring the tea, as if it and all things shared her scorn.

"Ma chère! mon chat!" said Mdlle. O'Faley, "you are quite right to spare yourself the trouble of guessing; for I give it you in two, I give it you in four, I give it you in eight, and you would never guess right. Figure to yourself only, that a man, who has the audacity to call himself a lover of Miss O'Shane's, could fold, could seal, could direct a letter in such a manner as this, which you here behold."

Dora, who during this speech had sat fishing for sugar in her tea-cup, raised her long eyelashes, and shot a scornful glance at the letter; but intercepting a crossing look of Ormond's, the expression of her countenance suddenly changed, and with perfect composure she observed, "A man may fold a letter badly, and be nevertheless a very good man."

"That nobody can possibly contradict," said her father; "and on all occasions 'tis a comfort to be able to say what no one can contradict."

"No well-bred person will never contradict nothing," said Miss O'Faley. "But, without contradicting you, my child." resumed Miss O'Faley, "I maintain the impossibility of his being a *gentleman* who folds a letter so."

"But if folding a letter is all a man wants of being a gentleman," said Dora, "it might be learnt, I should think; it might be taught—"

"If you were the teacher, Dora, it might, surely," said her father.

"But Heaven, I trust, will arrange that better," said mademoiselle.

"Whatever Heaven arranges must be best," said Dora.

"Heaven and your father, if you please, Dora," said her father: "put that and that together, like a dutiful daughter, as you must be."

"Must!" said Dora, angrily.

"That offensive *must* slipped out by mistake, darling; I meant only being *you*, you must be all that's dutiful and good."

"Oh!" said Dora, "that's another view of the subject."

"You have a very imperfect view of the subject, yet," said her father; "for you have both been so taken up with the manner, that you have never thought of inquiring into the matter of this letter."

"And what is the matter?" said Miss O'Faley.

"*Form!*" continued the father, addressing himself to his daughter; "*form,* I acknowledge, is one thing, and a great thing in a daughter's eyes."

Dora blushed. "But in a father's eyes substance is apt to be more."

Dora raised her cup and saucer together to her lips at this instant, so that the substance of the saucer completely hid her face from her father.

"But," said Miss O'Faley, "you have not told us yet what the man says."

"He says he will be here whenever we please."

"That's never," said Miss O'Faley: "never, I'd give for answer, if my pleasure is to be consulted."

"Luckily, there's another person's pleasure to be consulted here," said the father, keeping his eyes fixed upon his daughter.

"Another cup of tea, aunt, if you please."

"Then the sooner the better, I say," continued her father; "for when a disagreeable thing is to be done—that is, when a thing that's not quite agreeable to a young lady, such as marriage—" Dora took the cup of tea from her aunt's hand, Harry not interfering—"I say," persisted her father, "the sooner it's done and over, the better."

Dora saw that Ormond's eyes were fixed upon her: she suddenly tasted, and suddenly started back from her scalding tea; Harry involuntarily uttered some exclamation of pity; she turned, and seeing his eyes still fixed upon her, said, "Very rude, sir, to stare at any one so."

"I only thought you had scalded yourself."

"Then you only thought wrong."

"At any rate, there's no great occasion to be angry with me, Dora."

"And who is angry, pray, Mr. Ormond? What put it in your head that I was doing you the honour to be angry with you?"

"The cream! the cream!" cried Miss O'Faley.

A sudden motion, we must not say an angry motion of Dora's elbow, had at this moment overset the cream ewer; but Harry set it up again, before its contents poured on her new riding-habit.

"Thank you," said she, "thank you; but," added she, changing the places of the cream ewer and cups and saucers before her, "I'd rather manage my own affairs my own way, if you'd let me, Mr. Ormond—if you'd leave me—I can take care of myself my own way."

"I beg your pardon for saving your habit from destruction, for that is the only cause of offence that I am conscious of having given. But I leave you to your own way, as I am ordered," said he, rising from the breakfast table.

"Sparring! sparring again, you two!" said Dora's father: "but, Dora, I wonder whether you and White Connal were sparring that way when you met."

"Time enough for that, sir, after marriage," said Dora.

Our hero, who had stood leaning on the back of his chair, fearing that he had been too abrupt in what he had said, cast a lingering look at Dora, as her father spoke about White Connal, and as she replied; but there was something so unfeminine, so unamiable, so decided and bold, he thought, in the tone of her voice, as she pronounced the word *marriage*, that he then, without reluctance, and with a feeling of disgust, quitted the room, and left her "to manage her own affairs, and to take her own way."

CHAPTER XI.

Our young hero, hero-like, took a solitary walk to indulge his feelings; and as he rambled, he railed to his heart's content against Dora.

"Here all my plans of happiness and improvement are again overturned: Dora cannot improve me, can give me no motive for making myself any thing better than what I am. Polish my manners! no, when she has such rude, odious manners herself; much changed for the worse—a hundred times more agreeable when she was a child. Lost to me she is every way —no longer my playfellow—no chance of her being my friend. Her good father hoped she would be a sister to me—very sorry I should be to have such a sister: then I am to consider her as a married woman—pretty wife she will make! I am convinced she cares no more for that man she is going to marry than I do—marrying merely to be married, to manage her own affairs, and have her own way—so childish!—or marrying merely to get an establishment—so base! How women, and such young creatures, *can* bring themselves to make these venal matches—I protest Peggy Sheridan's worth a hundred of such. Moriarty may think himself a happy fellow—Suzy—Jenny, any body—only with dress and manner a little different—is full as good in reality. I question whether they'd give themselves, without liking, to any White Connal in their own rank, at the first offer, for a few sheep, or a cow, or to have their own way."

Such was the summing up of the topics of invective, which, during a two hours' walk, had come round and round continually in Ormond's indignant fancy. He went plucking off the hawthorn blossoms in his path, till at one desperate tug, that he gave to a branch which crossed his way, he opened to a bank that sloped down to the lake. At a little distance below him he saw old Sheelah sitting under a tree rocking herself backwards and forwards; while Dora stood motionless opposite to her, with her hand covering her eyes, and her head drooping. They neither of them saw Ormond, and he walked on pursuing his own path; it led close behind the hedge to the place where they were, so close, that the sounds "Willastrew! Willastrew!" from Old Sheelah, in her funereal tone, reached his ear, and then the words, "Oh, my heart's darling! so young to be a sacrifice—But what next did he say?"

Ormond's curiosity was strongly excited; but he was too honourable to listen or to equivocate with conscience: so to warn them that some one was within hearing, he began to whistle clear and strong. Both the old woman and the young lady started.

"Murder!" cried Sheelah, "it's Harry Ormond. Oh! did he overhear any thing—or all, think ye?"

"Not I," answered Ormond, leaping over the hedge directly, and standing firm before them: "I *overheard* nothing—I *heard* only your last words, Sheelah—you spoke so loud I could not help it. They are as safe with me as with yourself—but don't speak so loud another time, if you are talking secrets; and whatever you do, never suspect me of listening—I am incapable of *that*, or any other baseness."

So saying, he turned his back, and was preparing to vault over the hedge again, when he heard Dora, in a soft low voice, say, "I never suspected you, Harry, of that, or any other baseness."

"Thank you, Dora," said he, turning with some emotion, "thank you, Dora, for this first, this only kind word you've said to me since you came home."

Looking at her earnestly, as he approached nearer, he saw the traces of tears, and an air of dejection in her countenance, which turned all his anger to pity and tenderness in an instant. With a soothing tone he said, "Forgive my unseasonable reproach—I was wrong—I see you are not as much to blame as I thought you were."

"To blame!" cried Dora. "And pray how—and why—and for what did you think me to blame, sir?"

The impossibility of explanation, the impropriety of what he had said flashed suddenly on his mind; and in a few moments a rapid succession of ideas followed. "Was Dora to blame for obeying her father, for being ready to marry the man to whom her father had destined—promised her hand; and was he, Harry Ormond, the adopted child, the trusted friend of the family, to suggest to the daughter the idea of rebelling against her father's will, or disputing the propriety of his choice?"

Ormond's imagination took a rapid flight on Dora's side of the question, and he finished with the *conviction* that she was "a sacrifice, a martyr, and a miracle of perfection!" "Blame you, Dora!" cried he, "blame you! No—I admire, I esteem, I respect you. Did I say that I blamed you? I did not know what I said, or what I meant."

"And are you sure you know any better what you say or what you mean, now?" said Dora.

The altered look and tone of tartness in which this question was asked produced as sudden a change in Harry's *conviction*. He hesitatingly answered, "I am—"

"He is," said Sheelah, confidently.

"I did not ask your opinion, Sheelah: I can judge for myself," said Dora. "Your words tell me one thing, sir, and your looks another," said she, turning to Ormond; "which am I to believe, pray?"

"Oh! believe the young man any way, sure," said Sheelah; "silence speaks best for him."

"Best against him, in my opinion," said Dora.

"Dora, will you hear me?" Ormond began.

"No, sir, I will not," interrupted Dora. "What's the use of hearing or listening to a man who does not, by the confession of his own eyes, and his own tongue, know two minutes together *what* he means, or mean two minutes together the same thing? A woman might as well listen to a fool or a madman!"

"Too harsh, too severe, Dora," said he.

"Too true, too sincere, perhaps you mean."

"Since I am allowed, Dora, to speak to you as a brother—"

"Who allowed you, sir?" interrupted Dora.

"Your father, Dora."

"My father cannot, shall not! Nobody but nature can make any man my brother—nobody but myself shall allow any man to call himself my brother."

"I am sorry I presumed so far, Miss O'Shane—I was only going to offer one word of advice."

"I want no advice—I will take none from you, sir."

"You shall have none, madam, henceforward, from Harry Ormond."

"'Tis well, sir. Come away, Sheelah."

"Oh! wait, dear—Och! I am too old," said Sheelah, groaning as she rose slowly. "I'm too slow entirely for these quick passions."

"Passions!" cried Dora, growing scarlet and pale in an instant: "what do you mean by passions, Sheelah?"

"I mean *changes*," said Sheelah, "changes, dear. I am ready now—where's my stick? Thank you, Master Harry. Only I say I can't change my quarters and march so quick as you, dear."

"Well, well, lean on me," said Dora impatiently.

"Don't hurry, poor Sheelah—no necessity to hurry away from me," said Ormond, who had stood for a few moments like one transfixed. "'Tis for me to go—and I will go as fast and as far as you please, Dora, away from you and for ever."

"For ever!" said Dora: "what do you mean?"

"Away from the Black Islands? he can't mean that," said Sheelah.

"Why not?—Did not I leave Castle Hermitage at a moment's warning?"

"*Warning!* Nonsense!" cried Dora: "lean on him, Sheelah—he has frightened you; lean on him, can't you?—sure he's better than your stick. Warning!—where did you find that pretty word? Is Harry Ormond then turned footman?"

"Harry Ormond!—and a minute ago she would not let me—Miss O'Shane, I shall not forget myself again—amuse yourself with being as capricious as you please, but not at my expense; little as you think of me, I am not to be made your butt or your dupe: therefore, I must seriously beg, at once, that I may know whether you wish me to stay or to go."

"To stay, to be sure, when my father invites you. Would you expose me to his displeasure? you know he can't bear to be contradicted; and you know that he asked you to stay and live here."

"But without exposing you to any displeasure, I can," replied Ormond, "contrive—"

"Contrive nothing at all—do leave me to contrive for myself. I don't mean to say *leave* me—you take up one's words so quickly, and are so passionate, Mr. Ormond."

"If you would have me understand you, Dora, explain how you wish me to live with you."

"Lord bless me! what a fuss the man makes about living with one—one would think it was the most difficult thing in the world. Can't you live on like any body else? There's my aunt in the hedge-row walk, all alone—I must go and take care of her: I leave you to take care of Sheelah—you know you were always very good-natured when we were children."

Dora went off quick as lightning, and what to make of her, Ormond did not well know. Was it mere childishness, or affectation, or coquetry? No; the real tears, and real expression of look and word forbade each of these suppositions. One other cause for her conduct might have been suggested by a vain man. Harry Ormond was not a vain man; but a little fluttering delight was just beginning to play round his head, when Sheelah, leaning heavily on his arm as they ascended the bank, reminding him of her existence—"My poor old Sheelah!" said he, "are you not tired?"

"Not now, thanks to your arm, Master Harry, dear, that was always good to me—not now—I am not a whit tired; now I see all right again between my childer—and happy I was, these five minutes past, watching you smiling to yourself; and I don't doubt but all the world will smile on ye yet. If it was my world, it should. But I can only wish you my best wish, which I did long ago—*may you live to wonder at your own good luck!*"

Ormond looked as if he was going to ask some question that interested him much, but it ended by wondering what o'clock it was. Sheelah wondered at him for thinking what the hour was, when she was talking of Miss Dora. After a silence, which brought them to the chicken-yard door, where Sheelah was "to quit his arm," she leaned heavily again.

"The marriage—that they are all talking of in the kitchen, and every where through the country—Miss Dora's marriage with White Connal, is reprieved for the season. She axed time till she'd be seventeen—very rasonable. So it's to be in October—if we all live till those days—in the same mind. Lord, he knows—I know nothing at all about it; but I thank

100

you kindly, Master Harry, and wish you well, any way. Did you ever happen to see the bridegroom that is to be?"

"Never."

Harry longed to hear what she longed to say; but he did not deem it prudent, he did not think it honourable, to let her enter on this topic. The prudential consideration might have been conquered by curiosity; but the honourable repugnance to obtaining second-hand information, and encouraging improper confidence, prevailed. He deposited Sheelah safe on her stone bench at the chicken-yard door, and, much against her will, he left her before she had told or hinted to him all she did know—and all she did not know.

The flattering delight that played about our young hero's head had increased, was increasing, and ought to be diminished. Of this he was sensible. It should never come near his heart—of that he was determined; he would exactly follow the letter and spirit of his benefactor's commands—he would always consider Dora as a married woman; but the prospect of there being some temptation, and some struggle, was infinitely agreeable to our young hero—it would give him something to do, something to think of, something to feel.

It was much in favour of his resolution, that Dora really was not at all the kind of woman he had pictured to himself, either as amiable or charming: she was not in the least like his last patterns of heroines, or any of his approved imaginations of the *beau ideal*. But she was an exceedingly pretty girl; she was the only very pretty and tolerably accomplished girl immediately near him. A dangerous propinquity!

CHAPTER XII.

White Connal and his father—we name the son first, because his superior wealth inverting the order of nature, gave him, in his own opinion, the precedency on all occasions—White Connal and his father arrived at Corny Castle. King Corny rejoiced to see his old friend, the elder Connal; but through all the efforts that his majesty made to be more than civil to the son, the degenerate grazier, his future son-in-law, it was plain that he was only keeping his promise, and receiving such a guest as he ought to be received.

Mademoiselle decided that old Connal, the father, was quite a gentleman, for he handed her about, and in his way had some politeness towards the sex; but as for the son, her abhorrence must have burst forth in plain English, if it had not exhaled itself safely in French, in every exclamation of contempt which the language could afford. She called him *bête!* and *grand bête!* by turns, *butor! âne!* and *grand butor!*—*nigaud!* and *grand nigaud!*—pronounced him to be "Un homme qui ne dit rien—d'ailleurs un homme qui n'a pas l'air comme il faut—un homme, enfin, qui n'est pas présentable—même en fait de mari."

Dora looked unutterable things; but this was not unusual with her. Her scornful airs, and short answers, were not more decidedly rude to White Connal than to others; indeed she was rather more civil to him than to Ormond. There was nothing in her manner of keeping Connal at a distance, beyond what he, who had not much practice or skill in the language of female coquetry, might construe into maiden coyness to the acknowledged husband lover.

It seemed as if she had some secret hope, or fear, or reason, for not coming to open war: in short, as usual, she was odd, if not unintelligible. White Connal did not disturb himself at all to follow her doublings: his pleasure was not in the chase—he was sure the game was his own.

Be bold, but not too bold, White Connal!—be negligent, but not too negligent, of the destined bride. 'Tis bad, as you say, to be spoiling a *wife* before marriage; but what if she should never *be* your wife? thought some.

That was a contingency that never had occurred to White Connal. Had he not horses, and saddles, and bridles, and bits, finer than had ever been seen before in the Black Islands? And had he not thousands of sheep, and hundreds of oxen? And had he not the finest pistols, and the most famous fowling-pieces? And had he not thousands in paper, and thousands in gold; and if he lived, would he not have tens of thousands more? And had he not brought with him a plan of Connal's-town, the name by which he dignified a snug slated lodge he had upon one of his farms—an elevation of the house to be built, and of the offices that had been built?

He had so. But it happened one day, when Connal was going to ride out with Dora, that just as he mounted, her veil fluttering before his horse's eyes, startled the animal; and the awkward rider being unable to manage him, King Corny begged Harry Ormond to change horses with him, that Mr. Connal might go quietly beside Dora, "who was a bit of a coward."

Imprudent father! Harry obeyed—and the difference between the riders and the gentlemen was but too apparent. For what avails it that you have the finest horse, if another ride him better? What avails it that you have the finest saddle, if another become it better? What use to you your Wogden pistols, if another hit the mark you miss? What avails the finest fowling-piece to the worst sportsman? The thousands upon thousands to him who says but little, and says that little ill? What avail that the offices at Connal's town be finished, dog-kennel and all? or what boots it that the plan and elevation of Connal's-town be unrolled, and submitted to the fair one's inspection and remarks, if the fair disdain to inspect, and if she remark only that a cottage and love are more to her taste? White Connal put none of these questions to himself—he went on his own way. Faint heart never won fair lady. Then no doubt he was in a way to win, for his heart never quailed, his colour never changed when he saw his fair one's furtive smiles, or heard her aunt's open praises of the youth, by whom riding, dancing, shooting, speaking, or silent, he was always eclipsed. Connal of Connal's-town despised Harry Ormond of no-town —viewed him with scornful, but not with jealous eyes: idle jealousies were far from Connal's thoughts—he was intent upon the noble recreation of cock-fighting. Cock-fighting had been the taste of his boyish days, before he became a money-making man; and at every interval of business, at each intermission of the passion of avarice, when he had leisure to think of amusement, this his first idea of pleasure recurred. Since he came to Corny Castle, he had at sundry times expressed to his father his "hope in Heaven, that before they would leave the Black Islands, they should get some good *fun*, cock-fighting; for it was a poor case for a man that is not used to it, to be tied to a woman's apron-strings, twirling his thumbs all the mornings, for form's sake."

There was a strolling kind of gentleman in the Islands, a Mr. O'Tara, who was a famous cock-fighter. O'Tara came one day to dine at Corny Castle. The kindred souls found each other out, and an animated discourse across the table commenced concerning cocks. After dinner, as the bottle went round, the rival cock-fighters, warmed to enthusiasm in praise of their birds. Each relating wonders, they finished by proposing a match, laying bets and despatching messengers and hampers for their favourites. The cocks arrived, and were put in separate houses, under the care of separate feeders.

Moriarty Carroll, who was curious, and something of a sportsman, had a mind to have a peep at the cocks. Opening the door of one of the buildings hastily, he disturbed the cock, who taking fright, flew about the barn with such violence, as to tear off several of his feathers, and very much to deface his appearance. Unfortunately, at this instant, White Connal and Mr. O'Tara came by, and finding what had happened, abused Moriarty with all the vulgar eloquence which anger could supply. Ormond, who had been with Moriarty, but who had no share in the disaster, endeavoured to mitigate the fury of White Connal and apologized to Mr. O'Tara: O'Tara was satisfied!—shook hands with Ormond, and went off. But White Connal's anger lasted longer: for many reasons he disliked Ormond; and thinking from Harry's gentleness, that he might venture to insult him, returned to the charge, and becoming high and brutal in his tone, said that "Mr. Ormond had committed an ungentlemanlike action, which it was easier to apologize for than to defend." Harry took fire, and instantly was much more ready than his opponent wished to give any other satisfaction that Mr. Connal desired. Well, "Name his hour—his place." "To-morrow morning, six o'clock, in the east meadow, out of reach and sight of all," Ormond said; or he was ready at that instant, if Mr. Connal pleased: he hated, he said, to bear malice—he could not sleep upon it.

Moriarty now stepping up privately, besought Mr. Connal's "honour, for Heaven and earth's sake, to recollect, if he did not know it, what a desperate good shot Mr. Harry notoriously was always."

"What, you rascal! are you here still?" cried White Connal: "Hold your peace! How dare you speak between gentlemen?"

Moriarty begged pardon and departed. The hint he had given, however, operated immediately upon White Connal.

"This scattered-brained young Ormond," said he to himself, "desires nothing better than to fight. Very natural—he has nothing to lose in the world but his bare life: neither money, nor landed property as I have to quit, in leaving the world—unequal odds. Not worth my while to stand his shot, for the feather of a cock," concluded Connal, as he pulled to pieces one of the feathers, which had been the original cause of all the mischief.

Thus cooled, and suddenly become reasonable, he lowered his tone, declaring that he did not mean to say any thing in short that could give offence, nothing but what it was natural for any man in the heat of passion to say, and it was enough to put a man in a passion at first sight to see his favourite bird disfigured. If he had said any thing too strong, he hoped Mr. Ormond would excuse it.

Ormond knew what the heat of passion was, and was willing to make all proper allowances. White Connal made more than proper apologies; and Ormond rejoiced that the business was ended. But White Connal, conscious that he had first bullied, then quailed, and that if the story were repeated, it would tell to his disadvantage, made it his anxious request that he would say nothing to Cornelius O'Shane of what had passed between them, lest it should offend Cornelius, who he knew was so fond of Mr. Ormond. Harry eased the gentleman's mind, by promising that he would never say a word about the matter. Mr. Connal was not content till this promise was solemnly repeated. Even this, though it seemed quite to satisfy him at the time, did not afterwards relieve Connal from the uneasy consciousness he felt in Ormond's company. He could bear it only the remainder of this day. The next morning he left the Black Islands, having received letters of business, he said, which required his immediate presence at Connal's-town. Many at Corny Castle seemed willing to dispense with his further stay, but King Corny, true to his word and his character, took leave of him as his son-in-law, and only, as far as hospitality required, was ready to "speed the parting guest." At parting, White Connal drew his future father-in-law aside, and gave him a hint, that he had better look sharp after that youth he was fostering.

"Harry Ormond, do you mean?" said O'Shane.

"I do," said Connal: "but, Mr. O'Shane, don't go to mistake me, I am not jealous of the man—not capable—of such a fellow as that—a wild scatterbrains, who is not worth a sixpence scarce—I have too good an opinion of Miss Dora. But if I was in your place, her father, just for the look of the thing in the whole country, I should not like it: not that I mind what people say a potato skin; but still, if I was her father, I'd as soon have the devil an inmate and intimate in my house, muzzling in my daughter's ear behind backs."

Cornelius O'Shane stoutly stood by his young friend.

He never saw Harry Ormond *muzzling*—behind backs, especially—did not believe any such thing: all Harry said and did was always above-board, and before faces, any way. "In short," said Cornelius, "I will answer for Harry Ormond's honour with my own honour. After that, 'twould be useless to add with my life, if required—that of course; and this ought to satisfy any son-in-law, who was a gentleman—none such could glance or mean to reflect on Dora."

Connal, perceiving he had overshot himself, made protestations of his innocence of the remotest intention of glancing at, or reflecting upon, or imagining any thing but what was perfectly angelic and proper in Miss Dora—Miss O'Shane.

"Then that was all as it should be," Mr. O'Shane said, "so far: but another point he would not concede to mortal man, was he fifty times his son-in-law promised, that was, his own right to have who he pleased and *willed* to have, at his own castle, his inmate and his intimate."

"No doubt—to be sure," Connal said: "he did not mean—he only meant —he could not mean—in short, he meant nothing at all, only just to put Mr. O'Shane on his guard—that was all he meant."

"Phoo!" said Cornelius O'Shane; but checking the expression of his contempt for the man, he made an abrupt transition to Connal's horse, which had just come to the door.

"That's a handsome horse! certainly you are well mounted, Mr. Connal."

O'Shane's elision of contempt was beyond Mr. Connal's understanding or feeling.

"Well mounted! certainly I am *that*, and ever will be, while I can so well afford it," said Connal, mounting his horse; and identifying himself with the animal, he sat proudly, then bowing to the ladies, who were standing at an open window, "Good day to ye, ladies, till October, when I hope —"

But his horse, who did not seem quite satisfied of his identity with the man, would not permit him to say more, and off he went—half his hopes dispersed in empty air.

"I know I wish," said Cornelius O'Shane to himself, as he stood on the steps, looking after the man and horse, "I wish that that unlucky bowl of punch had remained for ever unmixed, at the bottom of which I found this son-in-law for my poor daughter, my innocent Dora, then unborn; but she must make the best of him for me and herself, since the fates and my word, irrevocable as the Styx, have bound me to him, the purse-proud grazier and mean man—not a remnant of a gentleman! as the father was. Oh, my poor Dora!"

As King Corny heaved a heartfelt sigh, very difficult to force from his anti-sentimental bosom, Harry Ormond, with a plate of meat in his hand, whistling to his dog to follow him, ran down the steps.

"Leave feeding that dog, and come here to me, Harry," said O'Shane, "and answer me truly such questions as I shall ask."

"*Truly*—if I answer at all," said Harry.

"Answer you must, when I ask you: every man, every gentleman, must answer in all honour for what he does."

"Certainly, answer *for* what he does," said Harry.

"*For!*—Phoo! Come, none of your tricks upon prepositions to gain time —I never knew you do the like—you'll give me a worse opinion. I'm no schoolmaster, nor you a grammarian, I hope, to be equivocating on monosyllables."

"Equivocate! I never equivocated, sir," said Harry.

"Don't begin now, then," said Cornelius: "I've enough to put me out of humour already—so answer straight, like yourself. What's this you've done to get the ill-will of White Connal, that's just gone?"

Surprised and embarrassed, Ormond answered, "I trust I have not his ill-will, sir."

"You have, sir," said O'Shane.

"Is it possible?" cried Harry, "when we shook hands; you must have misunderstood, or have been misinformed. How do you know, my dear sir?"

"I know it from the man's own lips, see! I can give you a straight answer at once. Now answer me, was there any quarrel between you? and what cause of offence did you give?"

"Excuse me, sir—those are questions which I cannot answer."

"Your blush, young man, answers me enough, and too much. Mark me, I thought I could answer for your honour with my own, and I did so."

"Thank you, sir, and you shall never have reason—"

"Don't interrupt me, young man. What reason can I have to judge of the future, but from the past? I am not an idiot to be bothered with fair words."

"Oh! sir, can you suspect?"

"I suspect nothing, Harry Ormond: I am, I thank my God, above suspicion. Listen to me. You know—whether I ever told it you before or not, I can't remember—but whether or not, you *know* as well as if you were withinside of me—that in my heart's core there's not a man alive I should have preferred for my son-in-law to the man I once thought Harry Ormond, without a penny—"

"Once thought!"

"Interrupt me again, and I'll lave you, sir. In confidence between ourselves, thinking as once I did, that I might depend on your friendship and discretion, equally with your honour, I confessed, I repented a rash promise, and let you see my regret deep enough that my son-in-law will never be what Dora deserves—I said, or let you see as much, no matter which; I am no equivocator, nor do I now unsay or retract a word. You have my secret; but remember when first I had the folly to tell it you, same time I warned you—I warned you, Harry, like the moth from the candle—I warned you in vain. In another tone I warn you now, young man, for the last time—I tell you my promise to me is sacred—she is as good as married to White Connal—fairly tied up neck and heels—and so am I, to all intents and purposes; and if I thought it were possible you could consider her, or make her by any means consider herself, in any other light, I will tell you what I would do—I would shoot myself; for one of us must fall, and I wouldn't choose it should be you, Harry. That's all."

"Oh! hear me, sir," cried Harry, seizing his arm as he turned away, "kill me if you will, but hear me—I give you my word you are from beginning to end mistaken. I cannot tell you the whole—but this much believe, Dora was not the cause of quarrel."

"Then there was a quarrel. Oh, for shame! for shame!—you are not used to falsehood enough yet—you can't carry it through—why did you attempt it with *me*?"

"Sir, though I can't tell you the truth, the foolish truth, I tell you no falsehood. Dora's name, a thought of Dora, never came in question between Mr. Connal and me, upon my honour."

"Your honour!" repeated Cornelius, with a severe look—severe more in its sorrow than its anger. "O Harry Ormond! what signifies whether the name was mentioned? You know she was the thing—the cause of offence. Stop! I charge you—equivocate no more. If a lie's beneath a gentleman, an equivocation is doubly beneath a man."

CHAPTER XIII.

Harry Ormond thought it hard to bear unmerited reproach and suspicion; found it painful to endure the altered eye of his once kind and always generous, and to him always dear, friend and benefactor. But Ormond had given a solemn promise to White Connal never to mention any thing that had passed between them to O'Shane; and he could not therefore explain these circumstances of the quarrel. Conscious that he was doing right, he kept his promise to the person he hated and despised, at the hazard, at the certainty, of displeasing the man he most loved in the world; and to whom he was the most obliged. While his heart yearned with tenderness towards his adopted father, he endured the reproach of ingratitude; and while he knew he had acted perfectly honourably, he suffered under the suspicion of equivocation and breach of confidence: he bore it all; and in reward he had the conviction of his own firmness, and an experience, upon trial, of his adherence to his word of honour. The trial may seem but trivial, the promise but weak: still it was a great trial to him, and he thought the promise as sacred as if it had been about an affair of state.

It happened some days after the conversation had passed between him and O'Shane, that Cornelius met O'Tara, the gentleman who had laid the bets about the cock-fight with Connal; and chancing to ask him what had prevented the intended battle, O'Tara told all he knew of the adventure. Being a good-natured and good-humoured man, he stated the matter as playfully as possible—acknowledged that they had all been foolish and angry; but that Harry Ormond and Moriarty had at last pacified them by proper apologies. Of what had passed afterwards, of the bullying, and the challenge, and the submission, O'Tara knew nothing; but King Corny having once been put on the right scent, soon made it all out. He sent for Moriarty, and cross-questioning him, heard the whole; for Moriarty had not been sworn to secrecy, and had very good ears. When he had been turned out of the stable, he had retreated only to the harness-room, and had heard all that had passed. King Corny was delighted with Harry's spirit—and now he was Prince Harry again, and the generous, warm-hearted Cornelius went, in impatience, to seek him out, and to beg his pardon for his suspicions. He embraced him, called him son, and dear son—said he had now found out, no thanks to him, Connal's cause of complaint, and it had nothing to do with Dora.—"But why could not you say so, man?"

He had said so repeatedly.

"Well, so I suppose it is to be made out clearly to be all my fault, that was in a passion, and could not hear, understand, or believe. Well, be it so; if I was unjust, I'll make it up to you, for I'll never believe my own ears, or eyes, against you, Harry, while I live, depend upon it:—if I heard you asking her to marry you, I would believe my ears brought me the words wrong; if I saw you even leading her into the church instead of the chapel, and the priest himself warning me of it, I'd say and think, Father Jos, 'tis a mistake—a vision—or a defect of vision. In short, I love and trust you as my own soul, Harry Ormond, for I did you injustice."

This full return of kindness and confidence, besides the present delight it gave him, left a permanent and beneficial impression upon our young hero's mind. The admiration he felt for O'Shane's generous conduct, and the self-approbation he enjoyed in consequence of his own honourable firmness, had a great effect in strengthening and forming his character: it also rendered him immediately more careful in his whole behaviour towards Miss O'Shane. He was prudent till both aunt and niece felt indignant astonishment. There was some young lady with whom Harry had danced and walked, and of whom he had, without any design, spoken as a pleasing *gentle* girl. Dora recollected this praise, and joining it with his present distant behaviour toward herself, she was piqued and jealous; and then she became, what probably she would never otherwise have been, quite decided in her partiality for Harry Ormond. The proofs of this were soon so manifest, that many thought, and Miss O'Faley in particular, that Harry was grown stupid, blind, and deaf. He was not stupid, blind, or deaf—he had felt the full power of Dora's personal charms, and his vanity had been flattered by the preference which Dora showed for him. Where vanity is the ruling passion, young men are easily flattered into being in love with any pretty, perhaps with any ugly girl, who is, or who affects to be, in love with them. But Harry Ormond had more tenderness of heart than vanity: against the suggestions of his vanity he had struggled successfully; but now his heart had a hard trial. Dora's spirits were failing, her cheek growing pale, her tone of voice was quite softened; sighs would sometimes break forth—persuasive sighs!— Dora was no longer the scornful lady in rude health, but the interesting invalid—the victim going to be sacrificed. Dora's aunt talked of the necessity of *advice* for her niece's health. Great stress was laid on air and exercise, and exercise on horseback. Dora rode every day on the horse Harry Ormond broke in for her, the only horse she could now ride; and

Harry understood *its ways*, and managed it so much better than any body else; and Dora was grown a coward, so that it was quite necessary he should ride or walk beside her. Harry Ormond's tenderness of heart increased his idea of the danger. Her personal charms became infinitely more attractive to him; her defects of temper and character were forgotten and lost in his sense of pity and gratitude; and the struggle of his feelings was now violent.

One morning our young hero rose early, for he could no longer sleep, and he walked out, or, more properly, he rambled, or he strolled, or *streamed* out, and he took his way—no, his steps were irresistibly led —to his accustomed haunt by the water side, under the hawthorn bank, and there he walked and picked daisies, and threw stones into the lake, and he loitered on, still thinking of Dora and death, and of the circles in the water, and again of the victim and of the sacrifice, when suddenly he was roused from his reverie by a shrill whistle, that seemed to come from the wood above, and an instant afterwards he heard some one shouting, "Harry Ormond!—Harry Ormond!"

"Here!" answered Harry; and as the shouts were repeated he recognized the voice of O'Tara, who now came, whip in hand, followed by his dogs, running down the bank to him.

"Oh! Harry Ormond, I've brought great news with me for all at Corny Castle; but the ladies are not out of their nests, and King Corny's Lord knows how far off. Not a soul or body to be had but yourself here, by good luck, and you shall have the first of the news, and the telling of it."

"Thank you," said Ormond; "and what is the news?"

"First and foremost," said O'Tara, "you know birds of a feather flock together. White Connal, though, except for the cock-fighting, I never relished him, was mighty fond of me, and invited me down to Connal's-town, where I've been with him this week—you know that much, I conclude."

Harry owned he did not.

O'Tara wondered how he could help knowing it. "But so it was; we had a great cock-fight, and White Connal, who knew none of my *secrets* in the feeding line, was bet out and out, and angry enough he was; and then I offered to change birds with him, and beat him with his own Ginger by my superiority o' feeding, which he scoffed at, but lookup the bet."

Ormond sighed with impatience in vain—he was forced to submit, and to go through the whole detail of the cock-fight. "The end of it was, that White Connal was *worsted* by his own bird, and then mad angry was he. So, then," continued O'Tara, "to get the triumph again on his side, one way or another, was the thing. I had the advantage of him in dogs, too, for he kept no hounds—you know he is close, and hounds lead to a gentlemanlike expense; but very fine horses he had, I'll acknowledge, and, Harry Ormond, you can't but remember that one which he could not manage the day he was out riding here with Miss Dora, and you changed with him."

"I remember it well," said Ormond.

"Ay, and he has got reason to remember it now, sure enough."

"Has he had a fall?" said Ormond, stopping.

"Walk on, can't ye—keep up, and I'll tell you all regular."

"There is King Corny!" exclaimed Ormond, who just then saw him come in view.

"Come on, then," cried O'Tara, leaping over a ditch that was between them, and running up to King Corny. "Great news for you, King Corny, I've brought—your son-in-law elect, White Connal, is off."

"Off—how?"

"Out of the world clean! Poor fellow, broke his neck with that horse he could never manage—on Sunday last. I left him for dead Sunday night—found him dead Monday morning—came off straight with the news to you."

"Dead!" repeated Corny and Harry, looking at one another. "Heaven forbid!" said Corny, "that I should—"

"Heaven forbid!" repeated Harry; "but—"

"But good morning to you both, then," said O'Tara: "shake hands either way, and I'll condole or congratulate to-morrow as the case may be, with more particulars if required."

O'Tara ran off, saying he would be back again soon; but he had great business to do. "I told the father last night."

"I am no hypocrite," said Corny. "Rest to the dead and all their faults! White Connal is out of my poor Dora's way, and I am free from my accursed promise!" Then clasping his hands, "Praised be Heaven for *that*!—Heaven is too good to me!—Oh, my child! how unworthy White Connal of her!—Thank Heaven on my knees, with my whole heart, thank Heaven that I am not forced to the sacrifice!—My child, my darling Dora, she is free!—Harry Ormond, my dear boy, I'm free," cried O'Shane, embracing Harry with all the warmth of paternal affection.

Ormond returned that embrace with equal warmth, and with a strong sense of gratitude: but was his joy equal to O'Shane's? What were his feelings at this moment? They were in such confusion, such contradiction, he could scarcely tell. Before he heard of White Connal's death, at the time when he was throwing pebbles into the lake, he desired nothing so much as to be able to save Dora from being sacrificed to that odious marriage; he thought, that if he were not bound in honour to his benefactor, he should instantly make that offer of his hand and heart to Dora, which would at once restore her to health, and happiness, and fulfil the wishes of her kind, generous father. But now, when all obstacles seemed to vanish—when his rival was no more—when his benefactor declared his joy at being freed from his promise—when he was embraced as O'Shane's *son*, he did not feel joy: he was surprised to find it; but he could not. Now that he could marry Dora, now that her father expected that he should, he was not clear that he wished it himself. Quick as obstacles vanished, objections recurred: faults which he had formerly seen so strongly, which of late compassion had veiled from his view, reappeared; the softness of manner, the improvement of temper, caused by love, might be transient as passion. Then her coquetry—her frivolity. She was not that superior kind of woman which his imagination had painted, or which his judgment could approve of in a wife. How was he to explain this confusion of feeling to Corny? Leaning on his arm, he walked on towards the house. He saw Corny, smiling at his own meditations, was settling the match, and anticipating the joy to all he loved. Harry sighed, and was painfully silent.

"Shoot across like an arrow to the house," cried Corny, turning suddenly to him, and giving him a kind push—"shoot off, Harry, and bring Dora to meet me like lightning, and the poor aunt, too—'twould be cruel else! But what stops you, son of my heart?"

"Stay!" cried Corny, a sudden thought striking him, which accounted for Harry Ormond's hesitation; "Stop, Harry! You are right, and I am a fool. There is Black Connal, the twin-brother—oh, mercy!—against us still. May be Old Connal will keep me to it still—as he couldn't, no more than I could, foresee that when I promised Dora that was not then born, it would be twins—and as I said son, and surely I meant the son that would be born then—and twins is all as one as one, they say. Promise fettering still! Bad off as ever, may be," said Cornelius. His whole countenance and voice changed; he sat down on a fallen tree, and rested his hands on his knees. "What shall we do now, Harry, with Black Connal?"

"He may be a very different man from White Connal—in every respect," said Ormond.

O'Shane looked up for a moment, and then interpreting his own way, exclaimed, "That's right, Harry—that thought is like yourself, and the very thought I had myself. We must make no declarations till we have cleared the point of honour. Not the most beautiful angel that ever took woman's beautiful form—and that's the greatest temptation man can meet—could tempt my Harry Ormond from the straight path of honour!"

Harry Ormond stood at this moment abashed by praise which he did not quite deserve. "Indeed, sir," said he, "you give me too much credit." "I cannot give you too much credit; you are an honourable young man, and I understand you through and through."

That was more than Harry himself did. Corny went on talking to himself aloud, "Black Connal is abroad these great many years, ever since he was a boy—never saw him since a child that high—an officer he is in the Irish brigade now—black eyes and hair; that was why they called him Black Connal—Captain Connal now; and I heard the father say he was come to England, and there was some report of his going to be married, if I don't mistake," cried Corny, turning again to Harry, pleasure rekindling in his eye. "If that should be! there's hope for us still; but I see you are right not to yield to the hope till we are clear. My first step, in honour, no doubt, must be across the lake this minute to the father—Connal of Glynn; but the boat is on the other side. The horn is with my fishing-tackle, Harry, down yonder—run, for you can run—horn the boat, or if the horn be not there, sign to the boat with your handkerchief—bring it up here, and I will put across before ten minutes shall be over—my horse I will have down to the water's edge by the time you have got the boat up—when an honourable tough job is to be done, the sooner the better."

The horse was brought to the water's edge, the boat came across, Corny and his horse were in; and Corny, with his own hands on the oar, pushed away from land: then calling to Harry, he bid him wait on the shore *by* such an hour, and he should have the first news.

"Rest on your oars, you, while I speak to Prince Harry.

"That you may know all, Harry, sooner than I can tell you, if all be safe, or as we wish it, see, I'll hoist my neckcloth, *white*, to the top of this oar; if not, the *black* flag, or none at all, shall tell you. Say nothing till then—God bless you, boy!" Harry was glad that he had these orders, for he knew that as soon as Mademoiselle should be up, and hear of O'Tara's early visit, with the message he said he had left at the house that he brought *great news*, Mademoiselle would soon sally forth to learn what that news might be. In this conjecture Ormond was not mistaken. He soon heard her voice "Mon-Dieu!-ing" at the top of the bank: he ducked —he dived—he darted through nettles and brambles, and escaped. Seen or unseen he escaped, nor stopped his flight even when out of reach of the danger. As to trusting himself to meet Dora's eyes, "'twas what he dared not."

He hid, and wandered up and down, till near dinner-time. At last, O'Shane's boat was seen returning—but no white flag! The boat rowed nearer and nearer, and reached the spot where Harry stood motionless.

"Ay, my poor boy, I knew I'd find you so," said O'Shane, as he got ashore. "There's my hand, you have my heart—I wish I had another hand to give you—but it's all over with us, I fear. Oh! my poor Dora!—and here she is coming down the bank, and the aunt!—Oh, Dora! you have reason to hate me!"

"To hate you, sir? Impossible!" said Ormond, squeezing his hand strongly, as he felt.

"Impossible!—true—for *her* to hate, who is all love and loveliness!—impossible too for *you*, Harry Ormond, who is all goodness!"

"Bon Dieu!" cried Mademoiselle, who was now within exclamation distance. "What a *course* we have had after you, gentlemen! Ladies looking for gentlemen!—C'est inouï!—What is it all? for I am dying with curiosity."

Without answering Mademoiselle, the father, and Harry's eyes, at the same moment, were fixed on one who was some steps behind, and who looked as if dying with a softer passion. Harry made a step forward to offer his arm, but stopped short; the father offered his, in silence.

"Can nobody speak to me?—Bien poli!" said Mademoiselle.

"If you please, Miss O'Faley, ma'am," cried a hatless footman, who had run after the ladies the wrong way from the house: "if you please, ma'am, will *she* send up dinner now?"

"Oui, qu'on serve!—Yes, she will. Let her dish—by that time she is dished, we shall be in—and have satisfied our curiosity, I hope," added she, turning to her brother-in-law.

"Let us dine first," said Cornelius, "and when the cloth is removed, and the waiting-ears out of hearing, time enough to have our talk to ourselves."

"Bien singulier, ces Anglois!" muttered Mademoiselle to herself, as they proceeded to the house. "Here is a young man, and the most polite of the silent company, who may well be in some haste for his dinner; for to my knowledge, he is without his breakfast."

Harry had no appetite for dinner, but swallowed as much as Mademoiselle O'Faley desired. A remarkably silent meal it would have been, but for her happy volubility, equal to all occasions. At last came the long expected words, "Take away." When all was taken away, and all were gone, but those who, as O'Shane said, would too soon wish unheard what they were dying to hear, he drew his daughter's chair close to him, placed her so as "to save her blushes," and began his story, by relating all that O'Tara had told.

"It was a sudden death—shocking!" Mademoiselle repeated several times; but both she and Dora recovered from the shock, or from the word "shocking!" and felt the delight of Dora's being no longer a sacrifice.

After a general thanksgiving having been offered for her escape from the *butor*, Mademoiselle, in transports, was going on to say that now her niece was free to make a suitable match, and she was just turning to wonder that Harry Ormond was not that moment at her niece's feet; and Dora's eyes, raised slowly towards him and suddenly retracted, abashed and perplexed Harry indescribably; when Corny continued thus: "Dora is not free, nor am I free in honour yet, nor can I give any body freedom of tongue or heart until I know farther."

Various exclamations of surprise and sorrow interrupted him.

"Am I never, never, to be free!" cried Dora: "Oh! am not I now at liberty?"

"Hear me, my child," said her father; "I feel it as you do."

"And what is it next—Qu'est-ce que c'est—this new obstacle?—What can it be?" said Mademoiselle.

The father then stated sorrowfully, that Old Connal of Glynn would by no means relinquish the promise, but considered it equally binding for the twin born with White Connal, considering both twins as coming under the promise to his *son* that was to be born. He said he would write immediately to his son, who was now in England.

"And now tell me what kind of a person is this new pretender, this Mr. Black Connal," cried Mademoiselle.

"Of him we know nothing as yet," said O'Shane; "but I hope, in Heaven, that the man that is coming is as different from the man that's gone as black from white."

Harry heard Dora breathe quick and quicker, but she said nothing.

"Then we shall get his answer to the father's letter in eight days, I count," said Mademoiselle; "and I have great hopes we shall never be troubled with him: we shall know if he will come or not, in eight days."

"About that time," said O'Shane: "but, sister O'Faley, do not nurse my child or yourself up with deceitful hopes. There's not a man alive—not a Connal, surely, hearing what happiness he is heir to, but would come flying over post-haste. So you may expect his answer, in eight days— Dora, my darling, and God grant he may be—"

"No matter what he is, sir—I'll die before I will see him," cried Dora, rising, and bursting into tears.

"Oh, my child, you won't die!—you can't—from me, your father!" Her father threw his arms round her, and would have drawn her to him, but she turned her face from him: Harry was on the other side—her eyes met his, and her face became covered with blushes.

"Open the window, Harry!" said O'Shane, who saw the conflict; "open the window!—we all want it."

Harry opened the window, and hung out of it gasping for breath.

"She's gone—the aunt has taken her off—it's over for this fit," said O'Shane. "Oh, my child, I must go through with it! My boy, I honour as I love you—I have a great deal to say about your own affairs, Harry."

"My affairs—oh! what affairs have I? Never think of me, dear sir—"

"I will—but can't now—I am spent for this day—leave out the bottle of claret for Father Jos, and I'll get to bed—I'll see nobody, tell Father Jos —I'm gone to my room."

The next morning O'Tara came to breakfast. Every person had a different question to ask him, except Dora, who was silent.

Corny asked what kind of man Black Connal was. Mademoiselle inquired whether he was most French or English; Ormond, whether he was going to be married.

To all these questions O'Tara pleaded ignorance: except with respect to the sports of the field, he had very little curiosity or intelligence.

A ray of hope again darted across the mind of Corny. From his knowledge of the world, he thought it very probable that a young officer in the French brigade would be well contented to be heir to his brother's fortune, without encumbering himself with an Irish wife, taken from an obscure part of the country. Corny, therefore, eagerly inquired from O'Tara what became of White Connal's property. O'Tara answered, that the common cry of the country was, that all White Connal's profitable farms were leasehold property, and upon his own life. Poor Corny's hopes were thus frustrated: he had nothing left to do for some days but to pity Harry Ormond, to bear with the curiosity and impatience of

Mademoiselle, and with the froward sullenness of Dora, till some intelligence should arrive respecting the new claimant to her destined hand.

CHAPTER XIV

A few days afterwards, Sheelah, bursting into Dora's room, exclaimed, "Miss Dora! Miss Dora! for the love of God, they are coming! They're coming down the avenue, *powdering* along! Black Connal himself flaming away, with one in a gold hat, this big, galloping after, and all gold over, he is entirely!—Oh! what will become of us, Master Harry, now! Oh! it took the sight out of my eyes!—And yours as red as ferrets, dear!—Oh! the *cratur*. But come to the window and look out—nobody will mind—stretch out the body, and I'll hold ye fast, never fear!—at the turn of the big wood do you see them behind the trees, the fir dales, glittering and flaming? Do you see them at all?"

"Too plainly," said Dora, sighing; "but I did not expect he would come in such a grand style. I wonder—"

"Oh! so do I, greatly—mostly at the carriage. Never saw the like with the Connals, so grand—but the queer thing—"

"Ah! my dear Dore, un cabriolet!" cried Mademoiselle, entering in ecstacy. "Here is Monsieur de Connal for you in a French cabriolet, and a French servant riding on to advertise you and all. Oh! what are you twisting your neck, child? I will have no toss at him now—he is all the gentleman, you shall see: so let me set you all to rights while your father is receive. I would not have him see you such a horrible figure—not presentable! you look—"

"I do not care how I look—the worse the better," said Dora: "I wish to look a horrible figure to him—to Black Connal."

"Oh! put your Black Connals out of your head—that is always in your mouth: I tell you he is call M. de Connal. Now did I not hear him this minute announced by his own valet?—Monsieur de Connal presents his compliments—he beg permission to present himself—and there was I, luckily, to answer for your father in French."

"French! sure Black Connal's Irish born!" said Sheelah: "that much I know, any way."

A servant knocked at the door with King Corny's request that the ladies would come down stairs, to see, as the footman added to his master's message, to see old Mr. Connal and the French gentleman.

"There! French, I told you," said Mademoiselle, "and quite the gentleman, depend upon it, my dear—come your ways."

"No matter what he is," said Dora, "I shall not go down to see him; so you had better go by yourself, aunt."

"Not one step! Oh! that would be the height of impolitesse and disobedience—you could not do that, my dear Dore; consider, he is not a man that nobody knows, like your old butor of a White Connal. Not signify how bad you treat him—like the dog; but here is a man of a certain quality, who knows the best people in Paris, who can talk, and tell every where. Oh! in conscience, my dear Dore, I shall not suffer these airs with a man who is somebody, and—"

"If he were the king of France," cried Dora, "if he were Alexander the Great himself, I would not be forced to see the man, or marry him against my will!"

"Marry! Who talk of marry? Not come to that yet; ten to one he has no thought of you, more than politeness require."

"Oh! as to that," said Dora, "aunt, you certainly are mistaken there. What do you think he comes over to Ireland, what do you think he comes here for?"

"Hark! then," said Sheelah, "don't I hear them out of the window? Faith! there they are, walking and talking and laughing, as if there was nothing at all in it."

"Just Heavens! What a handsome uniform!" said Miss O'Faley; "and a very proper-looking man," said Sheelah.

"Well, who'd have thought Black Connal, if it's him, would ever have turned out so fine a presence of a man to look at?"

"Very cavalier, indeed, to go out to walk, without waiting to see us," said Dora.

"Oh! I will engage it was that dear father of yours hoisted him out."

"Hoisted him out! Well, aunt, you do sometimes speak the oddest English. But I do think it strange that he should be so very much at his ease. Look at him—hear him—I wonder what he is saying—and Harry Ormond!—Give me my bonnet, Sheelah—behind you, quick. Aunt, let us go out of the garden door, and meet them out walking, by accident— that is the best way—I long to see how *somebody* will look."

"Very good—now you look all life and spirit—perfectly charming! Look that manner, and I'll engage he will fall in love with you."

"He had better not, I can tell him, unless he has a particular pleasure in being refused," said Dora, with a toss of her head and neck, and at the same time a glance at her looking-glass, as she passed quickly out of the room.

Dora and her aunt walked out, and accidentally met the gentlemen in their walk. As M. de Connal approached, he gave them full leisure to form their opinions as to his personal appearance. He had the air of a foreign officer—easy, fashionable, and upon uncommonly good terms with himself—conscious, but with no vulgar consciousness, of possessing a fine figure and a good face: his was the air of a French coxcomb, who in unconstrained delight, was rather proud to display, than anxious to conceal, his perfect self-satisfaction. Interrupting his conversation only when he came within a few paces of the ladies, he advanced with an air of happy confidence and Parisian gallantry, begging that Mr. O'Shane would do him the honour and pleasure to present him. After a bow, that said nothing, to Dora, he addressed his conversation entirely to her aunt, walking beside Mademoiselle, and neither approaching nor attempting to speak to Dora; he did not advert to her in the least, and seemed scarcely to know she was present. This quite disconcerted the young lady's whole plan of proceedings—no opportunity was afforded her of showing disdain. She withdrew her arm from her aunt's, though Mademoiselle held it as fast as she could—but Dora withdrew it resolutely, and falling back a step or two, took Harry Ormond's arm, and walked with him, talking with as much unconcern, and as loudly as she could, to mark her indifference. But whether she talked or was silent, walked on with Harry Ormond, or stayed behind, whispered or laughed aloud, it seemed to make no impression, no alteration whatever in Monsieur de Connal: he went on conversing with Mademoiselle, and with her father, alternately in French and English. In English he spoke with a native Irish accent, which seemed to have been preserved from childhood; but though the brogue was strong, yet there were no vulgar expressions: he spoke good English, but generally with somewhat of French idiom. Whether this was from habit or affectation it was not easy to decide. It seemed as if the person who was speaking, thought in French, and translated it into English as he went on. The peculiarity of manner and accent—for there was French mixed with the Irish—fixed attention; and besides Dora was really curious to hear what he was saying, for he was very entertaining. Mademoiselle was in raptures while he talked of Paris and Versailles, and various people of consequence and fashion at the court. The Dauphiness!—she was then but just married—de Connal had seen all the fêtes and the fireworks— but the beautiful Dauphiness!—In answering a question of Mademoiselle's about the colour of her hair, he for the first time showed that he had taken notice of Dora. "Nearly the colour, I think, of that young lady's hair, as well as one can judge; but powder prevents the possibility of judging accurately."

Dora was vexed to see that she was considered merely *as a young lady*: she exerted herself to take a part in the conversation, but Mr. Connal never joined in conversation with her—with the most scrupulous deference he stopped short in the middle of his sentence, if she began to speak. He stood aside, shrinking into himself with the utmost care, if she was to pass; he held the boughs of the shrubs out of her way, but continued his conversation with Mademoiselle all the time. When they came in from their walk, the same sort of thing went on. "It really is very extraordinary," thought she: "he seems as if he was spell-bound—obliged by his notions of politeness to let me pass incognita."

Mademoiselle was so fully engaged, chattering away, that she did not perceive Dora's mortification. The less notice Connal took of her, the more Dora wished to attract his attention: not that she desired to please him—no, she only longed to have the pleasure of refusing him. For this purpose the offer must be made—and it was not at all clear that any offer would be made.

When the ladies went to dress before dinner, Mademoiselle, while she was presiding at Dora's toilette, expressed how much she was delighted with M. de Connal, and asked what her niece thought of him? Dora replied that indeed she did not trouble herself to think of him at all—that she thought him a monstrous coxcomb—and that she wondered what could bring so prodigiously fine a gentleman to the Black Islands.

"Ask your own sense what brought him here! or ask your own looking-glass what shall keep him here!" said Miss O'Faley. "I can tell you he thinks you very handsome already; and when he sees you dress!"

"Really! he does me honour; he did not seem as if he had even seen me, more than any of the trees in the wood, or the chairs in the room."

"Chairs!—Oh, now you fish for *complimens!* But I shall not tell you how like he thinks you, if you were mise à la Françoise, to la belle Comtesse de Barnac."

"But is not it very extraordinary, he absolutely never spoke to me," said Dora: "a very strange manner of paying his court!"

Mademoiselle assured Dora "that this was owing to M. de Connal's French habits. The young ladies in Paris passing for nothing, scarcely ever appearing in society till they are married, the gentlemen have no intercourse with them, and it would be considered as a breach of respect due to a young lady or her mother, to address much conversation to her. And you know, my dear Dore, their marriages are all make up by the father, the mother, the friends—the young people themselves never speak, never know nothing at all about each one another, till the contract is sign: in fact, the young lady is the little round what you call cipher, but has no value in société at all, till the figure of de husband come to give it the value."

"I have no notion of being a cipher," said Dora: "I am not a French young lady, Monsieur de Connal."

"Ah, but my dear Dore, consider what is de French wife! Ah! then come her great glory; then she reign over all hearts, and is in full liberté to dress, to go, to come, to do what she like, with her own carriage, her own box at de opera, and—You listen well, and I shall draw all that out for you, from M. de Connal."

Dora languidly, sullenly begged her aunt would not give herself the trouble—she had no curiosity. But nevertheless she asked several questions about la Comtesse de Barnac; and all the time saying she did not in the least care what he thought or said of her, she drew from her aunt every syllable that M. de Connal had uttered, and was secretly mortified and surprised to find he had said so little. She could not dress herself to her mind to-day, and protesting she did not care how she looked, she resigned herself into her aunt's hands. Whatever he might think, she should take care to show him at dinner that young ladies in this country were not ciphers.

At dinner, however, as before, all Dora's preconcerted airs of disdain and determination to show that she was somebody, gave way, she did not know how, before M. de Connal's easy assurance and polite indifference. His knowledge of the world, and his talents for conversation, with the variety of subjects he had flowing in from all parts of the world, gave him advantages with which there was no possibility of contending.

He talked, and carved—all life, and gaiety, and fashion: he spoke of battles, of princes, plays, operas, wine, women, cardinals, religion, politics, poetry, and turkeys stuffed with truffles—and Paris for ever!—Dash on! at every thing!—hit or miss—sure of the applause of Mademoiselle—and, as he thought, secure of the admiration of the whole company of natives, from *le beau-père*, at the foot of the table, to the boy who waited, or who did not wait, opposite to him, but who stood entranced with wonder at all that M. de Connal said, and all that he did—even to the fashion in which he stowed trusses of salad into his mouth with a fork, and talked—through it all.

And Dora, what did she think?—she thought she was very much mortified that there was room for her to say so little. The question now was not what she thought of M. de Connal, but what he thought of her. After beginning with various little mock defences, avertings of the head, and twists of the neck, of the shoulders and hips, compound motions resolvable into *mauvaise honte* and pride, as dinner proceeded, and Monsieur de Connal's *success* was undoubted, she silently gave up her resolution "not to admire."

Before the first course was over, Connal perceived that he had her eye: "Before the second is over," thought he, "I shall have her ear; and by the time we come to the dessert, I shall be in a fair way for the heart."

Though he seemed to have talked without any design, except to amuse himself and the company in general, yet in all he had said there had been a prospective view to his object. He chose his means well, and in Mademoiselle he found, at once, a happy dupe and a confederate. Without previous concert, they raised visions of Parisian glory which were to prepare the young lady's imagination for a French lover or a French husband. M. de Connal was well aware that no matter who touched her heart, if he could pique her vanity.

After dinner, when the ladies retired, old Mr. Connal began to enter upon the question of the intended union between the families—Ormond left the room, and Corny suppressed a deep sigh. M. de Connal took an early opportunity of declaring that there was no truth in the report of his going to be married in England: he confessed that such a thing had been in question—he must speak with delicacy—but the family and connexions did not suit him; he had a strong prejudice, he owned, in favour of ancient family—Irish family; he had always wished to marry an Irish woman—for that reason he had avoided opportunities that might have occurred of connecting himself, perhaps advantageously, in France; he was really ambitious of the honour of an alliance with the O'Shanes. Nothing could be more fortunate for him than the friendship which had subsisted between his father and Mr. O'Shane.—And the promise?— Relinquish it!—Oh! that, he assured Mr. O'Shane, was quite impossible, provided the young lady herself should not make a decided objection— he should abide by her decision—he could not possibly think of pressing his suit, if there should appear any repugnance: in that case, he should be infinitely mortified—he should be absolutely in despair; but he should know how to submit—cost him what it would: he should think, as a man of honour, it was his part to sacrifice his wishes, to what the young lady might conceive to be for her happiness.

He added a profusion of compliments on the young lady's charms, with a declaration of the effect they had already produced on his heart.

This was all said with a sort of nonchalance, which Corny did not at all like. But Mademoiselle, who was summoned to Corny's private council, gave it as her opinion, that M. de Connal was already quite in love— quite as much as a French husband ever was. She was glad that her brother-in-law was bound by his promise to a gentleman who would really be a proper husband for her niece. Mademoiselle, in short, saw every thing *couleur de rose*; and she urged, that, since M. de Connal had come to Ireland for the express purpose of forwarding his present suit, he ought to be invited to stay at Corny Castle, that he might endeavour to make himself acceptable to Dora.

To this Corny acceded. He left Mademoiselle to make the invitation; for, he said, she understood French politeness, and *all that*, better than he did. The invitation was made and accepted, with all due expressions of infinite delight.

"Well, my dear Harry Ormond," said Corny, the first moment he had an opportunity of speaking to Harry in private, "what do you think of this man?"

"What Miss O'Shane thinks of him is the question," said Harry, with some embarrassment.

"That's true—it was too hard to ask you. But I'll tell you what I think: between ourselves, Black Connal is better than White, inasmuch as a puppy is better than a brute. We shall see what Dora will say or think soon—the aunt is over head and ears already: women are mighty apt to be taken, one way or other, with a bit of a coxcomb. Vanity—vanity! but still I know—I suspect, Dora has a heart: from me, I hope, she has a right to a heart. But I will say no more till I see which way the heart turns and *settles*, after all the little tremblings and variations: when it points steady, I shall know how to steer my course. I have a scheme in my head, but I won't mention it to you, Harry, because it might end in disappointment: so go off to bed and to sleep, if you can; you have had a hard day to go through, my poor honourable Harry."

And poor honourable Harry had many hard days to go through. He had now to see how Dora's mind was gradually worked upon, not by a new passion, for Mr. Connal never inspired or endeavoured to inspire passion, but by her own and her aunt's vanity. Mademoiselle with constant importunity assailed her: and though Dora saw that her aunt's only wish was to settle in Paris, and to live in a fine hotel; and though Dora was persuaded, that for this, her aunt would without scruple sacrifice her happiness and that of Harry Ormond; yet she was so dazzled by the splendid representation of a Parisian life, as not to see very distinctly what object she had herself in view. Connal's flattery, too, though it had scarcely any pretence to the tone of truth or passion, yet contrasting with his previous indifference, gratified her. She was sensible that he was not attached to her as Harry Ormond was, but she flattered herself that she should quite turn his head in time. She tried all her power of charming for this purpose, at first chiefly with the intention of exciting Harry's jealousy, and forcing him to break his honourable resolution. Harry continued her first object for some little time, but soon the idea of piquing him was merely an excuse for coquetry. She imagined that she could recede or advance with her new admirer, just as she thought proper; but she was mistaken: she had now to deal with a man practised in the game: he might let her appear to win, but not for nothing would he let her win a single move; yet he seemed to play so carelessly, as not in the least to alarm, or put her on her guard. The bystanders began to guess how the game would terminate: it was a game in which the whole happiness of Dora's life was at stake, to say nothing of his own, and Ormond could not look on without anxiety—and, notwithstanding his outwardly calm appearance, without strong conflicting emotions. "If," said he to himself, "I were convinced that this man would make her happy, I think I could be happy myself." But the more he saw of Connal, the less he thought him likely to make Dora happy; unless, indeed, her vanity could quite extinguish her sensibility: then, Monsieur de Connal would be just the husband to suit her.

Connal was exactly what he appeared to be—a gay young officer, who had made his own way up in the world—a petit-maître, who had really lived in good company at Paris, and had made himself agreeable to women of rank and fortune. He might, perhaps, as he said, with his figure, and fashion, and connexions, have made his fortune in Paris by marriage, had he had time to look about him—but a sudden run of ill-fortune at play had obliged him to quit Paris for a season. It was necessary to make his fortune by marriage in England or Ireland, and as expeditiously as possible. In this situation, Dora, with her own and her aunt's property, was, as he considered it, an offer not to be rashly slighted; nor yet was he very eager about the matter—if he failed here, he should succeed elsewhere. This real indifference gave him advantages with Dora, which a man of feeling would perhaps never have obtained, or never have kept. Her father, though he believed in the mutable nature of woman, yet could scarcely think that his daughter Dora was of this nature. He could scarcely conceive that her passion for Harry Ormond—

that passion which had, but a short time before, certainly affected her spirits, and put him in fear for her health—could have been conquered by a coxcomb, who cared very little whether he conquered or not.

How was this possible? Good Corny invented many solutions of the problem: he fancied one hour that his daughter was sacrificing herself from duty to him, or complaisance to her aunt; the next hour, he settled, and with more probability, that she was piqued by Harry Ormond's not showing more passion. King Corny was resolved to know distinctly how the matter really was: he therefore summoned his daughter and aunt into his presence, and the person he sent to summon them was Harry Ormond.

"Come back with them, yourself, Harry—I shall want you also."

Harry returned with both the ladies. By the countenance of Cornelius O'Shane, they all three augured that he had something of importance to say, and they stood in anxious expectation. He went to the point immediately.

"Dora, I know it is the custom on some occasions for ladies never to tell the truth—therefore I shall not ask any question that I think will put your truth to the test. I shall tell you my mind, and leave you to judge for yourself. Take as long or as short a time to know your own mind as you please—only know it clearly, and send me your answer by your aunt. All I beg is, that when the answer shall be delivered to me, this young man may be by. Don't interrupt me, Dora—I have a high opinion of him," said he, keeping his eye upon Dora's face.

"I have a great esteem, affection, love for him:" he pronounced the words deliberately, that he might see the effect on Dora; but her countenance was as undecided as her mind—no judgment could be formed from its changes. "I wish Harry Ormond," continued he, "to know all my conduct: he knows that, long ago, I made a foolish promise to give my daughter to a man I knew nothing about."

Mademoiselle was going to interrupt, but Cornelius O'Shane silenced her. "Mademoiselle—sister O'Faley, I will do the best I can to repair that folly—and to leave you at liberty, Dora, to follow the choice of your heart."

He paused, and again studied her countenance, which was agitated.

"Her choice is your choice—her father's choice is always the choice of the good daughter," said Mademoiselle.

"I believe she is a good daughter, and that is the particular reason I am determined to be as good a father as I can to her."

Dora wept in silence—and Mademoiselle, a good deal alarmed, wanted to remove Harry Ormond out of the young lady's sight: she requested him to go to her apartment for a smelling-bottle for her niece.

"No, no," said King Corny, "go yourself, sister O'Faley, if you like it, but I'll not let Harry Ormond stir—he is my witness present. Dora is not fainting—if you would only let her alone, she would do well. Dora, listen to me: if you don't really prefer this Black Connal for a husband to all other men, as you are to swear at the altar you do, if you marry him—"

Dora was strongly affected by the solemn manner of her father's appeal to her.

"If," continued her father, "you are not quite clear, my dear child, that you prefer him to other men, do not marry him. I have a notion I can bring you off without breaking my word: listen. I would willingly give half my fortune to secure your happiness, my darling. If I do not mistake him, Mr. Connal would, for a less sum, give me back my promise, and give you up altogether, my dear Dora."

Dora's tears stopped, Mademoiselle's exclamations poured forth, and they both declared they were certain that Mr. Connal would not, for any thing upon earth that could be offered to him, give up the match.

Corny said he was willing to make the trial, if they pleased. Mademoiselle seemed to hesitate; but Dora eagerly accepted the proposal, thanked her father for his kindness, and declared that she should be happy to have, and to abide by, this test of Mr. Connal's love. If he were so base as to prefer half her fortune to herself, she should, she said, think herself happy in having escaped from such a traitor.

Dora's pride was wakened, and she now spoke in a high tone: she always, even in the midst of her weaknesses, had an ambition to show spirit.

"I will put the test to him myself, within this hour," said Corny; "and before you go to bed this night, when the clock strikes twelve, all three of you be on this spot, and I will give you his answer. But stay, Harry Ormond, we have not had your opinion—would you advise me to make this trial?"

"Certainly, sir."

"But if I should lose half of Dora's fortune?"

"You would think it well bestowed, I am sure, sir, in securing her from an unhappy marriage."

"But then she might not, perhaps, so easily find another lover with half a fortune—that might make a difference, hey, Harry?"

"Impossible, I should think, sir, that it could make the least difference in the affection of any one who really—who was really worthy of Miss O'Shane."

The agitation into which Harry Ormond was thrown, flattered and touched Dora for the moment; her aunt hurried her out of the room.

Cornelius O'Shane rang, and inquired where Mr. Connal was? In his own apartment, writing letters, his servant believed. O'Shane sent to beg to see him, as soon as he was at leisure.

At twelve o'clock Dora, Mademoiselle, and Ormond, were all in the study, punctually as the clock was striking.

"Well, what is M. de Connal's answer?" cried Mademoiselle.

"If he hesitate, my dear Dore, give him up dat minute."

"Undoubtedly," said Dora: "I have too much spirit to do otherwise. What's his answer, father?"

"His answer, my dear child, has proved that you knew him better than I did—he scorns the offer of half your fortune—for your whole fortune he would not give you up."

"I thought so," cried Dora, triumphantly.

"I thought so," echoed Mademoiselle.

"I did him injustice," cried Ormond. "I am glad that M. de Connal has proved himself worthy of you, Dora, since you really approve of him— you have not a friend in the world, next to your father, who wishes your happiness more sincerely than I do."

He hurried out of the room.

"There's a heart for you!" said Corny.

"Not for me," said Mademoiselle: "he has no passion in him."

"I give you joy, Dora," said her father. "I own I misjudged the man—on account of his being a bit of a coxcomb. But if you can put up with that, so will I—when I have done a man injustice, I will make it up to him every way I can. Now let him, he has my consent, be as great a coxcomb as ever wore red heels. I'll put up with it all, since he really loves my child. I did not think he would have stood the test."

Nor would he, had not he been properly prepared by Mademoiselle—she had, before M. de Connal went to Corny, sent him a little billet, which told him the test that would be proposed, and thus prevented all possibility of her dear niece's being disappointed in her lover or her husband.

CHAPTER XV.

Vain of showing that he was not in the slightest degree jealous, Connal talked to Ormond in the freest manner imaginable, touching with indifference even on the very subject which Ormond, from feelings of delicacy and honour, had anxiously avoided. Connal seemed to be perfectly aware how matters had stood before his arrival between Dora and our young hero. "It was all very well," he said, "quite natural—in the common course of things—impossible it should have been otherwise. A young woman, who saw no one else, must inevitably fall in love with the first agreeable young man who made love to her, or who did not make love to her—it was quite equal to him which. He had heard wonders from his father-in-law elect on that last topic, and he was willing to oblige him, or any other gentleman or lady, by believing miracles."

Ormond, extremely embarrassed by the want of delicacy and feeling with which this polished coxcomb spoke, had, however, sufficient presence of mind to avoid, either by word or look, making any particular application of what was said.

"You have really prodigious presence of mind, and *discretion*, and *tact*, for a young man who has, I presume, had so little practice in these affairs," said Connal; "but don't constrain yourself longer. I speak frankly to take off all embarrassment on your part—you see there exists none on mine—never, for a moment: no, how can it possibly signify," continued he, "to any man of common sense, who, or what a woman liked before she saw him? You don't think a man, who has seen any thing of the world, would trouble himself to inquire whether he was, or was not, the first love of the woman he is going to marry. To *marry*—

observe the emphasis—distinguish—distinguish, and seriously let us calculate."

Ormond gave no interruption to his calculations, and the petit-maître, in a tone of philosophic fatuity, asked, "Of the numbers of your English or Irish wives—all excellent—how many, I pray you, do you calculate are now married to the man they first, *fell in love with*, as they call it? My good sir, not five per cent., depend on it. The thing is morally impossible, unless girls are married out of a convent, as with us in France, and very difficult even then; and after all, what are the French husbands the better for it? I understand English husbands think themselves best off. I don't pretend to judge; but they seem to prefer what they call domestic happiness to the French *esprit de société*. Still, this may be prejudice of education—of country: each nation has its taste. Every thing is for the best in this world, for people who know how to make the best of it. You would not think, to look at me, I was so philosophic: but even in the midst of my military career I have thought—thought profoundly. Every body in France *thinks* now," said M. de Connal, taking a pinch of snuff with a very pensive air.

"*Every body* in France *thinks* now!" repeated Ormond.

"Every man of a certain rank, that is to say."

"That is to say, of your rank," said Ormond.

"Nay, I don't give myself as an example; but—you may judge—I own I am surprised to find myself philosophizing here in the Black Islands—but one philosophizes every where." "And you would have more time for it here, I should suppose, than in Paris?"

"Time, my dear sir—no such thing! Time is merely in idea; but *Tais-toi Jean Jacques! Tais-toi Condillac!* To resume the chain of our reasoning —love and marriage—I say it all comes to much the same thing in France and in these countries—after all. There is more gallantry, perhaps, before marriage in England, more after marriage in France— which has the better bargain? I don't pretend to decide. Philosophic doubt for me, especially in cases where 'tis not worth while to determine; but I see I astonish you, Mr. Ormond."

"You do, indeed," said Ormond, ingenuously.

"I give you joy—I envy you," said M. de Connal, sighing.

"After a certain age, if one lives in the world, one can't be astonished—that's a lost pleasure."

"To me who have lived out of the world it is a pleasure, or rather a sensation—I am not sure whether I should call it a pleasure—that is not likely to be soon exhausted," said Ormond. "A sensation! and you are not sure whether you should call it a pleasure. Do you know you've a genius for metaphysics?"

"I!" exclaimed Ormond.

"Ah! now I have astonished you again. Good! whether pleasurable or not, trust me, nothing is so improving to a young man as to be well astonished. Astonishment I conceive to be a sort of mental electric shock—electric fire; it opens at once and enlightens the understanding: and really you have an understanding so well worth enlightening—I do assure you, that your natural acuteness will, whenever and wherever you appear, make you *un homme marquant.*"

"Oh! spare me, Mr. Connal," said Ormond. "I am not used to French compliment."

"No, upon my honour, without compliment, in all English *bonhommie,*" (laying his hand upon his heart)—"upon the honour of a gentleman, your remarks have sometimes perfectly astonished me."

"Really!" said Ormond; "but I thought you had lived so much in the world, you could not be astonished."

"I thought so, I own," said Connal; "but it was reserved for M. Ormond to convince me of my mistake, to revive an old pleasure—more difficult still than to invent a new one! In recompense I hope I give you some new ideas—just throw out opinions for you. Accept—reject—reject now—accept an hour, a year hence, perhaps—just as it strikes—merely materials for thinking, I give you."

"Thank you," said Ormond; "and be assured they are not lost upon me. You have given me a great deal to think of seriously."

"*Seriously!*—no; that's your fault, your national fault. Permit me: what you want chiefly in conversation—in every thing, is a certain degree of —of—you have no English word—*lightness.*"

"*Légèreté*, perhaps you mean," said Ormond.

"Precisely. I forgot you understood French so well. *Légèreté*—untranslatable!—You seize my idea."

He left Ormond, as he fancied, in admiration of the man who, in his own opinion, possessed the whole theory and practice of the art of pleasing, and the science of happiness.

M. de Connal's conversation and example might have produced a great effect on the mind of a youth of Ormond's strong passions, lively imagination, and total ignorance of the world, if he had met this brilliant officer in different society. Had he seen Connal only as a man shining in company, or considered him merely as a companion, he must have been dazzled by his fashion, charmed by his gaiety, and *imposed* upon by his decisive tone.

Had such a vision lighted on the Black Islands, and appeared to our hero suddenly, in any other circumstances but those in which it did appear, it might have struck and overawed him; and without inquiring "whether from heaven or hell," he might have followed wherever it led or pointed the way. But in the form of a triumphant rival—without delicacy, without feeling, neither deserving nor loving the woman he had won—not likely to make Dora happy—almost certain to make her father miserable—there was no danger that Black Connal could ever obtain any ascendancy over Ormond; on the contrary, Connal was useful in forming our hero's character. The electric shock of astonishment did operate in a salutary manner in opening Harry's understanding: the materials for thinking were not thrown away: he *did* think—even in the Black Islands; and in judging of Connal's character, he made continual progress in forming his own: he had motive for exercising his judgment—he was anxious to study the man's character on Dora's account.

Seeing his unpolished friend, old Corny, and this finished young man of the world, in daily contrast, Ormond had occasion to compare the real and the factitious, both in matter and manner: he distinguished, and felt often acutely, the difference between that politeness of the heart, which respects and sympathizes with the feelings of others, and that conventional politeness, which is shown merely to gratify the vanity of him by whom it is displayed. In the same way he soon discriminated, in conversation, between Corny's power of original thinking, and M. de Connal's knack of throwing old thoughts into new words; between the power of answering an argument, and the art of evading it by a repartee. But it was chiefly in comparing different ideas of happiness and modes of life, that our young hero's mind was enlarged by Connal's conversation—whilst the comparison he secretly made between this polished gentleman's principles and his own, was always more satisfactory to his pride of virtue, than Connal's vanity could have conceived to be possible.

One day some conversation passed between Connal and *his father-in-law elect*, as he now always called him, upon his future plans of life.

Good Corny said he did not know how to hope that, during the few years he had to live, Connal would not think of taking his daughter from him to Paris, as, from some words that had dropped from Mademoiselle, he had reason to fear.

"No," Connal said, "he had formed no such cruel intention: the Irish half of Mademoiselle must have blundered on this occasion. He would do his utmost, if he could with honour, to retire from the service; unless the service imperiously called him away, he should settle in Ireland: he should make it a point even, independently of his duty to his own father, not to take Miss O'Shane from her country and her friends."

The father, open-hearted and generous himself, was fond to believe what he wished: and confiding in these promises, the old man forgave all that he did not otherwise approve of in his future son-in-law, and thanked him almost with tears in his eyes; still repeating, as his natural penetration remonstrated against his credulity, "But I could hardly have believed this from such a young man as you, Captain Connal. Indeed, how you could ever bring yourself to think of settling in retirement is wonderful to me; but love does mighty things, brings about great changes."

French commonplaces of sentiment upon love, and compliments on Dora's charms and his own sensibility, were poured out by Connal, and the father left the room satisfied.

Connal then, throwing himself back in his chair, burst out a laughing, and turning to Ormond, the only person in the room, said, "Could you have conceived this?"

"Conceived what, sir?" said Ormond.

"Conceived this King Corny's capacity for belief? What!—believe that I will settle in his Black Islands!—I!—As well believe me to be half marble, half man, like *the unfortunate* in the Black Islands of the Arabian Tales. Settle in the Black Islands!—No: could you conceive a man on earth could be found so simple as to credit such a thing?"

"Here is another man on earth who was simple enough to believe it," said Ormond, "and to give you credit for it."

"You!" cried Connal—"That's too much!—Impossible!"

"But when you said it—when I heard you promise it to Mr. O'Shane—"

"Oh, mercy!—Don't kill me with laughing!" said he, laughing affectedly: "Oh! that face of yours—there is no standing it. You heard me *promise*—and the accent on *promise*. Why, even women, now-a-days, don't lay such an emphasis on *a promise*."

"That, I suppose, depends on who gives it." said Ormond.

"Rather on who receives it," said Connal: "but look here, you who understand the doctrine of promises, tell me what a poor conscientious man must do who has two pulling him different ways?"

"A conscientious man cannot have given two diametrically opposite promises."

"*Diametrically*!—Thank you for that word—it just saves my lost conscience. Commend me always to an epithet in the last resource for giving one latitude of conscience in these nice cases—I have not given two diametrically opposite—no, I have only given four that cross one another. One to your King Corny; another to my angel, Dora; another to the dear aunt; and a fourth to my dearer self. First promise to King Corny, to settle in the Black Islands; a gratuitous promise, signifying nothing—read Burlamaqui: second promise to Mademoiselle, to go and live with her at Paris; with *her*—on the face of it absurd! a promise extorted too under fear of my life, of immediate peril of being talked to death—see Vatel on extorted promises—void: third promise to my angel, Dora, to live wherever she pleases; but that's a lover's promise, made to be broken—see Love's Calendar, or, if you prefer the bookmen's authority, I don't doubt that, under the head of promises made when a man is not in his right senses, some of those learned fellows in wigs would bring me off *sain et sauf*: but now for my fourth promise—I am a man of honour—when I make a promise intending to keep it, no man so scrupulous; all promises made to myself come under this head; and I have promised myself to live, and make my wife live, wherever I please, or not to live with her at all. This promise I shall bold sacred. Oblige me with a smile, Mr. Ormond—a smile of approbation."

"Excuse me, Mr. Connal, that is impossible—I am sincere."

"So am I, and sincerely you are too romantic. See things as they are, as a man of the world, I beseech you."

"I am not a man of the world, and I thank God for it," cried Ormond.

"Thank your God for what you please," said Connal; "but in disdaining to be a man of the world, you will not, I hope, refuse to let me think you a man of common sense."

"Think what you please of me," said Ormond, rather haughtily; "what I think of myself is the chief point with me."

"You will lose this little brusquerie of manner," said Connal, "when you have mixed more with mankind. Providentially, we are all made dependent on one another's good opinion. Even I, you see, cannot live without yours."

Whether from vanity, from the habit of wishing to charm every body in every house he entered, especially any one who made resistance; or whether he was piqued and amused with Ormond's frank and natural character, and determined to see how far he could urge him, Connal went on, though our young hero gave him no encouragement to hope that he should win his good opinion.

"Candidly," said he, "put yourself in my place for a moment: I was in England, following my own projects; I was not in love with the girl as you—well, pardon—as anybody might have been—but I was at a distance, that makes all the difference: I am sent for over by two fathers, and I am told that in consequence of my good or evil fortune in being born a twin, and of some inconceivable promise between two Irish fathers over a punch-bowl, I am to have the refusal, I should rather say the acceptance, of a very pretty girl with a very pretty fortune. Now, except just at the moment when the overture reached me, it could not have been listened to for a moment by such a man as I am."

"Insufferable coxcomb," said Ormond to himself.

"But, to answer a question, which I omitted to answer just now to my father-in-law,—what could induce me to come over and think of settling in the Black Islands? I answer—for I am determined to win your confidence by my candour—I answer in one word, *un billard*—a billiard-table. To tell you all, I confess—"

"Confess nothing, I beg, Mr. Connal, to me, that you do not wish to be known to Mr. O'Shane: I am his friend—he is my benefactor."

"You would not repeat—you are a gentleman, and a man of honour."

"I am; and as such I desire, on this occasion, not to hear what I ought neither to repeat nor to keep secret. It is my duty not to leave my benefactor in the dark as to any point."

"Oh! come—come," interrupted Connal, "we had better not take it on this serious tone, lest, if we begin to talk of duty, we should presently conceive it to be our duty to run one another through the body, which would be no pleasure."

"No pleasure," said Ormond; "but if it became a duty, I hope, on all occasions, I should be able to do whatever I thought a duty. Therefore to avoid any misunderstanding, Mr. Connal, let me beg that you will not honour me farther with your confidence. I cannot undertake to be the confidant of any one, of whom I have never professed myself to be the friend."

"Ca suffit," said Connal, lightly. "We understand one another now perfectly'—you shall in future play the part of *prince*, and not of confidant. Pardon me, I forgot your highness's pretensions;" so saying, he gaily turned on his heel, and left the room.

From this time forward little conversation passed between Mr. Connal and Ormond—little indeed between Ormond and Dora. With Mademoiselle, Ormond had long ceased to be a favourite, and even her loquacity now seldom addressed itself to him. He was in a painful situation;—he spent as much of his time as he could at the farm his friend had given him. As soon as O'Shane found that there was no truth in the report of Black Connal's intended marriage in England, that he claimed in earnest his promise of his daughter, and that Dora herself inclined to the new love, his kind heart felt for poor Harry.

Though he did not know all that had passed, yet he saw the awkwardness and difficulty of Ormond's present situation, and, whatever it might cost him to part with his young friend, with his adopted son, Corny determined not to detain him longer.

"Harry Ormond, my boy," said he to him one day, "time for you to see something of the world, also for the world to see something of you; I've kept you here for my own pleasure too long: as long as I had any hope of settling you as I wished 'twas a sufficient excuse to myself; but now I have none left—I must part with you: and so, by the blessing, God helping me to conquer my selfishness, and the yearnings of my heart towards you, I will. I mean," continued he, "to send you far from me—to banish you for your good from the Black Islands entirely. Nay, don't you interrupt me, nor say a word; for if you do, I shall be too soft to have the heart to do you justice. You know you said yourself, and I felt it for you, that it was best you should leave this. Well, I have been thinking of you ever since, and licking different projects into shape for you—listening too to every thing Connal threw out; but all he says that way is in the air —no substance, when you try to have and to hold—too full of himself, that youngster, to be a friend to another."

"There is no reason why he should be my friend, sir," said Ormond—"I do not pretend to be his; and I rejoice in not being under any obligations to him."

"Right!—and high!—just as I feel for you. After all, I approve of your own wish to go into the British service in preference to any foreign service, and you could not be of the Irish brigade—Harry."

"Indeed, sir, I infinitely prefer," said Ormond, "the service of my own country—the service in which my father—I know nothing of my father, but I have always heard him spoken of as a good officer; I hope I shall not disgrace his name. The English service for me, sir, if you please."

"Why, then, I'm glad you see things as I do, and are not run away with by uniform, and *all that*. I have lodged the needful in the bank, to purchase a commission for you, my son. Now! no more go to thank me, if you love me, Harry, than you would your own father. I've written to a friend to choose a regiment in which there'd be as little danger as possible for you."

"As little danger as possible!" repeated Harry, surprised.

"Phoo! you don't think I mean as little danger of fighting. I would not wrong you so. No—but as little danger of gambling. Not that you're inclined to it, or any thing else that's bad—but there is no knowing what company might lead the best into; and it is my duty and inclination to look as close to all these things as if for my own son."

"My kind father—no father could be kinder," cried Harry, quite overpowered.

"So then you go as soon as the commission comes—that's settled; and I hope I shall be able to bear it, Harry, old as I am. There may perhaps be a delay of a little time longer than you could wish."

"Oh! sir, as long as you wish me to stay with you—"

"Not a minute beyond what's necessary. I mention the cause of delay, that you may not think I'm dallying for my own sake. You remember General Albemarle, who came here one day last year—election time, canvassing—the general that had lost the arm."

"Perfectly, sir, I remember your answer—'I will give my interest to this *empty sleeve*.'"

"Thank you—never a word lost upon you. Well, now I have hopes that this man—this general, will take you by the hand; for he has a hand left yet, and a powerful one to serve a friend; and I've requested him to keep his eye upon you, and I have asked his advice: so we can't stir till we get it, and that will be eight days, or ten, say. My boy, you must bear on as you are—we have the comfort of the workshop to ourselves, and some rational recreation; good shooting we will have soon too, for the first time this season."

Among the various circumstances which endeared Harry to our singular monarch, his skill and keenness as a sportsman were not inconsiderable: he knew where all the game in the island was to be found; so that, when his good old patron was permitted by the gout to take the field, Harry's assistance saved him a vast deal of unnecessary toil, and gratified him in his favourite amusement, whilst he, at the same time, sympathized in the sport. Corny, besides being a good shot, was an excellent mechanic: he beguiled the hours, when there was neither hunting nor shooting, in a workshop which was furnished with the best tools. Among the other occupations at the work-bench, he was particularly skilful in making and adjusting the locks of guns, and in boring and polishing the inside of their barrels to the utmost perfection: he had contrived and executed a tool for the enlarging the barrel of a gun in any particular part, so as to increase its effect in adding to the force of the discharge, and in preventing the shot from scattering too widely.

The hope of the success of his contrivance, and the prospect of going out with Harry on the approaching first of September, solaced King Corny, and seemed to keep up his spirits, through all the vexation he felt concerning Connal and this marriage, which evidently was not to his taste. It was to Dora's, however, and was becoming more evidently so every hour—and soon M. Connal pressed, and Mademoiselle urged, and Dora named—the happy day—and Mademoiselle, in transports, prepared to go to Dublin, with her niece, to choose the wedding-clothes, and, Connal to bespeak the equipages.

Mademoiselle was quick in her operations when dress was in question: the preparations for the delightful journey were soon made—the morning for their departure came—the carriage and horses were sent over the water early—and O'Shane and Harry afterwards accompanied the party in the boat to the other side of the lake, where the carriage waited with the door open. Connal, after handing in Mademoiselle, turned to look for his destined bride—who was taking leave of her father—Harry Ormond standing by. The moment she quitted her father's embrace, Father Jos poured with both his hands on her head the benedictions of all the saints. Released from Father Jos, Captain Connal hurried her on: Harry held out his hand to her as she passed. "Good bye, Dora—probably I shall never see you again."

"Oh, Harry!" said she, one touch of natural feeling stopping her short —"Oh, Harry!—Why?" Bursting into tears, she drew her hand from Connal, and gave it to Harry: Harry received the hand openly and cordially, shook it heartily, but took no advantage and no notice of the feelings by which he saw her at that moment agitated.

"*Forgive!*" she began.

"Good bye, *dear* Dora. God bless you—may you be as happy—half as happy, as I wish you to be!"

"To be sure she will—happy as the day is long," said Mademoiselle, leaning out of the carriage: "why will you make her cry, Mr. Ormond, spoiling her eyes at parting? Come in to me—Dora, M. de Connal is waiting to hand you, mon enfant."

"Is her dressing-box in, and all right?" asked Captain Connal, as he handed Dora into the carriage, who was still weeping.

"Bad compliment to M. de Connal, mon amie. Vrai scandale!" said Mademoiselle, pulling up the glass, while Dora sunk back in the carriage, sobbing without restraint.

"Good morning," said Connal, who had now mounted his Mr. Ormond, "Adieu, Mr. Ormond—command me in any way you please. Drive on!"

CHAPTER XVI.

The evening after the departure of the happy trio, who were gone to Dublin to buy wedding-dresses, the party remaining at Castle Corny consisted only of King Corny, Ormond, and Father Jos. When the candles were lighted, his majesty gave a long and loud yawn, Harry set the backgammon table for him, and Father Jos, as usual, settled himself in the chimney corner; "And now Mademoiselle's gone," said he, "I shall take leave to indulge myself in my pipe."

"You were on the continent this morning, Father Jos," said Cornelius. "Did ye learn any news for us? Size ace! that secures two points."

"News! I did," said Father Jos.

"Why not tell it us, then?"

"I was not asked. You both seemed so wrapped up, I waited my time and opportunity. There's a new parson come to Castle Hermitage."

"What new person?" said King Corny. "Doublets, aces, Harry."

"A new parson I'm talking of," said Father Jos, "that has just got the living there; and they say Sir Ulick's mad about it, in Dublin, where he is still."

"Mad!—Three men up—and you can't enter, Harry. Well, what is he mad about?"

"Because of the presentation to the living," replied the priest, "which government wouldn't make him a compliment of, as he expected."

"He is always expecting compliments from government," said Corny, "and always getting disappointments. Such throws as you have, Harry— Sixes! again—Well, what luck!—all over with me—It is only a hit at any rate! But what kind of man," continued he, "is this new clergyman?"

"Oh! them parsons is all one kind," said Father Jos.

"All one kind! No, no more than our own priests," said Corny. "There's good and bad, and all the difference in life."

"I don't know any thing at all about it," said Father Jos, sullenly; "but this I know, that no doubt he'll soon be over here, or his proctor, looking for the tithes."

"I hope we will have no quarrels," said Corny.

"They ought to be abolished," said Father Jos, "the tithes, that is, I mean."

"And the quarrels, too, I hope," said Ormond.

"Oh! It's not our fault if there's quarrels," said Father Jos.

"Faults on both sides generally in all quarrels," said Corny.

"In lay quarrels, like enough," said Father Jos. "In church quarrels, it don't become a good Catholic to say that."

"What?" said Corny.

"*That,*" said the priest.

"Which?" said Corny.

"That which you said, that there's faults on both sides; sure there's but one side, and that's our own side, can be in the right there can't be two *right sides,* can there? and consequently there won't be two wrong sides, will there?—Ergo, there cannot, by a parity of rasoning, be two sides in the wrong."

"Well, Harry, I'll take the black men now, and gammon you," said Corny. "Play away, man—what are you thinking of? is it of what Father Jos said? 'tis beyond the limits of the human understanding."

Father Jos puffed away at his pipe for some time.

"I was tired and ashamed of all the wrangling for two-pence with the last man," said King Corny, "and I believe I was sometimes too hard and too hot myself; but if this man's a gentleman, I think we shall agree. Did you hear his name, or any thing at all about him, Father?"

"He is one of them refugee families, the Huguenots, banished France by the adict of Nantz, they say, and his name's Cambray."

"Cambray!" exclaimed Ormond.

"A very good name," said O'Shane; "but what do you know of it, Harry?"

"Only, sir, I happened to meet with a Dr. Cambray the winter I was in Dublin, whom I thought a very agreeable, respectable, amiable man— and I wonder whether this is the same person."

"There is something more now, Harry Ormond, I know by your face," said Corny: "there's some story of or belonging to Dr. Cambray—what is it?"

"No story, only a slight circumstance—which, if you please, I'd rather not tell you, sir," said Ormond.

"That is something very extraordinary, and looks mysterious," said Father Jos.

"Nothing mysterious, I assure you," said Ormond,—"a mere trifle, which, if it concerned only myself, I would tell directly."

"Let him alone, father," said King Corny; "I am sure he has a good reason—and I'm not curious: only let me whisper this in your ear to show you my own penetration, Harry—I'd lay my life" (said he, stretching over and whispering), "I'd lay my life Miss Annaly has something to do with it."

"Miss Annaly!—nothing in the world—only—yes, I recollect she was present."

"There now—would not any body think I'm a conjuror? a physiognomist is cousin to (and not twice removed from) a conjuror."

"But I assure you, though you happened to guess right partly as to her being present, you are totally mistaken, sir, as to the rest."

"My dear Harry, *totally* means *wholly*: if I'm right in a part, I can't be mistaken in the whole. I am glad to make you smile, any way—and I wish I was right altogether, and that you was as rich as Croesus into the bargain; but stay a bit, if you come home a hero from the wars—that may do—ladies are mighty fond of heroes."

It was in vain that Ormond assured his good old imaginative friend that he was upon a wrong scent. Cornelius stopped to humour him; but was convinced that he was right: then turned to the still smoking Father Jos, and went on asking questions about Dr. Cambray.

"I know nothing at all about him," said Father Jos, "but this, that Father M'Cormuck has dined with him, if I'm not misinformed, oftener than I think becoming in these times—making too free! And in the chapel last Sunday, I hear he made a very extraordinary address to his flock—there was one took down the words, and handed them to me: after remarking on the great distress of the season—first and foremost about the keeping of fast days the year—he allowed the poor of his flock, which is almost all, to eat meat whenever offered to them, because, said he, many would starve—now mark the obnoxious word—'if it was not for their benevolent Protestant neighbours, who make soup and broth for them.'"

"What is there obnoxious in that?" said Cornelius.

"Wait till you hear the end—'and feed and clothe the distressed.'"

"That is not obnoxious either, I hope," said Ormond, laughing.

"Young gentleman, you belong to the establishment, and are no judge in this case, permit me to remark," said Father Jos; "and I could wish Mr. O'Shane would hear to the end, before he joins in a Protestant laugh."

"I've heard of a 'Protestant wind' before," said Harry, "but not of a Protestant laugh."

"Well, I'm serious, Father Jos," said Corny; "let me hear to the end what makes your face so long."

"'And, I am sorry to say, show more charity to them than their own people, the rich Catholics, sometimes do.' If that is not downright slander, I don't know what is," said Father Jos.

"Are you sure it is not truth, Father?" said Corny.

"And if it was, even, so much the worse, to be telling it in the chapel, and to his flock—very improper in a priest, very extraordinary conduct!"

Father Jos worked himself up to a high pitch of indignation, and railed and smoked for some time, while O'Shane and Ormond joined in defending M'Cormuck, and his address to his flock—and even his dining with the new clergyman of the parish. Father Jos gave up and had his punch. The result of the—whole was, that Ormond proposed to pay his respects the next morning to Dr. Cambray.

"Very proper," said O'Shane: "do so—fit you should—you are of his people, and you are acquainted with the gentleman—and I'd have you go and show yourself safe to him, that we've made no tampering with you."

Father Jos could not say so much, therefore he said nothing.

O'Shane continued, "A very exact church-goer at the little church there you've always been, at the other side of the lake—never hindered—make what compliment you will proper for me—say I'm too old and clumsy for morning visitings, and never go out of my islands. But still I can love my neighbour in or out of them, and hope, in the name of peace, to be on good terms. Sha'n't be my fault if them tithes come across. Then I wish that bone of contention was from between the two churches. Meantime, I'm not snarling, if others is not craving: and I'd wish for the look of it, for your sake, Harry, that it should be all smooth; so say any thing you will for me to this Dr. Cambray,—though we are of a different faith, I should do any thing in rason."

"Rason! what's that about rason?" said Father Jos: "I hope faith comes before rason."

"And after it, too, I hope, Father," said Corny.

Father Jos finished his punch, and went to sleep upon it.

Ormond, next morning, paid his visit—Dr. Cambray was not at home; but Harry was charmed with the neatness of his house, and with the amiable and happy appearance of his family. He had never before seen Mrs. Cambray or her daughters, though he had met the doctor in Dublin. The circumstance which Harry had declined mentioning, when Corny questioned him about his acquaintance with Dr. Cambray, was very slight, though Father Jos had imagined it to be of mysterious importance. It had happened, that among the dissipated set of young men with whom Marcus O'Shane and Harry had passed that winter in Dublin, a party had one Sunday gone to hear the singing at the Asylum, and had behaved in a very unbecoming manner during the service. Dr. Cambray preached—he spoke to the young gentlemen afterwards with mild but becoming dignity. Harry Ormond instantly, sensible of his error, made proper apologies, and erred no farther. But Marcus O'Shane in particular, who was not accustomed to endure anything, much less any person, that crossed his humour, spoke of Dr. Cambray afterwards with vindictive bitterness, and with all his talents of mimicry endeavoured to make him ridiculous. Harry defended him with a warmth of ingenuous eloquence which did him honour; and with truth, courage, and candour, that did him still more, corrected some of Marcus's mis-statements, declaring that they had all been much to blame. Lady Annaly and her daughter were present, and this was one of the circumstances to which her ladyship had alluded, when she said that some things had occurred that had prepossessed her with a favourable opinion of Ormond's character. Dr. Cambray knew nothing of the attack or the defence till some time afterwards; and it was now so long ago, and Harry was so much altered since that time, that it was scarcely to be expected the doctor should recollect even his person. However, when Dr. Cambray came to the Black Islands to return his visit, he did immediately recognize Ormond, and seemed so much pleased with meeting him again, and so much interested about him, that Corny's warm heart was immediately won. Independently of this, the doctor's persuasive benevolent politeness could not have failed to operate, as it usually did, even on a first acquaintance, in pleasing and conciliating even those who were of opposite opinions.

"There, now," said Corny, when the doctor was gone, "there, now, is a sincere minister of the Gospel for you, and a polite gentleman into the bargain. Now that's politeness that does not trouble me—that's not for show—that's for *us*, not *himself*, mark!—and conversation! Why that man has conversation for the prince and the peasant—the courtier and the anchorite. Did not he find plenty for me, and got more out of me than I thought was in me—and the same if I'd been a monk of La Trappe, he would have made me talk like a pie. Now there's a man of the high world that the low world can like, very different from—"

Poor Corny paused, checked himself, and then resumed—"Principles, religion, and all no hinderance!—liberal and sincere too! Well, I only wish—Father Jos, no offence—I only wish, for Dr. Cambray's sake, and the Catholic church's sake, I was, for one day, Archbishop of Canterbury, or Primate of all Ireland, or whatever else makes the bishops in your church, and I'd skip over dean and archdeacon, and all, and make that man—clean a bishop before night."

Harry smiled, and wished he had the power as well as the good-will.

Father Jos said, "A man ought to be ashamed not to think of his *own* first."

"Now, Harry, don't think I'd make a bishop lightly," continued King Corny; "I would not—I've been a king too long for that; and though only a king of my own fashion, I know what's fit for governing a country, observe me!—Cousin Ulick would make a job of a bishop, but I would not—nor I wouldn't to please my fancy. Now don't think I'd make that man a bishop just because he noticed and praised my gimcracks and inventions, and *substitutes*."

Father Jos smiled, and demurely abased his eye.

"Oh! then you don't know me as well as you think you do, father," said O'Shane. "Nor what's more, Harry, not his noting down the two regiments to make inquiry for friends for you, Harry, shouldn't have bribed me to partiality—though I could have kissed his shoe-ties for it."

"Mercy on you!" said Father Jos: "this doctor has bewitched you."

"But did you mind, then," persisted Corny, "the way he spoke of that cousin of mine, Sir Ulick, who he saw I did not like, and who has been, as you tell us, bitter against him, and even against his getting the living. Well, the way this Doctor Cambray spoke then pleased me—good morals without preaching—there's *do good to your enemies*—the true Christian doctrine—and the hardest point. Oh! let Father Jos say what he will, there's the man will be in heaven before many—heretic or no heretic, Harry!"

Father Jos shrugged up his shoulders, and then fixing the glass in his spectacles, replied, "We shall see better when we come to the tithes."

"That's true," said Corny.

He walked off to his workshop, and took down his fowling-piece to put the finishing stroke to his work for the next day, which was to be the first day of partridge-shooting: he looked forward with delight—anticipating the gratification he should have in going out shooting with Harry, and trying his new fowling-piece. "But I won't go out to-morrow till the post has come in; for my mind couldn't enjoy the sport till I was satisfied whether the answer could come about your commission, Harry: my mind misgives me—that is, my calculation tells me, that it will come to-morrow."

Good Corny's calculations were just: the next morning the little post-boy brought answers to various letters which he had written about Ormond—

one to Ormond from Sir Ulick O'Shane, repeating his approbation of his ward's going into the army, approving of all the steps Cornelius had taken—especially of his intention of paying for the commission.

"All's well," Cornelius said. The next letter was from Cornelius's banker, saying that the five hundred pound was lodged, ready. "All well." The army-agent wrote, "that he had commissions in two different regiments, waiting Mr. O'Shane's choice and orders per return of post, to purchase *in conformity*."—"That's all well." General Albemarle's answer to Mr. O'Shane's letter was most satisfactory: in terms that were not merely *officially* polite, but kind, "he assured Mr. O'Shane that he should, as far as it was in his power, pay attention to the young gentleman, whom Mr. O'Shane had so strongly recommended to his care, and by whose appearance and manner the general said he had been prepossessed, when he saw him some months ago at Corny Castle. There was a commission vacant in his son's regiment, which he recommended to Mr. Ormond."

"The very thing I could have wished for you, my dear boy—you shall go off the day after to-morrow—not a moment's delay—I'll answer the letters this minute."

But Harry reminded him that the post did not go out till the next day, and urged him not to lose this fine day—this first day of the season for partridge shooting.

"Time enough for my business after we come home—the post does not go out till morning."

"That's true: come off, then—let's enjoy the fine day sent us; and my gun, too—I forgot; for I do believe, Harry, I love you better even than my gun," said the warm-hearted Corny. "Call *Ormond*. Moriarty; let us have him with us—he'll enjoy it beyond all: one of the last day's shooting with his own Prince Harry!—but, poor fellow, we'll not tell him that."

Moriarty and the dogs were summoned, and the fineness of the day, and the promise of good sport, put Moriarty in remarkably good spirits. By degrees King Corny's own spirits rose, and he forgot that it was the last day with Prince Harry, and he enjoyed the sport. After various trials of his new fowling-piece, both the king and the prince agreed that it succeeded to admiration. But even in the midst of his pride in his success, and his joy in the sport, his superior fondness for Harry prevailed, and showed itself in little, almost delicate instances of kindness, which could hardly have been expected from his unpolished mind. As they crossed a bog, he stooped every now and then, and plucked different kinds of bog-plants and heaths.

"Here, Harry," said he, "mind these for Dr. Cambray. Remember yesterday his mentioning that a daughter of his was making a botanical collection, and there's Sheelah can tell you all the Irish names and uses. Some I can note for you myself; and here, this minute—by great luck! the very thing he wanted!—the andromeda, I'll swear to it: throw away all and keep this—carry it to her to-morrow—for I will have you make a friend of that Dr. Cambray; and no way so sure or fair to the father's heart as by proper attention to the daughter—I know that by myself. Hush, now, till I have that partridge!—Whirr!—Shot him clean, my dear gun!—Was not that good, Harry?"

Thus they continued their sport till late; and returning, loaded with game, had nearly reached the palace, when Corny, who had marked a covey, quitted Harry, and sent his dog to spring it, at a distance much greater than the usual reach of a common fowling-piece. Harry heard a shot, and a moment afterwards a violent shout of despair;—he knew the voice to be that of Moriarty, and running to the spot from whence it came, he found his friend, his benefactor, weltering in his blood. The fowling-piece, overloaded, had burst, and a large splinter of the barrel had fractured the skull, and had sunk into the brain. As Moriarty was trying to raise his head, O'Shane uttered some words, of which all that was intelligible was the name of Harry Ormond. His eye was fixed on Harry, but the meaning of the eye was gone. He squeezed Harry's hand, and an instant afterwards O'Shane's hand was powerless. The dearest, the only real friend Harry Ormond had upon earth was gone for ever!

CHAPTER XVII.

A boy passing by saw what had happened, and ran to the house, calling as he went to some workmen, who hastened to the place, where they heard the howling of the dogs. Ormond neither heard nor saw—till Moriarty said, "He must be carried home;" and some one approaching to lift the body, Ormond started up, pushed the man back, without uttering a syllable—made a sign to Moriarty, and between them they carried the body home. Sheelah and the women came out to meet them, wringing their hands, and uttering loud lamentations. Ormond, bearing his burden as if insensible of what he bore, walked onward, looking at no one, answering none, but forcing his way straight into the house, and on—till they came to O'Shane's bedchamber, which was upon the ground-floor —there laid him on his bed. The women had followed, and all those who had gathered on the way rushed in to see and to bewail. Ormond looked up, and saw the people about the bed, and made a sign to Moriarty to keep them away, which he did, as well as he could. But they would not be kept back—Sheelah, especially, pressed forward, crying loudly, till Moriarty, with whom she was struggling, pointed to Harry. Struck with his fixed look, she submitted at once. *"Best leave him!"* said she. She put every body out of the room before her, and turning to Ormond, said, they would leave him "a little space of time till the priest should come, who was at a clergy dinner, but was sent for."

When Ormond was left alone he locked the door, and kneeling beside the dead, offered up prayers for the friend he had lost, and there remained some time in stillness and silence, till Sheelah knocked at the door, to let him know that the priest was come. Then retiring, he went to the other end of the house, to be out of the way. The room to which he went was that in which they had been reading the letters just before they went out that morning. There was the pen which Harry had taken from his hand, and the answer just begun.

"Dear General, I hope my young friend, Harry Ormond—"

That hand could write no more!—that warm heart was cold! The certainty was so astonishing, so stupifying, that Ormond, having never yet shed a tear, stood with his eyes fixed on the paper, he knew not how long, till he felt some one touch his hand. It was the child, little Tommy, of whom O'Shane was so fond, and who was so fond of him. The child, with his whistle in his hand, stood looking up at Harry, without speaking. Ormond gazed on him for a few instants, then snatched him in his arms, and burst into an agony of tears. Sheelah, who had let the child in, now came and carried him away. "God be thanked for them tears," said she, "they will bring relief;" and so they did. The necessity for manly exertion —the sense of duty—pressed upon Ormond's recovered reason. He began directly, and wrote all the letters that were necessary to his guardian and to Miss O'Faley, to communicate the dreadful intelligence to Dora. The letters were not finished till late in the evening. Sheelah came for them, and leaving the door and the outer door to the hall open, as she came in, Ormond saw the candles lighted, and smelt the smell of tobacco and whiskey, and heard the sound of many voices.

"The wake, dear, which is beginning," said she, hastening back to shut the doors, as she saw him shudder. "Bear with it, Master Harry," said she: "hard for you!—but bear with us, dear; 'tis the custom of the country; and what else can we do but what the forefathers did?—how else for us to show respect, only as it would be expected, and has always been?—and great comfort to think we done our best for *him that is gone*, and comfort to know his wake will be talked of long hereafter, over the fires at night, of all the people that is there without—and that's all we have for it now: so bear with it, dear."

This night, and for two succeeding nights, the doors of Corny Castle remained open for all who chose to come.

Crowds, as many, and more, than the castle could hold, flocked to King Corny's wake, for he was greatly beloved.

There was, as Sheelah said, "plenty of cake, and wine, and tea, and tobacco, and snuff—every thing handsome as possible, and honourable to the deceased, who was always open-handed and open-hearted, and with open house too."

His praises, from time to time, were heard, and then the common business of the country was talked of—and jesting and laughter went on —and all night there were tea-drinkings for the women, and punch for the men. Sheelah, who inwardly grieved most, went about incessantly among the crowd, serving all, seeing that none, especially them who came from a distance, should be neglected—and that none should have to complain afterwards, "or to say that any thing at all was wanting or niggardly." Mrs. Betty, Sheelah's daughter, sat presiding at the tea-table, giving the keys to her mother when wanted, but never forgetting to ask for them again. Little Tommy took his cake and hid himself under the table, close by his mother, Mrs. Betty; and could not be tempted out but by Sheelah, whom he followed, watching for her to go in to Mr. Harry: when the door opened, he held by her gown, and squeezed in under her arm—and when she brought Mr. Harry his meals, she would set the child up at the table with him *for company*—and to tempt him to take something.

Ormond had once promised his deceased friend, that if he was in the country when he died, he would put him into his coffin. He kept his promise. The child hearing a noise, and knowing that Mr. Harry had gone into the room, could not be kept out; the crowd had left that room, and the child looked at the bed with the curtains looped up with black— and at the table at the foot of the bed, with the white cloth spread over it, and the seven candlesticks placed upon it. But the coffin fixed his attention, and he threw himself upon it, clinging to it, and crying bitterly upon King Corny, his dear King Corny, to come back to him.

It was all Sheelah could do to drag him away: Ormond, who had always liked this boy, felt now more fond of him than ever, and resolved that he should never want a friend.

"You are in the mind to attend the funeral, sir, I think you told me?" said Sheelah.

"Certainly," replied Ormond.

"Excuse me, then," said Sheelah, "if I mention—for you can't know what to do without. There will be high mass, may be you know, in the chapel. And as it's a great funeral, thirteen priests will be there, attending. And when the mass will be finished, it will be expected of you, as first of kin considered, to walk up first with your offering—whatsoever you think fit, for the priests—and to lay it down on the altar; and then each and all will follow, laying down their offerings, according as they can. I hope I'm not too bold or troublesome, sir."

Ormond thanked her for her kindness—and felt it was real kindness. He, consequently, did all that was expected from him *handsomely*. After the masses were over, the priests, who could not eat any thing before they said mass, had breakfast and dinner joined. Sheelah took care "the clergy was well served." Then the priests—though it was not essential that all should go, did all, to Sheelah's satisfaction, accompany the funeral the *whole way*, three long miles, to the burying-place of the O'Shanes; a remote old abbey-ground, marked only by some scattered trees, and a few sloping grave-stones. King Corny's funeral was followed by an immense concourse of people, on horseback and on foot; men, women, and children: when they passed by the doors of cabins, a set of the women raised the funeral cry—not a savage howl, as is the custom in some parts of Ireland, but chanting a melancholy kind of lament, not without harmony, simple and pathetic. Ormond was convinced, that in spite of all the festivity at the wake, which had so disgusted him, the poor people mourned sincerely for the friend they had lost.

We forgot to mention that Dr. Cambray went to the Black Islands the day after O'Shane's death, and did all he could to prevail upon Ormond to go to his house while the wake was going on, and till the funeral should be over. But Ormond thought it right to stay where he was, as none of the family were there, and there was no way in which he could so strongly mark, as Sheelah said, his respect for the dead. Now that it was all over, he had at least the consolation of thinking that he had not shrunk from any thing that was, or that he conceived to be, his duty. Dr. Cambray was pleased with his conduct, and at every moment he could spare went to see him, doing all he could to console him, by strengthening in Ormond's mind the feelings of religious submission to the will of Heaven, and of pious hope and confidence. Ormond had no time left him for the indulgence of sorrow—business pressed upon him.

Cornelius O'Shane's will, which Sir Ulick blamed Harry for not mentioning in the first letter, was found to be at his banker's in Dublin. All his property was left to his daughter, except the farm, which he had given to Ormond; this was specially excepted, with legal care: also a legacy of five hundred pounds was left to Harry; a trifling bequest to Sir Ulick, being his cousin; and legacies to servants. Miss O'Faley was appointed sole executrix—this gave great umbrage to Sir Ulick O'Shane, and appeared extraordinary to many people; but the will was in due form, and nothing could be done against it, however much might be said.

Miss O'Faley, without taking notice of any thing Ormond said of the money, which had been lodged in the bank to pay for his commission, wrote as executrix to beg of him to do various business for her—all which he did; and fresh letters came with new requests, inventories to be taken, things to be sent to Dublin, money to be received and paid, stewards' and agents' accounts to be settled, business of all kinds, in short, came pouring in—upon him, a young man unused to it, and with a mind peculiarly averse from it at this moment. But when he found that he could be of service to any one belonging to his benefactor, he felt bound in gratitude to exert himself to the utmost. These circumstances, however disagreeable, had an excellent effect upon his character, giving him habits of business which were ever afterwards of use to him. It was remarkable that the only point in his letters which had concerned his own affairs still continued unanswered. Another circumstance hurt his feelings—instead of Miss O'Faley's writing to make her own requests, Mr. Connal was soon deputed by Mademoiselle to write for her. He spoke of the shock the ladies had felt, and the distressing circumstances in which they were; all in commonplace phrases, which Ormond despised, and from which he could judge nothing of Dora's real feelings.

"The marriage must, of course," Mr. Connal said, "be put off for some time; and as it would be painful to the ladies to return to Corny Castle, he had advised their staying in Dublin; and they and he feeling assured that, from Mr. Ormond's regard for the family, they might take the liberty of troubling him, they requested so and so, and the *executrix*begged he would see this settled and that settled"—at last, with gradually forgotten apologies, falling very much into the style of a person writing to an humble friend or dependent, bound to consider requests as commands.

Our young hero's pride was piqued on the one side, as much as his gratitude was alive on the other.

Sir Ulick O'Shane wrote to Harry that he was at this time *peculiarly* engaged with affairs of his own. He said, that as to the material point of the money lodged for the commission, he would see the executrix, and do what he could to have that settled; but as to all lesser points, Sir Ulick said, he really had not leisure to answer letters at present. He enclosed a note to Dr. Cambray, whom he recommended it to his ward to consult, and whose advice and assistance he now requested for him in pressing terms.

In consequence of this direct application from the young gentleman's guardian, Dr. Cambray felt himself authorized and called upon to interfere, where, otherwise, delicacy might have prevented him. It was fortunate for Ormond that he had Dr. Cambray's counsel to guide him, or else he would, in the first moments of feeling, have yielded too much to the suggestions of both gratitude and pride.

In the first impulse of generous pride, Ormond wanted to give up the farm which his benefactor had left him, because he wished that no possible suspicion of interested motives having influenced his attachment to Cornelius O'Shane should exist, especially with Mr. Connal, who, as the husband of Dora, would soon be the lord of all in the Black Islands.

On the other hand, when Mr. Connal wrote to him, that the executrix, having no written order from the deceased to that effect, could not pay the five hundred pounds, lodged in the bank, for his commission, Ormond was on the point of flying out with intemperate indignation.

"Was not his own word sufficient? Was not the intention of his benefactor apparent from the letters? Would not this justify any executor, any person of common sense or honour?"

Dr. Cambray, his experienced and placid counsellor, brought all these sentiments to due measure by mildly showing what was law and justice, and what was fit and proper in each case; putting jealous honour, and romantic generosity, as they must be put, out of the question in business.

He prevented Ormond from embroiling himself with Connal about the legacy, and from giving up his farm. He persuaded him to decline having any thing to do with the affairs of the Black Islands.

A proper agent was appointed, who saw Ormond's accounts settled and signed, so that no blame or suspicion could rest upon him.

"There seems no probability, Mr. Ormond," said Dr. Cambray, "of your commission being immediately purchased. Your guardian, Sir Ulick O'Shane, will be detained some time longer, I understand, in Dublin. You are in a desolate situation here—you have now done all that you ought to do—leave these Black Islands, and come to Vicar's Dale: you will find there a cheerful family, and means of spending your time more agreeably, perhaps more profitably, than you can have here. I am sensible that no new friends *can* supply to you the place of him you have lost; but you will find pleasure in the perception, that you have, by your own merit, attached to you one friend in me, who will do all in his power to soothe and serve you.—Will you *trust* yourself to me?" added he, smiling, "You have already found that I do not flatter. Will you come to us?—The sooner the better—to-morrow, if you can."

It scarcely need be said, that this invitation was most cordially accepted. Next day Ormond was to leave the Black Islands. Sheelah was in despair when she found he was going: the child hung upon him so that he could hardly get out of the house, till Moriarty promised to return for the boy, and carry him over in the boat often, to see Mr. Ormond. Moriarty would not stay in the islands himself, he said, after Harry went: he let the cabin and little tenement which O'Shane had given him, and the rent was to be paid him by the agent. Ormond went, for the last time, that morning, to

Ormond's Vale, to settle his own affairs there: he and Moriarty took an unusual path across this part of the island to the waterside, that they might avoid that which they had followed the last time they were out, on the day of Corny's death. They went, therefore, across a lone tract of heath-bog, where, for a considerable time, they saw no living being.

On this bog, of which Cornelius O'Shane had given Moriarty a share, the grateful poor fellow had, the year before, amused himself with cutting in large letters of about a yard long the words

"LONG LIVE KING CORNY."

He had sowed the letters with broom-seed in the spring, and had since forgotten ever to look at them; but they were now green, and struck the eye.

"Think then of this being all the trace that's left of him on the face of the earth!" said Moriarty. "I'm glad that I did even that same."

After crossing this lone bog, when they came to the waterside, they found a great crowd of people, seemingly all the inhabitants of the islands, assembled there, waiting to take leave of Master Harry; and each of them was cheered by a kind word and a look, before they would let him step into the boat.

"Ay, go *to the continent*," said Sheelah, "ay, go to fifty continents, and in all Ireland you'll not find hearts warmer to you than those of the Black Islands, that knows you best from a child, Master Harry dear."

CHAPTER XVIII.

Ormond was received with much kindness in Dr. Cambray's family, in which he felt himself at ease, and soon forgot that he was a stranger: his mind, however, was anxious about his situation, as he longed to get into active life. Every morning, when the post came in, he hoped there would be a letter for him with his commission; and he was every morning regularly surprised and disappointed, on finding that there was none. In the course of each ensuing day, however, he forgot his disappointment, and said he believed he was happier where he was than he could be any where else. The regular morning question of "Any letters for me?" was at last answered by "Yes; one franked by Sir Ulick O'Shane." "Ah! no commission—I feel no enclosure—single letter—no! double." Double or single, it was as follows:—

"DEAR HARRY,

At last I have seen the executrix and son-in-law, whom that great genius deceased, my well-beloved cousin in folly, King Corny, chose for himself. As to that thing, half mud, half tinsel, half Irish, half French, Miss, or Mademoiselle, O'Faley, that jointed doll, is—all but the eyes, which move of themselves in a very extraordinary way—a mere puppet, pulled by wires in the hands of another. The master showman, fully as extraordinary in his own way as his puppet, kept, while I was by, as much as possible behind the scenes. The hand and ruffle of the French petit-maitre, and the prompter's voice, however, were visible and audible enough for me. In plain English, I suppose it is no news to you to hear that Mdlle. O'Faley is a fool, and Monsieur de Connal, Captain O'Connal, Black Connal, or by whatever other *alias* he is to be called, is *properly* a puppy. I am sorry, my dear boy, to tell you that the fool has let the rogue get hold of the five hundred pounds lodged in the bank—so no hopes of your commission for three months, or at the least two months to come. My dear boy, your much-lamented friend and benefactor (is not that the style?), King Corny, who began, I think, by being, years ago, to your admiration, his own tailor, has ended, I fear to your loss, by being his own lawyer: he has drawn his will so that any attorney could drive a coach and six through it—so ends 'every man his own lawyer.' Forgive me this laugh, Harry. By-the-bye, you, my dear ward, will be of age in December, I think—then all my legal power of interference ceases.

"Meantime, as I know you will be out of spirits when you read this, I have some comfort for you and myself, which I kept for a bonne-bouche —you will never more see Lady O'Shane, nor I either. Articles of separation—and I didn't trust myself to be my own lawyer—have been signed between us: so I shall see her ladyship sail for England this night —won't let any one have the pleasure of putting her on board but myself —I will see her safe off, and feel well assured nothing can tempt her to return—even to haunt me—or scold you. This was the business which detained me in Dublin—well worth while to give up a summer to secure, for the rest of one's days, liberty to lead a bachelor's merry life, which I mean to do at Castle Hermitage or elsewhere, now and from henceforth —Miss Black in no ways notwithstanding. Miss Black, it is but justice to tell you, is now convinced of my conjugal virtues, and admires my patience as much as she used to admire Lady O'Shane's. She has been very useful to me in arranging my affairs in this separation—*in consequence*, I have procured a commission of the peace for a certain Mr. M'Crule, a man whom you may remember to have seen or heard at the bottom or corner of the table at Castle Hermitage, one of the *Cromwellians*, a fellow with the true draw-down of the mouth, and who speaks, or snorts, through his nose. I have caused him, not without some difficulty, to ask Miss Black to be his helpmate (Lord *help* him and forgive me!); and Miss Black, preferring rather to stay in Ireland and become Mrs. M'Crule than to return to England and continue companion to Lady O'Shane, hath consented (who can blame her?) to marry on the spur of the occasion—to-morrow—I giving her away—you may imagine with what satisfaction. What with marriages and separations, the business of the nation, my bank, my canal, and my coal-mines, you may guess my hands have been full of business. Now, all for pleasure! next week I hope to be down enjoying my liberty at Castle Hermitage, where I shall be heartily glad to have my dear Harry again. Marcus in England still—the poor Annalys in great distress about the son, with whom, I fear, it is all over. No time for more. Measure my affection by the length of this, the longest epistle extant in my hand-writing.

"My dear boy, yours ever,

"Ulick O'Shane."

The mixed and crossing emotions which this letter was calculated to excite having crossed, and mixed, and subsided a little, the predominating feeling was expressed by our young hero with a sigh, and this reflection: "Two months at the least! I must wait before I can have my commission—two months more in idleness the fates have decreed."

"That last is a part of the decree that depends on yourself, not on the fates. Two months you must wait, but why in idleness?" said Dr. Cambray.

The kind and prudent doctor did not press the question—he was content with its being heard, knowing that it would sink into the mind and produce its effect in due season. Accordingly, after some time, after Ormond had exhaled impatience, and exhausted invective, and submitted to necessity, he returned to reason with the doctor. One evening, when the doctor and his family had returned from walking, and as the tea-urn was just coming in bubbling and steaming, Ormond set to work at a corner of the table, at the doctor's elbow.

"My dear doctor, suppose I was now to read over to you my list of books."

"Suppose you were, and suppose I was to fall asleep," said the doctor.

"Not the least likely, sir, when you are to do any thing kind for a friend— may I say friend?"

"You may. Come, read on—I am not proof against flattery, even at my age—well, read away."

Ormond began; but at that moment there drove past the windows a travelling chariot and four.

"Sir Ulick O'Shane, as I live!" cried Ormond, starting up. "I saw him—he nodded to me. Oh! no, impossible—he said he would not come till next week—Where's his letter?—What's the date?—Could it mean this week?—No, he says next week quite plainly—What can be the reason?"

A note for Mr. Ormond was brought in, which had been left by one of Sir Ulick O'Shane's servants as they went by.

"My commission, after all," cried Harry. "I always knew, I always said, that Sir Ulick was a good friend."

"Has he purchased the commission?" said Dr. Cambray.

"He does not actually say so, but that must be what his note means," said Ormond.

"Means! but what does it say?—May I see it?"

"It is written in such a hurry, and in pencil, you'll not be able to make it out."

The doctor, however, read aloud—

"If Mr. Harry Ormond will inquire at Castle Hermitage, he will hear of something to his advantage.

"U. O'SHANE."

"Go off this minute," said Mrs. Cambray, "and inquire at Castle Hermitage what Mr. Harry Ormond may hear to his advantage, and let us learn it as soon as possible."

"Thank you, ma'am," said Harry; and ere the words were well uttered, a hundred steps were lost.

With more than his usual cordiality, Sir Ulick O'Shane received him, came out into the hall to meet his dear Harry, his own dear boy, to welcome him again to Castle Hermitage.

"We did not expect you, sir, till next week—this is a most agreeable surprise. Did you not say—"

"No matter what I said—you see what I have done," interrupted Sir Ulick; "and now I must introduce you to a niece of mine, whom you have never yet seen—Lady Norton, a charming, well-bred, pleasant little widow, whose husband died, luckily for her and me, just when they had run out all their large fortune. She is delighted to come to me, and is just the thing to do the honours of Castle Hermitage—used to the style; but observe, though she is to rule my roast and my boiled, she is not to rule me or my friends—that is a preliminary, and a special clause for Harry Ormond's being a privileged *ami de la maison*. Now, my dear fellow, you understand how the land lies; and depend upon it, you'll like her, and find her every way of *great advantage to you*."

So, thought Harry, is this all the advantage I am to hear of?

Sir Ulick led on to the drawing-room, and presented him to a fashionable-looking lady, neither young nor old, nothing in any respect remarkable.

"Lady Norton, Harry Ormond—Harry Ormond, my niece, Lady Norton, who will make this house as pleasant to you, and to me, and to all my friends, as it has been unpleasant ever since—in short, ever since you were out of it, Harry."

Lady Norton, with gracious smile and well-bred courtesy, received Harry in a manner that promised the performance of all for which Sir Ulick had engaged. Tea came; and the conversation went on chiefly between Sir Ulick and Lady Norton on their own affairs, about invitations and engagements they had made, before they left Dublin, with various persons who were coming down to Castle Hermitage. Sir Ulick asked, "When are the Brudenells to come to us, my dear?—Did you settle with the Lascelles?—and Lady Louisa, she must be here with the vice-regal party—arrange that, my dear."

Lady Norton had settled every thing; she took out an elegant memorandum-book, and read the arrangements to Sir Ulick. Between whiles, Sir Ulick turned to Ormond and noted the claims of those persons to distinction, and as several ladies were named, exclaimed, "Charming woman!—delightful little creature!—The Darrells; Harry, you'll like the Darrells too!—The Lardners, all clever, pleasant, and odd, will entertain you amazingly, Harry!—But Lady Millicent is *the* woman—nothing at all has been seen in this country like her!—most fascinating! Harry, take care of your heart."

Then, as to the men—this man was clever—and the other was quite a hero—and the next the pleasantest fellow—and the best sportsman—and there were men of political eminence—men who had distinguished themselves on different occasions by celebrated speeches—and particularly promising rising young; men, with whom he must make Ormond intimately acquainted. Now Sir Ulick closed Lady Norton's book, and taking it from her hand, said, "I am tiring you, my dear—that's enough for to-night—we'll settle all the rest to-morrow: you must be tired after your journey—I whirled you down without mercy—you look fatigued and sleepy."

Lady Norton said, "Indeed, she believed she was a little tired, and rather sleepy."

Her uncle begged she would not sit up longer from compliment; accordingly, apologizing to Mr. Ormond, and "really much fatigued," she retired. Sir Ulick walked up and down the room, meditating for some moments, while Harry renewed his intimacy with an old dog, who, at every pause in the conversation, jumping up on him, and squealing with delight, had claimed his notice.

"Well, my boy," exclaimed Sir Ulick, stopping short, "aren't you a most extraordinary fellow? Pray did you get my note?"

"Certainly, sir, and came instantly in consequence."

"And yet you have never inquired what it is that you might hear to your advantage."

"I—I thought I had heard it, sir."

"Heard it, sir!" repeated Sir Ulick: "what *can* you mean?"

"Simply, sir, that I thought the advantage you alluded to was the introduction you did me just now the favour to give me to Lady Norton; you said, her being here would be *a great advantage to me*, and that led me to conclude—"

"Well, well! you were always a simple good fellow—confiding in my friendship—continue the same—you will, I am confident. But had you no other thought?"

"I had," said Harry, "when first I read your note, I had, I own, another thought."

"And what might it be?"

"I thought of my commission, sir."

"What of your commission?"

"That you had procured it for me, sir."

"Since you ask me, I tell you honestly, that if it had been for your interest, I would have purchased that commission long ago; but there is a little secret, a political secret, which I could not tell you before—those who are behind the scenes cannot always speak—I may tell it to you now confidentially, but you must not repeat it, especially from me—that peace is likely to continue; so the army is out of the question."

"Well, sir, if that be the case—you know best."

"I do—it is, trust me; and as things have turned out—though I could not possibly foresee what has happened—every thing is for the best: I have come express from town to tell you news that will surprise you beyond measure."

"What can you mean, sir?"

"Simply, sir, that you are possessed, or soon will be possessed of—But come, sit down quietly, and in good earnest let me explain to you. You know your father's second wife, the Indian woman, the governor's mahogany-coloured daughter—she had a prodigious fortune, which my poor friend, your father, chose, when dying, to settle upon her, and her Indian son; leaving you nothing but what he could not take from you, the little paternal estate of three hundred pounds a year. Well, it has pleased Heaven to take your mahogany-coloured step-mother and your Indian brother out of this world; both carried off within a few days of each other by a fever of the country—much regretted, I dare say, in the Bombay Gazette, by all who knew them.

"But as neither you nor I had that honour, we are not, upon this occasion, called upon for any hypocrisy, farther than a black coat, which I have ordered for you at my tailor's. *Have also noted* and answered, *in conformity*, the agent's letter of 26th July, received yesterday, containing the melancholy intelligence: farther, replied to that part of his last, which requested to know how and where to transmit the property, which, on the Indian mother and brother's demise, falls, by the will of the late Captain Ormond, to his European son, Harry Ormond, esq., now under the guardianship of Sir Ulick O'Shane, Castle Hermitage, Ireland."

As he spoke, Sir Ulick produced the agent's letter, and put it into his ward's hand, pointing to the "useful passages." Harry, glancing his eye over them, understood just enough to be convinced that Sir Ulick was in earnest, and that he was really heir to a very considerable property.

"Well! Harry Ormond, esq.," pursued Sir Ulick, "was I wrong when I told you that if you would inquire at Castle Hermitage you would hear of something to your advantage?"

"I *hope* in Heaven," said Ormond, "and *pray* to Heaven that it may be to my advantage!—I hope neither my head nor my heart may be turned by sudden prosperity."

"Your heart—oh! I'll answer for your heart, my noble fellow," said Sir Ulick; "but I own you surprise me by the coolness of head you show."

"If you'll excuse me," said Ormond, "I must run this minute to tell Dr. Cambray and all my friends at Vicar's Dale."

"Certainly—quite right," said Sir Ulick—"I won't detain you a moment," said he—but he still held him fast. "I let you go to-night, but you must come to me to-morrow."

"Oh! sir, certainly."

"And you will bid adieu to Vicar's Dale, and take up your quarters at Castle Hermitage, with your old guardian."

"Thank you, sir—delightful! But I need not bid adieu to Vicar's Dale—*they* are so near, I shall see them every day."

"Of course," said Sir Ulick, biting his lip; "*but* I was thinking of something."

"Pray," continued Sir Ulick, "do you like a gig, a curricle, or a phaeton best, or what carriage will you have? there is Tom Darrel's in London now, who can bring it over for you. Well, we can settle that to-morrow."

"If you please—thank you, kind Sir Ulick—how *can* you think so quickly of every thing?"

"Horses, too—let me see," said Sir Ulick, drawing Harry back to the fire-place—"Ay, George Beirne is a judge of horses—he can choose for you, unless you like to choose for yourself. What colour—black or bay?"

"I declare, sir, I don't know yet—my poor head is in such a state—and the horses happen not to be uppermost."

"I protest, Harry, you perfectly astonish me, by the sedateness of your mind and manner. You are certainly wonderfully formed and improved since I saw you last—but, how! in the name of wonder, in the Black Islands, *how* I cannot conceive," said Sir Ulick.

"As to sedateness, you know, sir, since I saw you last, I may well be sobered a little, for I have suffered—not a little," said Harry.

"Suffered! how?" said Sir Ulick, leaning his arm on the mantel-piece opposite to him, and listening with an air of sympathy—"suffered! I was not aware—"

"You know, sir, I have lost an excellent friend."

"Poor Corny—ay, my poor cousin, as far as he could, I am sure, he wished to be a friend to you."

"He wished to be, and *was*," said Ormond.

"It would have been better for him and his daughter too," resumed Sir Ulick, "if he had chosen you for his son-in-law, instead of the coxcomb to whom Dora is going to be married: yet I own, as your guardian, I am well pleased that Dora, though a very pretty girl, is out of your way—you must look higher—she was no match for you."

"I am perfectly sensible, sir, that we should never have been happy together."

"You are a very sensible young man, Ormond—you make me admire you, seriously—I always foresaw what you would be Ah! if Marcus—but we'll not talk of that now. Terribly dissipated—has spent an immensity of money already—but still, when he speaks in parliament he will make a figure. But good bye, good night; I see you are in a hurry to get away from me."

"*From you!* Oh! no, sir, you cannot think me so ungrateful. I have not expressed, because I have not words—when I feel much, I never can say any thing; yet believe me, sir, I do feel your kindness, and all the warm fatherly interest you have this night shown that you have for me:—but I am in a hurry to tell my good friends the Cambrays, who I know are impatient for my return, and I fear I am keeping them up beyond their usual hour."

"Not at all—besides—good Heavens! can't they sit up a quarter of an hour, if they are so much interested?—Stay, you really hurry my slow wits—one thing more I had to say—pray, may I ask to *which* of the Miss Cambrays is it that you are so impatient to impart your good fortune?"

"To both, sir," said Ormond—"equally."

"Both!—you unconscionable dog, polygamy is not permitted in these countries—Both! no, try again for a better answer; though that was no bad one at the first blush."

"I have no other answer to give than the plain truth, sir: I am thinking neither of polygamy nor even of marriage at present. These young ladies are both very amiable, very handsome, and very agreeable; but, in short, we are not thinking of one another—indeed, I believe they are engaged."

"Engaged!—Oh! then you have thought about these young ladies enough to find that out. Well, this saves your gallantry—good night."

Sir Ulick had this evening taken a vast deal of superfluous pains to sound a mind, which lay open before him, clear to the very bottom; but because it was so clear, he could not believe that he saw the bottom. He did not much like Dr. Cambray—Father Jos was right there. Dr. Cambray was one of those simple characters which puzzled Sir Ulick—the idea of these Miss Cambrays, of the possibility of his ward's having formed an attachment that might interfere with his views, disturbed Sir Ulick's rest this night. His first operation in the morning was to walk down unexpectedly early to Vicar's Dale. He found Ormond with Dr. Cambray, very busy, examining a plan which the doctor had sketched for a new cottage for Moriarty—a mason was standing by, talking of sand, lime, and stones. "But the young ladies, where are they?" Sir Ulick asked.

Ormond did not know. Mrs. Cambray, who was quietly reading, said she supposed they were in their gardens; and not in the least suspecting Sir Ulick's suspicions, she was glad to see him, and gave credit to his neighbourly good-will for the earliness of this visit, without waiting even for the doctor to pay his respects first, as he intended to do at Castle Hermitage.

"Oh! as to that," Sir Ulick said, "he did not intend to live on terms of ceremony with Dr. Cambray—he was impatient to take the first opportunity of thanking the doctor for his attentions to his ward."

Sir Ulick's quick eye saw on the table in Harry's handwriting the *list of books to be read*. He took it up, looked it over, and with a smile asked, "Any thoughts of the church, Harry?"

"No, sir; it would be rather late for me to think of the church. I should never prepare myself properly."

"Besides," said Sir Ulick, "I have no living in my gift; but if," continued he, in a tone of irony, "if, as I should opine from the list I hold in my hand—you look to a college living, my boy—if you are bent upon reading for a fellowship—I don't doubt but with Dr. Cambray's assistance, and with some *grinder* and *crammer*, we might get you cleverly through all the college examinations. And doctor, if he did not, in going through some of the college courses, die of a logical indigestion, or a classical fever, or a metaphysical lethargy, he might shine in the dignity of Trin. Coll. Dub., and, mad Mathesis inspiring, might teach eternally how the line AB is equal to the line CD,—or why poor X Y Z are unknown quantities. Ah! my dear boy, think of the pleasure, the glory of lecturing classes of *ignoramuses*, and dunces yet unborn!"

Harry, no way disconcerted, laughed good-humouredly with his guardian, and replied, "At present, sir, my ambition reaches no farther than to escape myself from the class of dunces and ignoramuses. I am conscious that at present I am very deficient."

"*In* what, my dear boy?—To make your complaint English, you must say deficient in some thing or other—'tis an *Iricism* to say in general that you are *very deficient*."

"There is one of my particular deficiencies then you see, sir—I am deficient in English."

"You are not deficient in temper, I am sure," said Sir Ulick: "come, come, you may be tolerably well contented with yourself."

"Ignorant as I am!—No," said Ormond, "I will never sit down content in ignorance. Now that I have the fortune of a gentleman, it would be so much the more conspicuous, more scandalous—now that I have every way the means, I will, by the blessing of Heaven, and with the help of kind friends, make myself something more and something better than I am."

"Gad! you are a fine fellow, Harry Ormond," cried Sir Ulick: "I remember having once, at your age, such feelings and notions myself."

"Very unlike the first thoughts and feelings many young men would have on coming into unexpected possession of a fortune," said Dr. Cambray.

"True," said Sir Ulick, "and we must keep his counsel, that he may not be dubbed a quiz—not a word of this sort, Harry, for the Darrells, the Lardners, or the Dartfords."

"I don't care whether they dub me a quiz or not," said Harry, hastily: "what are Darrells, Lardners, or Dartfords to me?"

"They are something to *me*," said Sir Ulick.

"Oh! I beg pardon, sir—I didn't know that—that makes it quite another affair."

"And, Harry, as you are to meet these young men, I thought it well to try how you could bear to be laughed at—I have tried you in this very conversation, and found you, to my infinite satisfaction, *ridicule proof*—better than even *bullet proof*—much better. No danger that a young man of spirit should be bullied out of his opinion and principles, but great danger that he might be *laughed* out of them—and I rejoice, my dear ward, to see that you are safe from this peril."

Benevolent pleasure shone in Dr. Cambray's countenance, when he heard Sir Ulick speak in this manner.

"You will dine with us, Dr. Cambray?" said Sir Ulick. "Harry, you will not forget Castle Hermitage?"

"Forget Castle Hermitage! as if I could, where I spent my happy childhood—that paradise, as it seemed to me the first time—when, a poor little orphan boy, I was brought from my smoky cabin. I remember the day as well as if it were this moment—when you took me by the hand, and led me in, and I clung to you."

"Cling to me still! cling to me ever," interrupted Sir Ulick, "and I will never fail you—no, never," repeated he, grasping Harry's hand, and looking upon him with an emotion of affection, strongly felt, and therefore strongly expressed.

"To be sure I will," said Harry.

"And I hope," added Sir Ulick, recovering the gaiety of his tone, "that at Castle Hermitage a paradise will open for your youth as it opened for your childhood."

Mrs. Cambray put in a word of hope and fear about Vicar's Dale. To which Ormond answered, "Never fear, Mrs. Cambray—trust me—I know my own interest too well."

Sir Ulick turning again as he was leaving the room, said with an air of frank liberality, "We'll settle that at once—we'll divide Harry between us—or we'll divide his day thus: the mornings I leave you to your friends and studies for an hour or two Harry, in this Vale of Eden—the rest of the day we must have you—men and books best mixed—see Bacon, and see every clever man that ever wrote or spoke. So here," added Sir Ulick, pointing to a map of history, which lay on the table, "you will have *The Stream of Time*, and with us *Le Courant du Jour.*"

Sir Ulick departed. During the whole of this conversation, and of that of the preceding night, while he seemed to be talking at random of different things, unconnected and of opposite sorts, he had carefully attended to one object. Going round the whole circle of human motives—love, ambition, interest, ease, pleasure, he had made accurate observation on his ward's mind; and reversing the order, he went round another way, and repeated and corrected his observations. The points he had strongly noted for practical use were, that for retaining influence over his ward, he must depend not upon interested motives of any kind, nor upon the force of authority or precedent, nor yet on the power of ridicule, but principally upon feelings of honour, gratitude, and generosity. Harry now no longer crossed any of his projects, but was become himself the means of carrying many into execution. The plan of a match for Marcus with Miss Annaly was entirely at an end. That young lady had given a decided refusal; and some circumstances, which we cannot here stop to explain, rendered Marcus and his father easy under that disappointment. No jealousy or competition existing, therefore, any longer between his son and ward, Sir Ulick's affection for Ormond returned in full tide; nor did he reproach himself for having banished Harry from Castle Hermitage, or for having formerly neglected, and almost forgotten him for two or three years. Sir Ulick took the matter up just as easily as he had laid it down—he now looked on Harry not as the youth whom he had deserted, but as the orphan boy whom he had cherished in adversity, and whom he had a consequent right to produce and patronize in prosperity. Beyond, or beneath all this, there was another reason why Sir Ulick took so much pains, and felt so much anxiety, to establish his influence over his ward. This reason cannot yet be mentioned—he had hardly revealed it to himself—it was deep down in his soul—to be or not to be—as circumstances, time, and the hour, should decide.

CHAPTER XIX.

After having lived so long in retirement, our young hero, when he was to go into company again, had many fears that his manners would appear rustic and unfashioned. With all these apprehensions as to his manners there was mixed a large proportion of pride of character, which tended rather to increase than to diminish his apparent timidity. He dreaded that people would value him, or think that he valued himself, for his newly acquired fortune, instead of his good qualities: he feared that he should be flattered; and he feared that he should like flattery. In the midst of all these various and contradictory apprehensions, he would perhaps have been awkward and miserable, had he been introduced into society by one who had less knowledge of the world, or less knowledge of the human heart, than Sir Ulick O'Shane possessed. Sir Ulick treated him as if he had always lived in good company. Without presupposing any ignorance, he at the same time took care to warn him of any etiquette or modern fashion, so that no one should perceive the warning but themselves. He neither offended Ormond's pride by seeming to patronize or *produce* him, nor did he let his timidity suffer from uncertainty or neglect. Ormond's fortune was never adverted to, in any way that could hurt his desire to be valued for his own sake; but he was made to feel that it was a part, and a very agreeable part, of his personal merit. Managed in this kind and skilful manner, he became perfectly at ease and happy. His spirits rose, and he enjoyed every thing with the warmth of youth, and with the enthusiasm of his natural character.

The first evening that "the earthly paradise" of Castle Hermitage re-opened upon his view, he was presented to all the well-dressed, well-bred belles. Black, brown, and fair, for the first hour appeared to him all beautiful. His guardian standing apart, and seeming to listen to a castle secretary, who was whispering to him of state affairs, observed all that was passing.

Contrary to his guardian's expectations, however, Ormond was the next morning faithful to his resolution, and did not appear among the angels at the breakfast-table at Castle Hermitage. "It won't last a good week," said Sir Ulick to himself. But that good week, and the next, it lasted. Harry's studies, to be sure, were sometimes interrupted by floating visions of the Miss Darrells, Dartfords, and Lardners. He every now and then sung bits of their songs, repeated their bon-mots, and from time to time laying down his book, started up and practised quadrille steps, to refresh himself, and increase his attention. His representations of all he saw and heard at Castle Hermitage, and his frank and natural description of the impression that every thing and every body made upon him, were amusing and interesting to his friends at Vicar's Dale. It was not by satire that he amused them, but by simplicity mixed with humour and good sense—good sense sometimes half opening his eyes, and humour describing what he saw with those eyes, half open, half shut.

"Pray what sort of people are the Darrells and Dartfords?" said Mrs. Cambray.

"Oh! delightful—the girls especially—sing like angels."

"Well, the ladies I know are all angels with you at present—that you have told us several times."

"It's really true, I believe—at least as far as I can see: but you know I have not had time to see farther than the outside yet."

"The gentlemen, however—I suppose you have seen the inside of some of them?"

"Certainly—those who have any thing inside of them—Dartford, for instance."

"Well, Mr. Dartford, he is the man Sir Ulick said was so clever."

"Very clever—he is—I suppose, though I don't really recollect any thing remarkable that I have heard him say. But the wit must be *in* him—and he lets out a good deal of his opinions—of his opinion of himself a little too much. But he is much admired."

"And Mr. Darrell—what of him?"

"Very fashionable. But indeed all I know about him is, that his dress is *quite the thing*, and that he knows more about dishes and cooks than I could have conceived any man upon earth of his age could know—but they say it's the fashion—he is very fashionable, I hear."

"But is he conceited?"

"Why, I do not know—his manner might appear a little conceited—but in reality he must be wonderfully humble—for he certainly values his horses far above himself—and then he is quite content if his boot-tops are admired. By-the-bye, there is a *famous invaluable* receipt he has for polishing those boot-tops, which is to make quite another man of me—if I don't forget to put him in mind about it."

"And Mr. Lardner?"

"Oh! a pleasant young man—has so many good songs, and good stories, and is so good-natured in repeating them. But I hope people won't make him repeat them too often, for I can conceive one might be tired, in time."

During the course of the first three weeks, Harry was three times in imminent danger of falling in love—first, with the beautiful, and beautifully dressed, Miss Darrell, who danced, sung, played, rode, did every thing charmingly, and was universally admired. She was remarkably good-humoured, even when some of her companions were rather cross. Miss Darrell reigned queen of the day, and queen of the ball, for three days and three nights, unrivalled in our young hero's eyes; but on the fourth night, Ormond chancing to praise the fine shape of one of her very dear friends, Miss Darrell whispered, "She owes that fine shape to a finely padded corset. Oh! I am clear of what I tell you—she is my intimate friend."

From that moment Ormond was cured of all desire to be the intimate friend of this fair lady. The second peerless damsel, whose praises he sounded to Dr. Cambray, between the fits of reading Middleton's Cicero, was Miss Eliza Darrell, the youngest of the three sisters: she was not yet *come out*, though in the mean time allowed to appear at Castle Hermitage; and she was so *naïve*, and so timid, and so very bashful, that Sir Ulick was forced always to bring her into the room leaning on his arm;—she could really hardly walk into a room—and if any body looked at her, she was so much distressed—and there were such pretty confusions and retreatings, and such a manoeuvring to get to the side-table every day, and "Sir Ulick so terribly determined it should not be." It was all naturally acted, and by a young pretty actress. Ormond, used only to the gross affectation of Dora, did not suspect that there was any affectation in the case. He pitied her so much, that Sir Ulick was certain "love was in the next degree." Of this the young lady herself was still more secure; and in her security she forgot some of her graceful timidity. It happened that, in standing up for country dances one night, some dispute about precedency occurred. Miss Eliza Darrell was the *honourable* Eliza Darrell; and some young lady, who was not honourable, in contempt, defiance, neglect, or ignorance, stood above her. The timid Eliza remonstrated in no very gentle voice, and the colour came into her face—"the eloquent blood spoke" too plainly. She!—the gentle Eliza!—pushed for her place, and with her honourable elbows made way for herself; for what will not even well-bred belles do in a crowd? Unfortunately, well-bred beaux are bound to support them. Ormond was on the point of being drawn into a quarrel with the partner of the offending party, when Sir Ulick appearing in the midst, and not seeming to know that any thing was going wrong, broke up the intended set of country dances, by insisting upon it that the Miss Darrells had promised him a quadrille, and that they must dance it then, as there was but just time before supper. Harry, who had seen how little his safety was in the eye of the gentle Eliza, in comparison with the most trifling point of her offended pride, was determined in future not to expose himself to similar danger. The next young lady who took his fancy was of course as unlike the last as possible: she was one of the remarkably pleasant, sprightly, clever, most agreeable Miss Lardners. She did not interest him much, but she amused him exceedingly. Her sister had one day said to her, "Anne, you can't be pretty, so you had better be odd." Anne took the advice, set up for being odd, and succeeded. She was a mimic, a wit, and very satirical; and as long as the satire touched only those for whom he did not care, Ormond was extremely diverted. He did not think it quite feminine or amiable, but still it was entertaining: there was also something flattering in being exempted from this general reprobation and ridicule. Miss Lardner was intolerant of all insipid people—*flats*, as she called them. How far Ormond might have been drawn on by this laughing, talking, satirical, flattering wit, there is no saying; but luckily they fell out one evening about old Lady Annaly. Miss Lardner was not aware that Ormond knew, much less could she have conceived, that he liked her ladyship. Miss Lardner was mimicking her, for the amusement of a set of young ladies who were standing round the fire after dinner, when Harry Ormond came in: he was not quite as much diverted as she expected.

"Mr. Ormond does not know the *original*—the copy is lost upon him," said Miss Lardner; "and happy it is for you," continued she, turning to him, "that you do not know her, for Lady Annaly is as stiff and tiresome an original as ever was seen or heard of;—and the worst of it is, she is an original without originality."

"Lady Annaly!" cried Ormond, with surprise, "surely not the Lady Annaly I know."

"There's but one that I know of—Heaven forbid that there were two! But I beg your pardon, Mr. Ormond, if she is a friend of yours—I humbly beg your forgiveness—I did not know your taste was so *very good!* Lady Annaly is a fine old lady, certainly—vastly respectable; and I so far agree with Mr. Ormond, that of the two paragons, mother and daughter, I prefer the mother. Paragons in their teens are insufferable: patterns of perfection are good for nothing in society, except to be torn to pieces."

Miss Lardner pursued this diversion of tearing them to pieces, still flattering herself that her present wit and drollery would prevail with Ormond, as she had found it prevail with most people against an absent friend. But Ormond thought upon this occasion she showed more flippancy than wit, and more ill-nature than humour. He was shocked at the want of feeling and reverence for age with which she, a young girl, just entering into the world, spoke of a person of Lady Annaly's years and high character. In the heat of attack, and in her eagerness to carry her point against the Annalys, the young lady, according to custom, proceeded from sarcasm to scandal. Every ill-natured report she had ever heard against any of the family, she now repeated with exaggeration and asseverations—vehement in proportion to the weakness of proof. She asserted that Lady Annaly, with all her high character, was very hard-

hearted to some of her nearest family connexions. Sweet Lady Millicent!
—Oh! how barbarously she used her!—Miss Annaly too she attacked, as
a cold-blooded jilt. If the truth must be told, she had actually broken the
heart of a young nobleman, who was fool enough to be taken in by her
sort of manner: and the son, the famous Sir Herbert Annaly! he was an
absolute miser: Miss Lardner declared that she knew, from the best
authority, most shameful instances of his shabbiness.

The instances were stated, but Ormond could not believe these stories;
and what was more, he began to doubt the good faith of the person by
whom they were related. He suspected that she uttered these slanders,
knowing them to be false.

Miss Lardner observing that Ormond made no farther defence, but now
stood silent, and with downcast eyes, flattered herself that she had
completely triumphed. Changing the subject, she would have resumed
with him her familiar, playful tone; but all chance of her ever triumphing
over Ormond's head or heart was now at an end: so finished the third of
his three weeks' *fancies*. Such evanescent fancies would not have been
worth mentioning, but for the effect produced on his mind; though they
left scarcely any individual traces, they made a general and useful
impression. They produced a permanent contempt for *scandal*, that
common vice of idle society. He determined to guard against it
cautiously himself; and ever after, when he saw a disposition to it in any
woman, however highly-bred, highly-accomplished, or highly-gifted, he
considered her as a person of mean mind, with whom he could never
form any connexion of friendship or love.

The Lardners, Darrells, Dartfords, vanished, and new figures were to
appear in the magic lantern at Castle Hermitage. Sir Ulick thought a few
preliminary observations necessary to his ward. His opinion of Ormond's
capacity and steadiness had considerably diminished, in consequence of
his various mistakes of character, and sudden changes of opinion; for Sir
Ulick, with all his abilities, did not discriminate between want of
understanding, and want of practice. Besides, he did not see the whole:
he saw the outward boyish folly—he did not see the inward manly sense;
he judged Ormond by a false standard, by comparison with the young

men of the world of his own age. He knew that none of these, even of moderate capacity, could have been three times in three weeks so near being *taken in*—not one would have made the sort of blunders, much less would any one, having made them, have acknowledged them as frankly as Ormond did. It was this *imprudent* candour which lowered him most in his guardian's estimation. From not having lived in society, Harry was not aware of the signs and tokens of folly or wisdom by which the world judge; the opinion of the bystanders had not habitual power over him. While the worldly young men guarded themselves with circumspect self-love against every external appearance of folly, Harry was completely unguarded: they lived cheaply upon borrowed wisdom; he profited dearly, but permanently, by his own experience.

"My dear boy," said Sir Ulick, "are you aware that his Excellency the Lord Lieutenant is coming to Castle Hermitage to-morrow?"

"Yes, sir; so I heard you say," replied Harry. "What sort of a man is he?"

"*Man!*" repeated Sir Ulick, smiling. "In the first place, he is a very *great* man, and may be of great service to you."

"How so, sir? I don't want any thing from him. Now I have a good fortune of my own, what can I want from any man—or if I must not say *man*, any *great* man?"

"My dear Harry, though a man's fortune is good, it may be better for pushing it."

"And worse, may it not, sir? Did not I hear you speaking last night of Lord Somebody, who had been pushing his fortune all his life, and died pennyless?"

"True, because he pushed ill; if he had pushed well, he would have got into a good place."

"I thank Heaven, I can get that now without any pushing."

"You can!—yes, by my interest perhaps you mean."

"No; by my own money, I mean."

"Bribery and corruption! Harry, places are not in this country to be bought—openly—these are things one must not talk of: and pray, with your own money—if you could—what place upon earth would you purchase?"

"The only place in the world I should wish for, sir, would be a place in the country."

Sir Ulick was surprised and alarmed; but said not a word that could betray his feelings.

"A place of my own," continued Ormond, "a comfortable house and estate, on which I could live independently and happily, with some charming amiable woman."

"Darrell, Dartford, Lardner, which?" said Sir Ulick, with a sarcastic smile.

"I am cured of these foolish fancies, sir."

"Well, there is another more dangerous might seize you, against which I must warn you, and I trust one word of advice you will not take amiss."

"Sir, I am very much obliged to you: how could I take advice from you as any thing but a proof of friendship?"

"Then, my dear boy, I must tell you, *in confidence*, what you will find out the first night you are in his company, that his Excellency drinks hard."

"No danger of my following his example," said Harry. "Thank you, sir, for the warning; but I am sure enough of myself on this point, because I have been tried—and when I would not drink to please my own dear King Corny, there is not much danger of my drinking to please a Lord Lieutenant, who, after all, is nothing to me."

"After all," said Sir Ulick; "but you are not come to *after all* yet—you know nothing about his Excellency yet."

"Nothing but what you have told me, sir: if he drinks hard, I think he sets no very good example as a Lord Lieutenant of Ireland."

"What oft was thought, perhaps, but ne'er so bluntly expressed," said Sir Ulick.

Sir Ulick was afterwards surprised to see the firmness with which his ward, when in company with persons of the first rank and fashion, resisted the combined force of example, importunity, and ridicule. Dr. Cambray was pleased, but not surprised; for he had seen in his young friend other instances of this adherence to whatever he had once been convinced was right. Resolution is a quality or power of mind totally independent of knowledge of the world. The habit of self-control can be acquired by any individual, in any situation. Ormond had practised and strengthened it, even in the retirement of the Black Islands.

Other and far more dangerous trials were now preparing for him; but before we go on to these, it may be expected that we should not pass over in silence the vice-regal visit—and yet what can we say about it? All that Ormond could say was, that "he supposed it was a great honour, but it was no great pleasure."

The mornings, two out of five, being rainy, hung very heavily on hand in spite of the billiard-room. Fine weather, riding, shooting, or boating, killed time well enough till dinner; and Harry said he liked this part of the business exceedingly, till he found that some great men were very cross, if they did not shoot as many little birds as he did. Then came dinner, the great point of relief and reunion!—and there had been late dinners, and long dinners, and great dinners, fine plate, good dishes, and plenty of wine, but a dearth of conversation—the natural topics chained up by etiquette. One half of the people at table were too prudent, the other half too stupid, to talk. Sir Ulick talked away indeed; but even he was not half so entertaining as usual, because he was forced to bring down his wit and humour to *court quality*. In short, till the company had drunk a certain quantity of wine, nothing was said worth repeating, and afterwards nothing repeatable.

After the vice-regal raree show was over, and that the grand folk had been properly bowed into their carriages, and had fairly driven away, there was some diversion to be had. People, without yawning, seemed to recover from a dead sleep; the state of the atmosphere was changed; there was a happy thaw; the frozen words and bits and ends of conversations were repeated in delightful confusion. The men of wit, in revenge for their prudent silence, were now happy and noisy beyond measure. Ormond was much entertained: he had an opportunity of being not only amused but instructed by conversation, for all the great dealers in information, who had kept up their goods while there was no market, now that there was a demand, unpacked, and brought them out in profusion. There was such a rich supply, and such a quick and happy intercourse of wit and knowledge, as quite delighted, almost dazzled, his eyes; but his eyes were strong. He had a mind untainted with envy, highly capable of emulation. Much was indeed beyond, or above, the reach of his present powers; but nothing was beyond his generous admiration—nothing above his future hopes of attainment. The effect and more than the effect, which Sir Ulick had foreseen, was produced on Ormond's mind by hearing the conversation of some of those who had distinguished themselves in political life; he caught their spirit—their ambition: his wish was no longer merely to see the world, but to distinguish himself in it. His guardian saw the noble ambition rising in his mind. Oh! at that instant, how could he think of debasing it to servile purposes—of working this great power only for paltry party ends?

CHAPTER XX.

New circumstances arose, which unexpectedly changed the course of our hero's mind. There was a certain Lady Millicent, whose name Lady Norton had read from her memorandum-book among the list of guests expected at Castle Hermitage. Sir Ulick, as Ormond recollected, had pronounced her to be a charming, elegant, fascinating creature. Sir Ulick's praise was sometimes exaggerated, and often lavished from party motives, or given half in jest and half in earnest, against his conscience. But when he did speak sincerely, no man's taste or judgment as to female beauty, manners, and character, could be more safely trusted.

He was sincere in all he said of Lady Millicent's appearance and manners; but as to the rest, he did not think himself bound to tell all he knew about her.

Her ladyship arrived at Castle Hermitage. Ormond saw her, and thought that his guardian had not in the least exaggerated as to her beauty, grace, or elegance.

She was a very young widow, still in mourning for her husband, a gallant officer, who had fallen the preceding year at a siege in Flanders.

Lady Millicent, as Lady Norton said, had not recovered, and she feared never would recover from the shock her health had received at the time of her husband's death. This account interested Ormond exceedingly for the young widow.

There was something peculiarly engaging in the pensive softness and modesty of her manner. It appeared free from affectation. Far from making any display of her feelings, she seemed as much as possible to repress them, and to endeavour to be cheerful, that she might not damp the gaiety of others. Her natural disposition, Lady Norton said, was very sprightly; and however passive and subdued she might appear at present, she was of a high independent spirit, that would, on any great occasion, think and act for itself. Better and better—each trait suited Ormond's character more and more: his own observation confirmed the high opinion which the praises of her friend tended to inspire. Ormond was particularly pleased with the indulgent manner in which Lady Millicent spoke of her own sex; she was free from that propensity to detraction which had so disgusted him in his last love. Even of those by whom, as it had been hinted to him, she had been hardly treated, she spoke with gentleness and candour. Recollecting Miss Lardner's assertion, that "Lady Annaly had used Lady Millicent barbarously," he purposely mentioned Lady Annaly, to hear what she would say. "Lady Annaly," said she, "is a most respectable woman—she has her prejudices—who is there that has not?—It is unfortunate for me that she has been prepossessed against *me*. She is one of my nearest connexions by marriage—one to whom I might have looked in difficulty and distress— one of the few persons whose assistance and interference I would willingly have accepted, and would even have stooped to ask; but unhappily—I can tell you no more," said she, checking herself: "it is every way an unfortunate affair; and," added she, after a deep sigh, "the most unfortunate part of it is, that it is my own fault."

That Ormond could hardly believe; and whether it were or not, whatever the unfortunate affair might be, the candour, the gentleness, with which she spoke, even when her feelings were obviously touched and warm, interested him deeply in her favour. He had heard that the Annalys were just returning to Ireland, and he determined to go as soon as possible to see them: he hoped they would come to Castle Hermitage, and that this coolness might be made up. Meantime the more he saw of Lady Millicent, the more he was charmed with her. Sir Ulick was much engaged with various business in the mornings, and Lady Norton, Lady Millicent, and Ormond, spent their time together: walking, driving in the sociable, or boating on the lake, they were continually together. Lady Norton, a very good kind of well-bred little woman, was a nonentity in conversation; but she never interrupted it, nor laid the slightest restraint on any one by her presence, which, indeed, was usually forgotten by Ormond. His conversation with Lady Millicent generally took a sentimental turn. She did not always speak sense, but she talked elegant nonsense with a sweet persuasive voice and eloquent eyes: hers was a kind of exalted sentimental morality, referring every thing to feeling, and to the notion of *sacrifice*, rather than to a sense of duty, principle, or reason. She was all for sensibility and enthusiasm—enthusiasm in particular—with her there was no virtue without it. Acting from the hope of making yourself or others happy, or from any view of utility, was acting merely from low selfish motives. Her "point of virtue was so high, that ordinary mortals might well console themselves by perceiving the impossibility of ever reaching it." Exalted to the clouds, she managed matters as she pleased there, and made charming confusion. When she condescended to return to earth, and attempted to define—no, not to define—definitions were death to her imagination!—but to *describe* her notions, she was nearly unintelligible. She declared, however, that she understood herself perfectly well; and Ormond, deceived by eloquence, of which he was a passionate admirer, thought that he understood when he only *felt*. Her ideas of virtue were carried to such extremes, that they touched the opposite vices—in truth, there was nothing to prevent them; for the line between right and wrong, that line which should be strongly marked, was effaced: so delicately had sentiment shaded off its boundaries. These female metaphysics, this character of exalted imagination and sensitive softness, was not quite so cheap and common some years ago, as it has lately become. The consequences to which it practically leads were not then fully foreseen and understood. At all times a man experienced in female character, who had any knowledge of the world, even supposing he had no skill in metaphysics, would easily have seen to what all this tends, and where it usually terminates; and such a man would never have thought of marrying Lady Millicent. But Ormond was inexperienced: the whole, matter and manner, was new to him; he was struck with the delicacy and sensibility of the fair sophist, and with all that was ingenious and plausible in the doctrine, instead of being alarmed by its dangerous tendency. It should be observed, in justice to Lady Millicent, that she was perfectly sincere—if we may use the expression *of good faith* in absurdities. She did not use this sentimental sophistry, as it has since been too often employed by many, to veil from themselves the criminality of passion, or to mask the deformity of vice: there was, perhaps, the more immediate hazard of her erring from ignorance and rashness; but there was also, in her youth and innocence, a chance that she might instinctively start back the moment she should see the precipice.

One evening Sir Ulick was talking of Lord Chesterfield's Letters, a book at that time much in vogue, but which the good sense and virtue of England soon cast into disrepute; and which, in spite of the charms of wit and style, in spite of many sparkling and some valuable observations mixed with its corruption, has since sunk, fortunately for the nation, almost into oblivion. But when these *private* letters were first published, and when my lord, who now appears so stiff and awkward, was in the fashion of the day, there was no withstanding it. The book was a manual of education—with the vain hope of getting cheaply second-hand knowledge of the world, it was read universally by every young man entering life, from the nobleman's son, while his hair was powdering, to the 'prentice thumbing it surreptitiously behind the counter. Sir Ulick O'Shane, of course, recommended it to his ward: to Lady Millicent's credit, she inveighed against it with honest indignation.

"What!" said Sir Ulick, smiling, "you are shocked at the idea of Lord Chesterfield's advising his pupil at Paris to prefer a reputable affair with a married woman, to a disreputable intrigue with an opera girl! Well, I believe you are right as an Englishwoman, my dear Lady Millicent; and I am clear, at all events, that you are right, as a woman, to blush so eloquently with virtuous indignation:—Lady Annaly herself could not have spoken and looked the thing better."

"So I was just thinking," said Ormond.

"Only the difference, Harry, between a young and an elderly woman," said Sir Ulick. "Truths divine come mended from the lips of youth and beauty."

His compliment was lost upon Lady Millicent. At the first mention of Lady Annaly's name she had sighed deeply, and had fallen into reverie—and Ormond, as he looked at her, fell into raptures at the tender expression of her countenance. Sir Ulick tapped him on the shoulder, and drawing him a little on one side, "Take care of your heart, young man," whispered he: "no serious attachment here—remember, I warn you." Lady Norton joined them, and nothing more was said.

"Take care of my heart," thought Ormond: "why should I guard it against such a woman?—what better can I do with it than offer it to such a woman?"

A thought had crossed Ormond's mind which recurred at this instant. From the great admiration Sir Ulick expressed for Lady Millicent, and the constant attention—more than gallant—tender attention, which Sir Ulick paid her, Ormond was persuaded that, but for that half of the broken chain of matrimony which still encumbered him whom it could not bind, Sir Ulick would be very glad to offer Lady Millicent not only his heart but his hand. Suspecting this partiality, and imagining a latent jealousy, Ormond did not quite like to consult his guardian about his own sentiments and proceedings. He wished previously to consult his impartial and most safe friend, Dr. Cambray. But Dr. Cambray had been absent from home ever since the arrival of Lady Millicent. The doctor and his family had been on a visit to a relation at a distance. Ormond, impatient for their return, had every day questioned the curate; and at last, in reply to his regular question of "When do you expect the doctor, sir?" he heard the glad tidings of "We expect him to-morrow, or next day, sir, positively."

The next day, Ormond, who was now master of a very elegant phaeton and beautiful gray horses, and, having for some time been under the tuition of that knowing whip Tom Darrell, could now drive to admiration, prevailed upon Lady Millicent to trust herself with him in his phaeton—Sir Ulick came up just as Ormond had handed Lady Millicent into the carriage, and, pressing on his ward's shoulder, said, "Have you the reins safe?"

"Yes."

"That's well—remember now, Harry Ormond," said he, with a look which gave a double meaning to his words, "remember, I charge you, the warning I gave you last night—drive carefully—pray, young sir, look before you—no rashness!—young horses these," added he, patting the horses—"pray be careful, Harry."

Ormond promised to be very careful, and drove off.

"I suppose," thought he, "my guardian must have some good reason for this reiterated caution; I will not let her see my sentiments till I know his reasons; besides, as Dr. Cambray returns to-morrow, I can wait another day."

Accordingly, though not without putting considerable restraint upon himself, Ormond talked of the beauties of nature, and of indifferent matters. The conversation rather flagged, and sometimes on her ladyship's side as well as on his. He fancied that she was more reserved than usual, and a little embarrassed. He exerted himself to entertain her —that was but common civility;—he succeeded, was pleased to see her spirits rise, and her embarrassment wear off. When she revived, her manner was this day so peculiarly engaging, and the tones of her voice so soft and winning, that it required all Ormond's resolution to refrain from declaring his passion. Now, for the first time, he conceived a hope that he might make himself agreeable to her; that he might, in time, soothe her grief, and restore her to happiness. Her expressions were all delicately careful to imply nothing but friendship—but a woman's friendship insensibly leads to love. As they were returning home after a delightful drive, they entered upon this subject, so favourable to the nice casuistry of sentiment, and to the enthusiastic eloquence of passion—when, at an opening in the road, a carriage crossed them so suddenly, that Ormond had but just time to pull up his horses.

"Dr. Cambray, I declare: the very man I wished to see."

The doctor, whose countenance had been full of affectionate pleasure at the first sight of his young friend, changed when he saw who was in the phaeton with him. The doctor looked panic-struck.

"Lady Millicent, Dr. Cambray," Ormond began the introduction; but each bowing, said, in a constrained voice, "I have the honour of knowing —" "I have the pleasure of being acquainted—"

The pleasure and honour seemed to be painful and embarrassing to both.

"Don't let us detain you," said the doctor; "but I hope, Mr. Ormond, you will let me see you as soon as you can at Vicar's Dale."

"You would not doubt that, my dear doctor," said Ormond, "if you knew how impatient I have been for your return—I will be with you before you are all out of the carriage."

"The sooner the better," said the doctor.

"The sooner the better," echoed the friendly voices of Mrs. Cambray and her daughter.

Ormond drove on; but from this moment, till they reached Castle Hermitage, no more agreeable conversation passed between him and his fair companion. It was all constrained.

"I was not aware that Dr. Cambray had the honour of being acquainted with Lady Millicent," said Ormond.

"O yes! I had the pleasure some time ago," replied Lady Millicent, "when he was in Dublin—not lately—I was a great favourite of his once."

"Once, and always, I should have thought."

"Dr. Cambray's a most amiable, respectable man," said her ladyship: "he must be a great acquisition in this neighbourhood—a good clergyman is valuable every where; in Ireland most especially, where the spirit of conciliation is much wanted. 'Tis unknown how much a good clergyman may do in Ireland."

"Very true—certainly."

So with a repetition of truisms, interspersed with reflections on the state of Ireland, tithes, and the education of the poor, they reached Castle Hermitage.

"Lady Millicent, you look pale," said Sir Ulick, as he handed her out.

"Oh, no, I have had a most delightful drive."

Harry just stayed to say that Dr. Cambray was returned, and that he must run to see him, and off he went. He found the doctor in his study.

"Well, my dear doctor," said Ormond, in breathless consternation, "what is the matter?"

"Nothing, I hope," said the doctor, looking earnestly in Ormond's face; "and yet your countenance tells me that my fears are well founded."

"What is it you fear, sir?"

"The lady who was in the phaeton with you, Lady Millicent, I fear—"

"Why should you fear, sir?—Oh! tell me at once—what do you know of her?"

"At once, then, I know her to be a very imprudent, though hope she is still an innocent woman."

"Innocent!" repeated Ormond. "Good Heavens! is it possible that there can be any doubt? Imprudent! My dear doctor, perhaps you have been misinformed."

"All I know on the subject is this," said Dr. Cambray: "during Lord Millicent's absence on service, a gentleman of high rank and gallantry paid assiduous attention to Lady Millicent. Her relation and friend, Lady Annaly, advised her to break off all intercourse with this gentleman in such a decided manner, as to silence scandal. Lady Millicent followed but half the advice of her friend; she discountenanced the public attentions of her admirer, but she took opportunities of meeting him at private parties: Lady Annaly again interfered—Lady Millicent was offended: but the death of her husband saved her from farther danger, and opened her eyes to the views of a man, who thought her no longer worthy his pursuit, when he might have her for life."

Ormond saw that there was no resource for him but immediately to quit Castle Hermitage; therefore, the moment he returned, he informed Sir Ulick of his determination, pointing out to him the impropriety of his remaining in the society of Lady Millicent, when his opinion of her character and the sentiments which had so strongly influenced his behaviour, were irrevocably changed. This was an unexpected blow upon Sir Ulick: he had his private reasons for wishing to detain Ormond at Castle Hermitage till he was of age, to dissipate his mind by amusement and variety, and to obtain over it an habitual guidance.

Ormond proposed immediately to visit the continent: by the time he should arrive at Paris, Dora would be settled there, and he should be introduced into the best company. The subtle Sir Ulick, perceiving that Ormond must change his quarters, advised him to see something of his own country before he went abroad. In the course of a few days, various letters of recommendation were procured for him from Sir Ulick and his connexions; and, what was of still more consequence, from Dr. Cambray and his friends.

During this interval, Ormond once more visited the Black Islands; scenes which recalled a thousand tender, and a few embittering, recollections. He was greeted with heartfelt affection by many of the inhabitants of the island, with whom he had passed some of his boyish days. Of some scenes he had to be ashamed, but of others he was justly proud; and from every tongue he heard the delightful praises of his departed friend and benefactor.

His little farm had been well managed during his absence; the trees he had planted began to make some appearance; and, upon the whole, his visit to the Black Islands revived his generous feelings, and refreshed those traces of early virtue which had been engraven on his heart.

At Castle Hermitage every thing had been prepared for his departure; and upon visiting his excellent friend at the vicarage, he found the whole family heartily interested in his welfare, and ready to assist him, by letters of introduction to the best people in every part of Ireland which Ormond intended to visit.

CHAPTER XXI.

During the course of Ormond's tour through Ireland, he frequently found himself in company with those who knew the history of public affairs for years past, and were but too well acquainted with the political profligacy and shameful jobbing of Sir Ulick O'Shane.

Some of these gentlemen, knowing Mr. Ormond to be his ward, refrained, of course, from touching upon any subject relative to Sir Ulick; and when Ormond mentioned him, evaded the conversation, or agreed in general terms in praising his abilities, wit, and address. But, after a day or two's journey from Castle Hermitage, when he was beyond his own and the adjoining counties, when he went into company with those who happened to know nothing of his connexion with Sir Ulick O'Shane, then he heard him spoken of in a very different manner. He was quite astonished and dismayed by the general abuse, as he thought it, which was poured upon him.

"Well, every man of abilities excites envy—every man who takes a part in politics, especially in times when parties run high, must expect to be abused: they must bear it; and their friends must learn to bear it for them."

Such were the reflections with which Ormond at first comforted himself. As far as party abuse went, this was quite satisfactory; even facts, or what are told as facts, are so altered by the manner of seeing them by an opposite party, that, without meaning to traduce, they calumniate. Ormond entrenched himself in total disbelief, and cool assertion of his disbelief, of a variety of anecdotes he continually heard discreditable to Sir Ulick. Still he expected that, when he went into other company, and met with men of Sir Ulick's own party, he should obtain proofs of the falsehood of these stories, and by that he might be able, not only to contradict, but to confute them. People, however, only smiled, and told him that he had better inquire no farther, if he expected to find Sir Ulick an immaculate character. Those who liked him best, laughed off the notorious instances of his public defection of principle, and of his private jobbing, as good jokes; proofs of his knowledge of the world—his address, his frankness, his being "not a bit of a hypocrite." But even those who professed to like him best, and to be the least scrupulous with regard to public virtue, still spoke with a sort of facetious contempt of Sir Ulick, as a thorough-going friend of the powers that be—as a hack of administration—as a man who knew well enough what he was about. Ormond was continually either surprised or hurt by these insinuations. The concurrent testimony of numbers who had no interest to serve, or prejudice to gratify, operated upon him by degrees, so as to enforce conviction, and this was still more painful.

Harry became so sore and irritable upon this subject, that he was now every day in danger of entangling himself in some quarrel in defence of his guardian. Several times the master of the house prevented this, and brought him to reason, by representing that the persons who talked of Sir Ulick were quite ignorant of his connexion with him, and spoke only according to general opinion, and to the best of their belief, of a public character, who was fair game. It was, at that time, much the fashion among a certain set in Dublin, to try their wit upon each other in political and poetical squibs—the more severe and bitter these were, the more they were applauded: the talent for invective was in the highest demand at this period in Ireland; it was considered as the unequivocal proof of intellectual superiority. The display of it was the more admired, as it could not be enjoyed without a double portion of that personal promptitude to give the *satisfaction of a gentleman*, on which the Irish pride themselves: the taste of the nation, both for oratory and manners, has become of late years so much more refined, that when any of the lampoons of that day are now recollected, people are surprised at the licence of abuse which was then tolerated, and even approved of in fashionable society. Sir Ulick O'Shane, as a well-known public character, had been the subject of a variety of puns, bon-mots, songs, and epigrams, which had become so numerous as to be collected under the title of Ulysseana. Upon the late separation of Sir Ulick and his lady, a new edition, with a caricature frontispiece, had been published; unfortunately for Ormond, this had just worked its way from Dublin to this part of the country.

It happened one day, at a gentleman's house where this Ulysseana had not yet been seen, that a lady, a visitor and a stranger, full of some of the lines which she had learned by heart, began to repeat them for the amusement of the tea-table. Ladies do not always consider how much mischief they may do by such imprudence; nor how they may hazard valuable lives, for the sake of producing a *sensation*, by the repetition of *a severe thing*. Ormond came into the room after dinner, and with some other gentlemen gathered round the tea-table, while the lady was repeating some extracts from the new edition of the Ulysseana. The master and mistress of the house made reiterated attempts to stop the lady; but, too intent upon herself and her second-hand wit to comprehend or take these hints, she went on reciting the following lines:—

> To serve in parliament the nation,
> Sir Ulick read his recantation:
>   At first he joined the patriot throng,
>   But soon perceiving he was wrong,
>   He ratted to the courtier tribe,
>   Bought by a title and a bribe;
>   But how that new found friend to bind,
>   With any oath—of any kind,
>   Disturb'd the premier's wary mind.
>   "Upon his faith.—Upon his word,"
>   Oh! that, my friend, is too absurd.
>   "Upon his honour."—Quite a jest.
>   "Upon his conscience."—No such test.
>   "By all he has on earth."—'Tis gone.
>   "By all his hopes of Heaven."—They're none.
>   "How then secure him in our pay—
>   He can't be trusted for a day?"
>   How?—When you want the fellow's throat—
>   Pay by the job—you have his vote.

Sir Ulick himself, had he been present, would have laughed off the epigram with the best grace imaginable, and so, in good policy, ought Ormond to have taken it. But he felt it too much, and was not in the habit of laughing when he was vexed. Most of the company, who knew any thing of his connexion with Sir Ulick, or who understood the agonizing looks of the master and mistress of the house, politely refrained from smiles or applause; but a cousin of the lady who repeated the lines, a young man who was one of the hateful tribe of *quizzers*, on purpose to *try* Ormond, praised the verses to the skies, and appealed to him for his opinion.

"I can't admire them, sir," replied Ormond.

"What fault can you find with them?" said the young man, winking at the bystanders.

"I think them *incorrect*, in the first place, sir," said Ormond, "and altogether indifferent."

"Well, at any rate, they can't be called *moderate*," said the gentleman; "and as to incorrect, the substance, I fancy, is correctly true."

"*Fancy*, sir!—It would be hard if character were to be at the mercy of fancy," cried Ormond, hastily; but checking himself, he, in a mild tone, added, "before we go any farther, sir, I should inform you that I am a ward of Sir Ulick O Shane's."

"Oh! mercy," exclaimed the lady, who had repeated the verses; "I am sure I did not know that, or I would not have said a word—I declare I beg your pardon, sir."

Ormond's bow and smile spoke his perfect satisfaction with the lady's contrition, and his desire to relieve her from farther anxiety. So the matter might have happily ended; but her cousin, though he had begun merely with an intention to try Ormond's temper, now felt piqued by his spirit, and thought it incumbent upon him to persist. Having drunk enough to be ill-humoured, he replied, in an aggravating and ill-bred manner, "Your being Sir Ulick O'Shane's ward may make a difference in your feelings, sir, but I don't see why it should make any in my opinion."

"In the expression of that opinion at least, sir, I think it ought."

The master of the house now interfered, to explain and pacify, and Ormond had presence of mind and command enough over himself, to say no more while the ladies were present: he sat down, and began talking about some trifle in a gay tone; but his flushed cheek, and altered manner, showed that he was only repressing other feelings. The carriages of the visitors were announced, and the strangers rose to depart. Ormond accompanied the master of the house to hand the ladies to their carriages. To mark his being in perfect charity with the fair penitent, he showed her particular attention, which quite touched her; and as he put her into her carriage, she, all the time, repeated her apologies, declared it should be a lesson to her for life, and cordially shook hands with him at parting. For her sake, he wished that nothing more should be said on the subject.

But, on his return to the hall, he found there the cousin, buttoning on his great coat, and seeming loath to depart: still in ill-humour, the gentleman said, "I hope you are satisfied with that lady's apologies, Mr. Ormond."

"I am, sir, perfectly."

"That's lucky: for apologies are easier had from ladies than gentlemen, and become them better."

"I think it becomes gentlemen as well as ladies to make candid apologies, where they are conscious of being wrong—if there was no intention to give offence."

"*If* is a great peace-maker, sir; but I scorn to take advantage of an *if.*"

"Am I to suppose then, sir," said Ormond, "that it was your intention to offend me?"

"Suppose what you please, sir—I am not in the habit of explanation or apology."

"Then, sir, the sooner we meet the better," said Ormond. In consequence Ormond applied to an officer who had been present during the altercation, to be his second. Ormond felt that he had restrained his anger sufficiently—he was now as firm as he had been temperate. The parties met and fought: the man who deserved to have suffered, by the chance of this rational mode of deciding right and wrong, escaped unhurt; Ormond received a wound in his arm. It was only a flesh wound. He was at the house of a very hospitable gentleman, whose family were kind to him; and the inconvenience and pain were easily borne. In the opinion of all, in that part of the world, who knew the facts, he had conducted himself as well as the circumstances would permit; and, as it was essential, not only to the character of a hero, but of a gentleman at that time in Ireland, to fight a duel, we may consider Ormond as fortunate in not having been in the wrong. He rose in favour with the ladies, and in credit with the gentlemen, and he heard no more of the Ulysseana; but he was concerned to see paragraphs in all the Irish papers, about the duel that had been fought between M. N. Esq. jun. of ——, and H. O. Esq., in consequence of a dispute that arose about some satirical verses, repeated by a lady on a certain well-known character, nearly related to one of the parties. A flaming account of the duel followed, in which there was the usual newspaper proportion of truth and falsehood: Ormond knew and regretted that this paragraph must meet the eyes of his guardian; and still more he was sorry that Dr. Cambray should see it. He knew the doctor's Christian abhorrence of the whole system of duelling; and, by the statement in the papers, it appeared that that gallant youth, H. O. Esq., to whom the news-writer evidently wished to do honour, had been far more forward to provoke the fight than he had been, or than he ought to have been:—his own plain statement of facts, which he wrote to Dr. Cambray, would have set every thing to rights, but his letter crossed the doctor's on the road. As he was now in a remote place, which the delightful mail coach roads had not then reached—where the post came in only three days in the week—and where the mail cart either broke down, lost a wheel, had a tired horse, was overturned, or robbed, at an average once a fortnight—our hero had no alternative but patience, and the amusement of calculating dates and chances upon his restless sofa. His taste for reading enabled him to pass agreeably some of the hours of bodily confinement, which men, and young men especially, accustomed to a great deal of exercise, liberty, and locomotion, generally find so intolerably irksome. At length his wound was well enough for him to travel—letters for him arrived: a warm, affectionate one from his guardian; and one from Dr. Cambray, which relieved his anxiety.

"I must tell you, my dear young friend," said Dr. Cambray, "that while you have been defending Sir Ulick O'Shane's public character (of which, by-the-by, you know nothing), I have been defending your private character, of which I hope and believe I know something. The truth is always known in time, with regard to every character; and therefore, independently of other motives, moral and religious, it is more prudent to trust to time and truth for their defence, than to sword and pistol. I know you are impatient to hear what were the reports to your disadvantage, and from whom I had them. I had them from the Annalys; and they heard them in England, through various circuitous channels of female correspondents in Ireland. As far as we can trace them, we think that they originated with your old friend Miss Black. The first account Lady Annaly heard of you after she went to England, was, that you were living a most dissolute life in the Black Islands, with King Corny, who was described to be a profligate rebel, and his companion an ex-communicated catholic priest; king, priest, and *Prince Harry*, getting drunk together regularly every night of their lives. The next account which Lady Annaly received some months afterwards, in reply to inquiries she had made from her agent, was, that it was impossible to know any thing for certain of Mr. Harry Ormond, as he always kept in the Black Islands. The report was, that he had lately seduced a girl of the name of Peggy Sheridan, a respectable gardener's daughter, who was going to be married to a man of the name of Moriarty Carroll, a person whom Mr. Ormond had formerly shot in some unfortunate drunken quarrel. The match between her and Moriarty had been broken off in consequence. The following year accounts were worse and worse. This Harry Ormond had gained the affections of his benefactor's daughter, though, as he had been warned by her father, she was betrothed to another man. The young lady was afterwards, by her father's anger, and by Ormond's desertion of her, thrown into the arms of a French adventurer, whom Ormond brought into the house under pretence of learning French from him. Immediately after the daughter's elopement with the French master, the poor father died suddenly, in some extraordinary manner, when out shooting with this Mr. Ormond; to whom a considerable landed property, and a large legacy in money, were, to every body's surprise, found to be left in a will which *he* produced, and which the family did not think fit to dispute. There were strange circumstances told concerning the wake and burial, all tending to prove that this Harry Ormond had lost all feeling. Hints were further given that he had renounced the Protestant religion, and had turned Catholic for the sake of absolution."

Many times during the perusal of this extravagant tissue of falsehoods, Ormond laid down and resumed the paper, unable to refrain from exclamations of rage and contempt; sometimes almost laughing at the absurdity of the slander. "After this," thought he, "who can mind common reports?—and yet Dr. Cambray says that these excited some prejudice against me in the mind of Lady Annaly. With such a woman I should have thought it impossible. Could she believe me capable of such crimes?—*me*, of whom she had once a good opinion?—*me*, in whose fate she said she was interested?"

He took Dr. Cambray's letter again, and read on: he found that Lady Annaly had not credited these reports as to the atrocious accusations; but they had so far operated as to excite doubts and suspicions. In some of the circumstances, there was sufficient truth to colour the falsehood. For example, with regard both to Peggy Sheridan, and Dora, the truth had been plausibly mixed with falsehood. The story of Peggy Sheridan, Lady Annaly had some suspicion might be true. Her ladyship, who had seen Moriarty's generous conduct to Ormond, was indignant at his ingratitude. She was a woman prompt to feel strong indignation against all that was base; and, when her indignation was excited, she was sometimes incapable of hearing what was said on the other side of the question. Her daughter Florence, of a calmer temper and cooler judgment, usually acted as moderator on these occasions. She could not believe that Harry Ormond had been guilty of faults that were so opposite to those which they had seen in his disposition:—violence, not treachery, was his fault. But why, if there were nothing wrong, Lady Annaly urged—why did not he write to her, as she had requested he would, when his plans for his future life were decided?—She had told him that her son might probably be able to assist him. Why could not he write one line?

Ormond had heard that her son was ill, and that her mind was so absorbed with anxiety, that he could not at first venture to intrude upon her with his selfish concerns. This was his first and best reason; but afterwards, to be sure, when he heard that the son was better, he might have written. He wrote at that time such a sad scrawl of a hand—he was so little used to letter-writing, that he was ashamed to write. Then it was *too late* after so long a silence, &c. Foolish as these reasons were, they had, as we have said before, acted upon our young hero; and have, perhaps, in as important circumstances, prevented many young men from writing to friends, able and willing to serve them. It was rather fortunate for Ormond that slander did not stop at the first plausible falsehoods: when the more atrocious charges came against him, Miss Annaly, who had never deserted his cause, declared her absolute disbelief. The discussions that went on, between her and her mother, kept alive their interest about this young man. He was likely to have been forgotten during their anxiety in the son's illness; but fresh reports had brought him to their recollection frequently; and when their friend, Dr. Cambray, was appointed to the living of Castle Hermitage, his evidence perfectly reinstated Harry in Lady Annaly's good opinion. As if to make amends for the injustice she had done him by believing any part of the evil reports, she was now anxious to see him again. A few days after Dr. Cambray wrote, Ormond received a very polite and gratifying letter from Lady Annaly, requesting that, as "Annaly" lay in his route homewards, he would spend a few days there, and give her an opportunity of making him acquainted with her son. It is scarcely necessary to say that this invitation was eagerly accepted.

CHAPTER XXII.

Upon his arrival at Annaly, Ormond found that Dr. Cambray and all his family were there.

"Yes, all your friends," said Lady Annaly, as Ormond looked round with pleasure, "all your friends, Mr. Ormond—you must allow me an old right to be of that number—and here is my son, who is as well inclined, as I hope you feel, to pass over the intermediate formality of new acquaintanceship, and to become intimate with you as soon as possible."

Sir Herbert Annaly confirmed, by the polite cordiality of his manner, all that his mother promised; adding that their mutual friend Dr. Cambray had made him already so fully acquainted with Mr. Ormond, that though he had never had the pleasure of seeing him before, he could not consider him as a stranger.

Florence Annaly was beautiful, but not one of those beauties who strike at first sight. Hers was a face which neither challenged nor sued for admiration. There was no expression thrown into the eyes or the eyebrows, no habitual smile on the lips—the features were all in natural repose; the face never expressed any thing but what the mind really felt. But if any just observation was made in Miss Annaly's company, any stroke of genius, that countenance instantly kindled into light and life: and if any noble sentiment was expressed, if any generous action was related, then the soul within illumined the countenance with a ray divine. When once Ormond had seen this, his eye returned in hopes of seeing it again—he had an indescribable interest and pleasure in studying a countenance, which seemed so true an index to a noble and cultivated mind, to a heart of delicate, but not morbid sensibility. His manners and understanding had been formed and improved, beyond what could have been expected, from the few opportunities of improvement he had till lately enjoyed. He was timid, however, in conversation with those of whose information and abilities he had a high opinion, so that at first he did not do himself justice; but in his timidity there was no awkwardness; it was joined with such firmness of principle, and such a resolute, manly character, that he was peculiarly engaging to women.

During his first visit at Annaly he pleased much, and was so much pleased with every individual of the family, with their manners, their conversation, their affection for each other, and altogether with their mode of living, that he declared to Dr. Cambray he never had been so happy in his whole existence. It was a remarkable fact, however, that he spoke much more of Lady Annaly and Sir Herbert than of Miss Annaly.

He had never before felt so very unwilling to leave any place, or so exceedingly anxious to be invited to repeat his visit. He did receive the wished-for invitation; and it was given in such a manner as left him no doubt that he might indulge his own ardent desire to return, and to cultivate the friendship of this family. His ardour for foreign travel, his desire to see more of the world, greatly abated; and before he reached Castle Hermitage, and by the time he saw his guardian, he had almost forgotten that Sir Ulick had traced for him a course of travels through the British islands and the most polished parts of the Continent.

He now told Sir Ulick that it was so far advanced in the season, that he thought it better to spend the winter in Ireland.

"In Dublin instead of London?" said Sir Ulick, smiling; "very patriotic, and very kind to me, for I am sure I am your first object; and depend upon it few people, ladies always excepted, will ever like your company better than I do."

Then Sir Ulick went rapidly over every subject, and every person, that could lead his ward farther to explain his feelings; but now, as usual, he wasted his address, for the ingenuous young man directly opened his whole heart to him.

"I am impatient to tell you, sir," said he, "how very kindly I was received by Lady Annaly."

"She is very kind," said Sir Ulick: "I suppose, in general, you have found yourself pretty well received wherever you have gone—not to flatter you too much on your mental or personal qualifications, and, no disparagement to Dr. Cambray's letters of introduction or my own, five or six thousand a-year are, I have generally observed, a tolerably good passport into society, a sufficient passe-partout." "Passe-partout!—not *partout*—not quite sufficient at Annaly, you cannot mean, sir—"

"Oh! I cannot mean any thing, but that Annaly is altogether the eighth wonder of the world," said Sir Ulick, "and all the men and women in it absolutely angels—perfect angels."

"No, sir, if you please, not perfect; for I have heard—though I own I never saw it—that perfection is always stupid: now certainly *that* the Annalys are not."

"Well, well, they shall be as imperfect as you like—any thing to please you."

"But, sir, you used to be so fond of the Annalys. I remember."

"True, and did I tell you that I had changed my opinion?"

"Your manner, though not your words, tells me so."

"You mistake: the fact is—for I always treat you, Harry, with perfect candour—I was hurt and vexed by their refusal of my son. But, after all," added he, with a deep sigh, "it was Marcus's own fault—he has been very dissipated. Miss Annaly was right, and her mother quite right, I own. Lady Annaly is one of the most respectable women in Ireland—and Miss Annaly is a charming girl—I never saw any girl I should have liked so much for my daughter-in-law. But Marcus and I don't always agree in our tastes—I don't think the refusal there, was half as great a mortification and disappointment to him, as it was to me."

"You delight me, dear sir," cried Ormond; "for then I may feel secure that if ever in future—I don't mean in the least that I have any present thought—it would be absurd—it would be ridiculous—it would be quite improper—you know I was only there ten days; but I mean if, in future, I should ever have any thoughts—any serious thoughts—"

"Well, well," said Sir Ulick, laughing at Ormond's hesitation and embarrassment, "I can suppose that you will have thoughts of some kind or other, and serious thoughts in due course; but, as you justly observe, it would be quite ridiculous at present."

"I beg your pardon, sir," interrupted Harry, "but it would even at present be an inexpressible satisfaction to me to know, that if in future such a thing should occur, I should be secure, in the first place, of your approbation."

"As to that, my dear boy," said Sir Ulick, "you know in a few days you will be at years of discretion—then my control ceases."

"Yes, sir; but not my anxiety for your approbation, and my deference for your opinion."

"Then," said Sir Ulick, "and without circumlocution or nonsense, I tell you at once, Harry Ormond, that Florence Annaly is the woman in the world I should like best to see your wife."

"Thank you, sir, for this explicit answer—I am sure towards me nothing can have been more candid and kind than your whole conduct has ever been."

"That's true, Harry," exclaimed Sir Ulick. "Tell me about this duel—you have fought a duel in defence of my conduct and character, I understand, since I saw you. But, my dear fellow, though I am excessively obliged to you, I am exceedingly angry with you: how could you possibly be so hot-heated and silly as to *take up* any man for relishing the Ulysseana? Bless ye! I relish it myself—I only laugh at such things: believe me, 'tis The best way."

"I am sure of it, sir, if one can; and, indeed, I have had pretty good proof that one should despise reports and scandal of all kinds—easier for oneself sometimes than for one's friends."

"Yes, my dear Ormond, by the time you have been half as long living in the great and the political world as I have been, you will be quite case-hardened, and will hear your friends abused, without feeling it in the least. Believe me, I once was troubled with a great deal of susceptibility

like yours—but after all, 'tis no bad thing for you to have fought a duel
—a feather in your cap with the ladies, and a warning to all impertinent
fellows to let you alone—but you were wounded, the newspaper said—I
asked you where, three times in my letters—you never condescended to
answer me—answer me now, I insist upon it."

"In my arm, sir—a slight scratch."

"Slight scratch or not, I must hear all about it—come, tell me exactly
how the thing began and ended—tell me all the rascals said of me.—You
won't?—then I'll tell you: they said, 'I am the greatest jobber in Ireland
—that I do not mind how I throw away the public money—in short, that
I am a sad political profligate.'—Well! well! I am sure, after all, they did
me the justice to acknowledge, that in private life no man's honour is
more to be depended on."

"They did do you that justice, sir," said Ormond; "but pray ask me no
farther questions—for, frankly, it is disagreeable to me—and I will tell
you no more."

"That's frank," said Sir Ulick, "and I as frankly assure you I am perfectly
satisfied."

"Then, to return to the Annalys," said Ormond, "I never saw Sir Herbert
till now—I like him—I like his principles—his love of his country—and
his attachment to his family."

"He's a very fine fellow—no better fellow than Herbert Annaly. But as
for his attachment to his family, who thanks him for that? Who could
help it, with such a family? And his love for his country—every body
loves his country."

"More or less, I suppose," said Ormond.

"But, upon my word, I entirely agree with you about Sir Herbert, though
I know he is prejudiced against me to the last degree."

"If he be, I don't know it, sir—I never found it out."

"He will let it out by and by—I only hope he will not prejudice you against me."

"That is not very easily done, sir."

"As you have given some proof, my dear boy, and I thank you for it. But the Annalys would go more cautiously to work—I only put you on your guard—Marcus and Sir Herbert never could hit it off together; and I am afraid the breach between us and the Annalys must be widened, for Marcus must stand against Sir Herbert at the next election, if he live— Pray how is he?"

"Not strong, sir—he has a hectic colour—as I was very sorry to see."

"Ay, poor fellow—he broke some blood-vessel, I think Marcus told me, when they were in England."

"Yes, sir—so Lady Annaly told me—it was in over-exerting himself to extinguish a fire."

"A very fine spirited fellow he is, no doubt," said Sir Ulick; "but, after all, that was rather a foolish thing, in his state of health. By-the-by, as your guardian, it is my duty to explain the circumstances of this family— in case you should hereafter *have any serious thoughts*; as you say, you should know what comforted Marcus in his disappointment there. There is, then, some confounded flaw in that old father's will, through which the great Herbert estate slips to an heir-at-law, who has started up within this twelvemonth. Miss Annaly, who was to have been a nonpareil of an heiress in case of the brother's death, will have but a moderate fortune; and the poor dowager will be but scantily provided for, after all the magnificence which she has been used to, unless he lives to make up something handsome for them. I don't know the particulars, but I know that a vast deal depends on his living till he has levied certain fines, which he ought to have levied, instead of amusing himself putting out other people's fires. But I am excessively anxious about it, and now on your account as well as theirs; for it would make a great difference to you, if you seriously have any *thoughts* of Miss Annaly."

Ormond declared this could make no difference to him, since his own fortune would be sufficient for all the wishes of such a woman as he supposed Miss Annaly to be. The next day Marcus O'Shane arrived from England. This was the first time that Ormond and he had met since the affair of Moriarty, and the banishment from Castle Hermitage. The meeting was awkward enough, notwithstanding Sir Ulick's attempts to make it otherwise: Marcus laboured under the double consciousness of having deserted Harry in past adversity, and of being jealous of his present prosperity. Ormond at first went forward to meet him more than half way with great cordiality, but the cold politeness of Marcus chilled him; and the heartless congratulations, and frequent allusions in the course of the first hour, to Ormond's new fortune and consequence, offended our young hero's pride. He grew more reserved, the more complimentary Marcus became, especially as in all his compliments there was a mixture of *persiflage*, which Marcus supposed, erroneously, that Ormond's untutored, unpractised ear would not perceive.

Harry sat silent, proudly indignant. He valued himself on being something, and somebody, independently of his fortune—he had worked hard to become so—he had the consciousness about him of tried integrity, resolution, and virtue; and was it to be implied that he was *somebody*, only in consequence of his having chanced to become heir to so many thousands a year? Sir Ulick, whose address was equal to most occasions, was not able to manage so as to make these young men like one another. Marcus had an old jealousy of Harry's favour with his father, of his father's affection for Harry: and at the present moment, he was conscious that his father was with just cause much displeased with him. Of this Harry knew nothing, but Marcus suspected that his father had told Ormond every thing, and this increased the awkwardness and ill-humour that Marcus felt; and notwithstanding all his knowledge of the world, and conventional politeness, he showed his vexation in no very well-bred manner. He was now in particularly bad humour, in consequence of a *scrape*, as he called it, which he had got into, during his last winter in London, respecting an intrigue with a married lady of rank. Marcus, by some intemperate expressions, had brought on the discovery, of which, when it was too late, he repented. A public trial was likely to be the consequence—the damages would doubtless be laid at the least at ten thousand pounds. Marcus, however, counting, as sons sometimes do in calculating their father's fortune, all the credit, and knowing nothing of the debtor side of the account, conceived his father's wealth to be inexhaustible. Lady O'Shane's large fortune had cleared off all debts, and had set Sir Ulick up in a bank, which was in high credit; then he had shares in a canal and in a silver mine—he held two lucrative sinecure places—and had bought estates in three counties: but the son did not know, that for the borrowed purchase-money of two of the estates Sir Ulick was now paying high and accumulating interest; so that the prospect of being called upon for ten thousand pounds was most alarming. In this exigency Sir Ulick, who had long foreseen how the affair was likely to terminate, had his eye upon his ward's ready money. It was for this he had been at such peculiar pains to ingratiate himself with Ormond. Affection, nevertheless, made him hesitate; he was unwilling to injure or to hazard his property—very unwilling to prey upon his generosity—still more so after the late handsome manner in which Ormond had hazarded his life in defence of his guardian's honour.

Sir Ulick, who perceived the first evening that Marcus and Ormond met, that the former was not going the way to assist these views, pointed out to him how much it was for his interest to conciliate Ormond, and to establish himself in his good opinion; but Marcus, though he saw and acknowledged this, could not submit his pride and temper to the necessary restraint. For a few hours he would display his hereditary talents, and all his acquired graces; but the next hour his ill-humour would break out towards his inferiors, his father's tenants and dependents, in a way which Ormond's generous spirit could not bear. Before he went to England, even from his boyish days, his manners had been habitually haughty and tyrannical to the lower class of people. Ormond and he had always differed and often quarrelled on this subject. Ormond hoped to find his manners altered in this respect by his residence in a more polished country. But the external polish he had acquired had not reached the mind: high-bred society had taught him only to be polite to his equals; he was now still more disposed to be insolent to his inferiors, especially to his Irish inferiors. He affected to consider himself as more than half an Englishman; and returning from London in all the distress and disgrace to which he had reduced himself by criminal indulgence in the vices of fashionable, and what he called *refined*, society, he vented his ill-humour on the poor Irish peasants—the *natives*, as he termed them in derision. He spoke to them as if they were slaves— he considered them as savages. Marcus had, early in life, almost before he knew the real distinctions, or more than the names of the different parties in Ireland, been a strong party man. He called himself a government man; but he was one of those partisans, whom every wise and good administration in Ireland has discountenanced and disclaimed. He was, in short, one of those who make their politics an excuse to their conscience for the indulgence of a violent temper.

Ormond was indignant at the inveterate prejudice that Marcus showed against a poor man, whom he had injured, but who had never injured him. The moment Marcus saw Moriarty Carroll again, and heard his name mentioned, he exclaimed and reiterated, "That's a bad fellow—I know him of old—all those Carrolls are rascals and rebels."

Marcus looked with a sort of disdainful spleen at the house which Ormond had fitted up for Moriarty.

"So, you stick to this fellow still!—What a dupe, Ormond, this Moriarty has made of you!" said Marcus; "but that's not my affair. I only wonder how you wheedled my father out of the ground for the garden here."

"There was no wheedling in the case," said Ormond: "your father gave it freely, or I should not have accepted it."

"You were very good to accept it, no doubt," said Marcus, in an ironical tone: "I know I have asked my father for a garden to a cottage before now, and have been refused."

Sir Ulick came up just as this was said, and, alarmed at the tone of voice, used all his address to bring his son back to good temper; and he might have succeeded, but that Peggy Carroll chanced to appear at that instant.

"Who is that?" cried Marcus—"Peggy Sheridan, as I live! is it not?"

"No, please your honour, but Peggy Sheridan that was—Peggy Carroll *that is*," said Peggy, curtsying, with a slight blush, and an arch smile.

"So, you have married that Moriarty at last."

"I have, please your honour—he is a very honest boy—and I'm very happy—if your honour's pleased."

"Who persuaded your father to this, pray, contrary to my advice?"

"Nobody at all, plase your honour," said Peggy, looking frightened.

"Why do you say that, Peggy," said Ormond, "when you know it was I who persuaded your father to give his consent to your marriage with Moriarty?"

"You! Mr. Ormond!—Oh, I comprehend it all now," said Marcus, with his sneering look and tone: "no doubt you had good reasons."

Poor Peggy blushed the deepest crimson.

"I understand it all now," said Marcus—"I understand you now, Harry."

Ormond's anger rose, and with a look of high disdain, he replied, "You understand me, now! No, nor ever will, nor ever can. Our minds are unintelligible to each other."

Then turning from him, Ormond walked away with indignant speed.

"Peggy, don't I see something like a cow yonder, *getting her bread* at my expense?" said Sir Ulick, directing Peggy's eye to a gap in the hedge by the road-side. "Whose cow is that at the top of the ditch, half through my hedge?"

"I can't say, please your honour," said Peggy, "if it wouldn't be Paddy M'Grath's—Betty M'Gregor!" cried she, calling to a bare-footed girl, "whose cow is yonder?"

"Oh, marcy! but if it isn't our own red rogue—and when I tied her legs three times myself, the day!" said the girl, running to drive away the cow.

"Oh! she strays and trespasses strangely, the red cow, for want of the little spot your honour promised her," said Peggy.

"Well, run and save my hedge from her now, my pretty Peggy, and I will find the little spot for her to-morrow," said Sir Ulick.

Away ran Peggy after the cow—while lowering Marcus cursed them all three. Pretty Peg he swore ought to be banished the estate—the cow ought to be hamstrung instead of having *a spot* promised her; "but this is the way, sir, you ruin the country and the people," said he to his father.

"Be that as it may, I do not ruin myself as you do, Marcus," replied the cool Sir Ulick. "Never mind the cow—nonsense! I am not thinking of a cow."

"Nor I neither, sir."

"Then follow Harry Ormond directly, and make him understand that he misunderstood you," said Sir Ulick.

"Excuse me, sir—I cannot bend to him," said Marcus.

"And you expect that he will lend you ten thousand pounds at your utmost need?"

"The money, with your estate, can be easily raised elsewhere, sir," said Marcus.

"I tell you it cannot, sir," said the father.

"I cannot bend to Ormond, sir: to any body but him—any thing but that —my pride cannot stoop to that."

"Your pride!—'pride that licks the dust,'" thought Sir Ulick. It was in vain for the politic father to remonstrate with the headstrong son. The whole train which Sir Ulick had laid with so much skill, was, he feared, at the moment when his own delicate hand was just preparing to give the effective touch, blown up by the rude impatience of his son. Sir Ulick, however, never lost time or opportunity in vain regret for the past. Even in the moment of disappointment, he looked to the future. He saw the danger of keeping two young men together, who had such incompatible tempers and characters. He was, therefore, glad when he met Ormond again, to hear him propose his returning to Annaly, and he instantly acceded to the proposal.

"Castle Hermitage, I know, my dear boy, cannot be as pleasant to you just now, as I could wish to make it: we have nobody here now, and Marcus is not all I could wish him," said Sir Ulick, with a sigh. "He had always a jealousy of my affection for you, Harry—it cannot be helped—we do not choose our own children—but we must abide by them—you must perceive that things are not going on quite rightly between my son and me."

"I am sorry for it, sir; especially as I am convinced I can do no good, and therefore wish not to interfere."

"I believe you are right—though I part from you with regret."

"I shall be within your reach, sir, you know: whenever you wish for me, if ever I can be of the least use to *you*, summon me, and I am at your orders."

"Thank you! but stay one moment," said Sir Ulick, with a sudden look of recollection: "you will be of age in a few days, Harry—we ought to settle accounts, should not we?"

"Whenever you please, sir—no hurry on my part—but you have advanced me a great deal of money lately—I ought to settle that."

"Oh, as to that—a mere trifle. If you are in no hurry, I am in none; for I shall have business enough on my hands during these few days, before

Lady Norton fills the house again with company—I am certainly a little hurried now."

"Then, sir, do not think of my business—I cannot be better off, you know, than I am—I assure you I am sensible of that. Never mind the accounts—only send for me whenever I can be of any use or pleasure to you. I need not make speeches: I trust, my dear guardian—my father, when I was left fatherless—I trust you believe I have some gratitude in me."

"I do," cried Sir Ulick, much moved; "and, by Heaven, it is impossible to —I mean—in short, it is impossible not to love you, Harry Ormond."

CHAPTER XXIII.

There are people who can go on very smoothly with those whose principles and characters they despise and dislike. There are people who, provided they live in *company*, are happy, and care but little of what the company is composed. But our young hero certainly was not one of these contented people. He was perhaps too much in the other extreme. He could not, without overt words or looks of indignation, endure the presence of those whose characters or principles he despised—he could not, even without manifest symptoms of restlessness or ennui, submit long to live with mere companions; he required to have friends; nor could he make a friend from ordinary materials, however smooth the grain, or however fine the polish they might take. Even when the gay world at Castle Hermitage was new to him—amused and enchanted as he was at first with that brilliant society, he could not have been content or happy without his friends at Vicar's Dale, to whom, once at least in the four-and-twenty hours, he found it necessary to open his heart. We may then judge how happy he now felt in returning to Annaly: after the sort of moral constraint which he had endured in the company of Marcus O'Shane, we may guess what an expansion of heart took place.

The family union and domestic happiness which he saw at Annaly, certainly struck him at this time more forcibly, from the contrast with what he had just seen at Castle Hermitage. The effect of contrast, however, is but transient. It is powerful as a dramatic resource, but in real life it is of no permanent consequence. There was here a charm which operates with as great certainty, and with a power secure of increasing instead of diminishing from habit—the charm of *domestic politeness*, in the every day manners of this mother, son, and daughter, towards each other, as well as towards their guests. Ormond saw and felt it irresistibly. He saw the most delicate attentions combined with entire sincerity, perfect ease, and constant respect; the result of the early habits of good-breeding acting upon the feelings of genuine affection. The external polish, which Ormond now admired, was very different from that varnish which often is hastily applied to hide imperfections. This polish was of the substance itself, to be obtained only by long use; but, once acquired, lasting for ever: not only beautiful, but serviceable, preserving from the injuries of time and from the dangers of familiarity.

What influence the sister's charms might have to increase Ormond's admiration of the brother, we shall not presume to determine; but certainly he liked Sir Herbert Annaly better than any young man he had ever seen. Sir Herbert was some years older than Ormond; he was in his twenty-seventh year: but at this age he had done more good in life than many men accomplish during their whole existence. Sir Herbert's principal estates were in another part of Ireland. Dr. Cambray had visited them. The account he gave Ormond of what had been done there, to improve the people and to make them happy; of the prosperous state of the peasantry; their industry and independence; their grateful, not servile, attachment to Sir Herbert Annaly and his mother; the veneration in which the name of Annaly was held; all delighted the enthusiastic Ormond.

The name of Annaly was growing wonderfully dear to him; and, all of a sudden, the interest he felt in the details of a country gentleman's life was amazingly increased. At times, when the ladies were engaged, he accompanied Sir Herbert in visiting his estate. Sir Herbert had never till lately resided at Annaly, which had, within but a short time, reverted to his possession, in consequence of the death of the person to whom it had been let. He found much that wanted improvement in the land, and more in the people.

This estate stretched along the sea-shore: the tenants whom he found living near the coast were an idle, profligate, desperate set of people; who, during the time of the late middle landlord, had been in the habit of *making their rents* by nefarious practices. The best of the set were merely idle fishermen, whose habits of trusting to their *luck* incapacitated them from industry: the others were illicit distillers—smugglers—and miscreants who lived by *waifs* and *strays*; in fact, by the pillage of vessels on the coast. The coast was dangerous—there happened frequent shipwrecks; owing partly, as was supposed, to the false lights hung out by these people, whose interest it was that vessels should be wrecked. Shocked at these practices, Sir Herbert Annaly had, from the moment he came into possession of the estate, exerted himself to put a stop to them, and to punish, where he could not reform the offenders. The people at first pleaded a sort of *tenant's right*, which they thought a landlord could scarcely resist. They protested that they could not make *the rent*, if they were not allowed to make it in their own way; and showed, beyond a doubt, that Sir Herbert could not get half as much rent for his land in those parts, if he looked too scrupulously into the means by which it was made. They brought, in corroboration of their arguments or assertions, the example and constant practice of "many as good a jantleman as any in Ireland, who had his rent made up for him that ways, very ready and punctual. There was his honour, Mr. Such-a-one, and so on; and there was Sir Ulick O'Shane, sure! Oh! he was the man to live under—he was the man that knew when to wink and when to blink; and if he shut his eyes *properly*, sure his tenants filled his fist. Oh! Sir Ulick was the great man for *favour and purtection*, none like him at all!—He is the good landlord, that will fight the way clear for his own tenants through thick and thin—none dare touch them. Oh! Sir Ulick's the kind jantleman that understands the law for the poor, and could bring them off at every turn, and show them the way through the holes in an act of parliament, asy as through a *riddle!*

"Oh, and if he could but afford to be half as good as his promises, Sir Ulick O'Shane would be too good entirely!"

Now Sir Ulick O'Shane had purchased a tract of ground adjoining to Sir Herbert's, on this coast; and he had bought it on the speculation that he could let it at a very high rent to these people, of whose *ways and means* of paying it he chose to remain in ignorance. All the tenants whom Sir Herbert *banished* from his estate flocked to Sir Ulick's.

By the sacrifice of his own immediate interest, and by great personal exertion, strict justice, and a generous and well secured system of reward, Sir Herbert already had produced a considerable change for the better in the morals and habits of the people. He was employing some of his tenants on the coast, in building a lighthouse, for which he had a grant from parliament; and he was endeavouring to establish a manufacture of sail-cloth, for which there was sufficient demand. But almost at every step of his progress, he was impeded by the effects of the bad example of his neighbours on Sir Ulick's estate; and by the continual quarrels between the idle, discarded tenants, and their industrious and now prosperous successors.

Whenever a vessel in distress was seen off the coast, there was a constant struggle between the two parties who had opposite interests; the one to save, the other to destroy. In this state of things, causes of complaint perpetually occurred; and Ormond who was present, when the accusers and the accused appealed to their landlord, sometimes as lord of the manor, sometimes as magistrate, had frequent opportunities of seeing both Sir Herbert's principles and temper put to the test. He liked to compare the different modes in which King Corny, his guardian, and Sir Herbert Annaly managed these things. Sir Herbert governed neither by threats, punishments, abuse, nor tyranny; nor yet did he govern by promises nor bribery, *favour* and *protection*, like Sir Ulick. He neither cajoled nor bullied—neither held it as a principle, as Marcus did, that the people must be kept down, or that the people must be deceived. He treated them neither as slaves, subject to his will; nor as dupes, or objects on which to exercise his wit or his cunning. He treated them as reasonable beings, and as his fellow-creatures, whom he wished to improve, that he might make them and himself happy. He spoke sense to them; and he mixed that sense with wit and humour, in the proportion necessary to make it palatable to an Irishman.

In generosity there was a resemblance between the temper of Sir Herbert and of Corny; but to Ormond's surprise, and at first to his disappointment, Sir Herbert valued justice more than generosity. Ormond's heart on this point was often with King Corny, when his head was forced to be with Sir Herbert; but, by degrees, head and heart came together. He became practically convinced that justice is the virtue that works best for a constancy, and best serves every body's interest in time and in turn. Ormond now often said to himself, "Sir Herbert Annaly is but a few years older than I am; by the time I am of his age, why should not I become as useful, and make as many human beings happy as he does?" In the meantime, the idea of marrying and settling in Ireland became every day more agreeable to Ormond; and France and Italy, which he had been so eager to visit, faded from his imagination. Sir Herbert and Lady Annaly, who had understood from Dr. Cambray that Ormond was going to commence his grand tour immediately, and who heard him make a number of preparatory inquiries when he had been first at Annaly, naturally turned the conversation often to the subject. They had looked out maps and prints, and they had taken down from their shelves the different books of travels, which might be most useful to him, with guides, and post-road books, and all that could speed the parting guest. But the guest had no mind to part—every thing, every body at Annaly, he found so agreeable and so excellent.

It must be a great satisfaction to a young man who has a grain of sense, and who feels that he is falling inevitably and desperately in love, to see that all the lady's family, as well as the object of his passion, are exactly the people whom he should wish of all others to make his friends for life. Here was every thing that could be desired, suitability of age, of fortune, of character, of temper, of tastes—every thing that could make a marriage happy, could Ormond but win the heart of Florence Annaly. Was that heart disengaged?—He resolved to inquire first from his dear friend, Dr. Cambray, who was much in the confidence of this family, a great favourite with Florence, and consequently dearer than ever to Ormond. He went directly to Vicar's Dale to see and consult him, and Ormond thought he was confiding a profound secret to the doctor, when first he spoke to him of his passion for Miss Annaly; but to his surprise, the doctor told him he had seen it long ago, and his wife and daughters had all discovered it, even when they were first with him at Annaly.

"Is it possible?—and what do you all think?"

"We think that you would be a perfectly happy man, if you could win Miss Annaly; and we wish you success most sincerely. But—"

"*But*—Oh, my dear doctor, you alarm me beyond measure."

"What! by wishing you success?"

"No, but by something in your look and manner, and by that terrible *but*: you think that I shall never succeed—you think that her heart is engaged. If that be the case, tell me so at once, and I will set off for France to-morrow."

"My good sir, you are always for desperate measures—you are in too great a hurry to come to a conclusion, before you have the means of forming a just conclusion. Remember, I tell you, this precipitate temper will some time or other bring some great evil upon you."

"I will be patient all my life afterwards, if you will only this instant tell me whether she is engaged."

"I do not know whether Miss Annaly's heart be disengaged or not—I can tell you only that she has had a number of brilliant offers, and that she has refused them all."

"That proves that she had not found one amongst them that she liked," said Ormond.

"Or that she liked some one better than all those whom she refused," said Dr. Cambray.

"That is true—that is possible—that is a dreadful possibility," said Ormond. "But do you think there is any probability of that?"

"There is, I am sorry to tell you, my dear Ormond, a probability against you—but I can only state the facts in general. I can form no opinion, for I have had no opportunity of judging—I have never seen the two young people together. But there is a gentleman of great merit, of suitable family and fortune, who is deeply in love with Miss Annaly, and who I presume has not been refused, for I understand he is soon to be here."

"To be here!" cried Ormond: "a man of great merit!—I hope he is not an agreeable man."

"That's a vain hope," said Dr. Cambray; "he is a very agreeable man."

"*Very* agreeable!—What sort of person—grave or gay?—Like any body that I ever saw?"

"Yes, like a person that you have seen, and a person for whom I believe you have a regard—like his own father, your dear King Corny's friend, General Albemarle."

"How extraordinary!—how unlucky!" said Ormond. "I would rather my rival were any one else than the son of a man I am obliged to; and a most dangerous rival he must be, if he have his father's merit, and his father's manners. Oh! my dear Dr. Cambray, I am sure she likes him—and yet she could not be so cheerful in his absence, if she were much in love—I defy her; and it is impossible that he can be as much in love with her as I am, else nothing could keep him from her."

"Nothing but his duty, I suppose you mean?"

"Duty!—What duty?"

"Why, there really are duties in this world to be performed, though a man in love is apt to forget it. Colonel Albemarle, being an officer, cannot quit his regiment till he has obtained leave of absence."

"I am heartily glad of it," cried Ormond—"I will make the best use of my time before he comes. But, my dear doctor, do you think Lady Annaly—do you think Sir Herbert wish it to be?"

"I really cannot tell:—I know only that he is a particular friend of Sir Herbert, and that I have heard Lady Annaly speak of him as being a young man of excellent character and high honour, for whom she has a great regard."

Ormond sighed.

"Heaven forgive me that sigh!" said he: "I thought I never should be brought so low as to sigh at bearing of any man's excellent character and high honour: but I certainly wish Colonel Albemarle had never been born. Heaven preserve me from envy and jealousy!"

Our young hero had need to repeat this prayer the next morning at breakfast, when Sir Herbert, on opening his letters, exclaimed, "My friend, Colonel Albemarle—"

And Lady Annaly, in a tone of joy, "Colonel Albemarle!—I hope he will soon be here."

Sir Herbert proceeded: "Cannot obtain leave of absence yet—but lives *in hopes*," said Sir Herbert, reading the letter, and handing it to his mother.

Ormond did not dare, did not think it honourable, to make use of his eyes, though there now might have been a decisive moment for observation. No sound reached his ear from Miss Annaly's voice; but Lady Annaly spoke freely and decidedly in praise of Colonel Albemarle. As she read the letter, Sir Herbert, after asking Ormond three times whether he was not acquainted with General Albemarle, obtained for answer, that he "really did not know." In truth, Ormond did not know any thing at that moment. Sir Herbert, surprised, and imagining that Ormond had not yet heard him, was going to repeat his question—but a look from his mother stopped him. A sudden light struck Lady Annaly. Mothers are remarkably quick-sighted upon these occasions. There was a silence of a few minutes, which appeared to poor Ormond to be a silence that would never be broken; it was broken by some slight observation which the brother and sister made to each other upon a paragraph in the newspaper, which they were reading together. Ormond took breath.

"She cannot love him, or she could not be thinking of a paragraph in the newspaper at this moment."

From this time forward Ormond was in a continual state of agitation, reasoning, as the passions reason, as ill as possible, upon even the slightest circumstances that occurred, from whence he might draw favourable or unfavourable omens. He was resolved—and that was prudent—not to speak of his own sentiments, till he was clear how matters stood about Colonel Albemarle: he was determined not to expose himself to the useless mortification of a refusal. While in this agony of uncertainty, he went out one morning to take a solitary walk, that he might reflect at leisure. Just as he was turning from the avenue to the path that led to the wood, a car full of morning visitors appeared. Ormond endeavoured to avoid them, but not before he had been seen. A servant rode after him to beg to know "if he were Mr. Harry Ormond—if he were, one of the ladies on the car, Mrs. M'Crule, sent her compliments to him, and requested he would be so good as to let her speak with him at the house, as she had a few words of consequence to say."

"Mrs. M'Crule!" Ormond did not immediately recollect that he had the honour of knowing any such person, till the servant said, "Miss Black, sir, that was—formerly at Castle Hermitage."

His old enemy, Miss Black, he recollected well. He obeyed the lady's summons, and returned to the house.

Mrs. M'Crule had not altered in disposition, though her objects had been changed by marriage. Having no longer Lady O'Shane's quarrels with her husband to talk about, she had become the pest of the village of Castle Hermitage and of the neighbourhood—the Lady Bluemantle of the parish. Had Miss Black remained in England, married or single, she would only have been one of a numerous species too well known to need any description; but transplanted to a new soil and a new situation, she proved to be a variety of the old species, with peculiarly noxious qualities, which it may be useful to describe, as a warning to the unwary. It is unknown how much mischief the Lady Bluemantle class may do in Ireland, where parties in religion and politics run high; and where it often happens, that individuals of the different sects and parties actually hate without knowing each other, watch without mixing with one another, and consequently are prone reciprocally to believe any stories or reports, however false or absurd, which tend to gratify their antipathies. In this situation it is scarcely possible to get the exact truth as to the words, actions, and intentions, of the nearest neighbours, who happen to be of opposite parties or persuasions. What a fine field is here for a mischief-maker! Mrs. M'Crule had in her parish done her part; she had gone from rich to poor, from poor to rich, from catholic to protestant, from churchman to dissenter, and from dissenter to methodist, reporting every idle story, and repeating every ill-natured thing that she heard said—things often more bitterly expressed than thought, and always exaggerated or distorted in the repetition. No two people in the parish could have continued on speaking terms at the end of the year, but that, happily, there were in this parish both a good clergyman and a good priest; and still more happily, they both agreed in labouring for the good of their parishioners. Dr. Cambray and Mr. M'Cormuck made it their business continually to follow after Mrs. M'Crule, healing the wounds which she inflicted, and pouring into the festering heart the balm of

Christian charity: they were beloved and revered by their parishioners; Mrs. M'Crule was soon detected, and universally avoided. Enraged, she attacked, by turns, both the clergyman and the priest; and when she could not separate them, she found out that it was very wrong that they should agree. She discovered that she was a much better protestant, and a much better Christian, than Dr. Cambray, because she hated her catholic neighbours.

Dr. Cambray had taken pains to secure the co-operation of the catholic clergyman, in all his attempts to improve the lower classes of the people. His village school was open to catholics as well as protestants; and Father M'Cormuck, having been assured that their religion would not be tampered with, allowed and encouraged his flock to send their children to the same seminary.

Mrs. M'Crule was, or affected to be, much alarmed and scandalized at seeing catholic and protestant children mixing so much together; she knew that opinions were divided among some families in the neighbourhood upon the propriety of this *mixture*, and Mrs. M'Crule thought it a fine opportunity of making herself of consequence, by stirring up the matter into a party question. This bright idea had occurred to her just about the time that Ormond brought over little Tommy from the Black Islands. During Ormond's absence upon his tour, Sheelah and Moriarty had regularly sent the boy to the village school; exhorting him to mind his *book* and his *figures*, that he might surprise Mr. Ormond with his *larning* when he should come back. Tommy, with this excitation, and being a quick, clever little fellow, soon got to the head of his class, and kept there; and won all the school-prizes, and carried them home in triumph to his grandame, and to his dear Moriarty, to be treasured up, that he might show them to Mr. Ormond at his return home. Dr. Cambray was pleased with the boy, and so was every body, except Mrs. M'Crule. She often visited the school for the pleasure of finding fault; and she *wondered* to see this little Tommy, who was a catholic, carrying away the prizes from all the others. She thought it her duty to inquire farther about him; and as soon as she discovered that he came from the Black Islands, that he lived with Moriarty, and that Mr. Ormond was interested about him, she said she knew there was something wrong—

therefore, she set her face against the child, and against the shameful partiality that *some people* showed.

Dr. Cambray pursued his course without attending to her; and little Tommy pursued his course, improving rapidly in his *larning*.

Now there was in that county an excellent charitable institution for the education of children from seven to twelve years old; an apprentice fee was given with the children when they left the school, and they had several other advantages, which made parents of the lower classes extremely desirous to get their sons into this establishment.

Before they could be admitted, it was necessary that they should have a certificate from their parish minister and catholic clergyman, stating that they could read and write, and that they were well-behaved children. On a certain day, every year, a number of candidates were presented. The certificates from the clergyman and priest of their respective parishes were much attended to by the lady patronesses, and by these the choice of the candidate to be admitted was usually decided. Little Tommy had an excellent certificate both from Father M'Cormuck and from Dr. Cambray. Sheelah and Moriarty were in great joy, and had "all the hopes in life" for him; and Sheelah, who was very fond of *surprises*, had cautioned Moriarty, and begged the doctor not to tell Mr. Harry a word about it, *till all was fixed*, "for if the boy should not have the luck to be chose at last, it would only be breaking his little heart the worse, that Mr. Harry should know any thing at all about it, sure."

Meantime, Mrs. M'Crule was working against little Tommy with all her might.

Some of the lady patronesses were of opinion, that it would be expedient in future, to confine their bounty to the children of protestants only.

Mrs. M'Crule, who had been deputed by one of the absent ladies to act for her, was amazingly busy, visiting all the patronesses, and talking, and fearing, and "hoping to heaven!" and prophesying, canvassing, and collecting opinions and votes, as for a matter of life and death. She hinted that she knew that the greatest interest was making to get in this year a catholic child, and there was no knowing, if this went on, what the consequence might be. In short Ireland would be ruined, if little Tommy should prove the successful candidate. Mrs. M'Crule did not find it difficult to stir up the prejudices and passions of several ladies, whose education and whose means of information might have secured them from such contemptible influence.

Her present business at Annaly was to try what impression she could make on Lady and Miss Annaly, who were both patronesses of the school. As to Ormond, whom she never had liked, she was glad of this opportunity of revenging herself upon his little protégé; and of making Mr. Ormond sensible, that she was now a person of rather more consequence than she had been, when he used formerly to defy her at Castle Hermitage. She little thought that, while she was thus pursuing the dictates of her own hate, she might serve the interests of Ormond's love.

CHAPTER XXIV.

When Ormond returned, in obedience to Mrs. M'Crule's summons, he found in the room an unusual assemblage of persons—a party of morning visitors, the unmuffled contents of the car. As he entered, he bowed as courteously as possible to the whole circle, and advanced towards Mrs. M'Crule, whose portentous visage he could not fail to recognize. That visage was nearly half a yard long, thin out of all proportion, and dismal beyond all imagination; the corners of the mouth drawn down, the whites or yellows of the eyes upturned, while with hands outspread she was declaiming, and in a lamentable tone deploring, as Ormond thought, some great public calamity; for the concluding words were "The danger, my dear Lady Annaly—the danger, my dear Miss Annaly—oh! the danger is imminent. We shall all be positively undone, ma'am; and Ireland—oh! I wish I was once safe in England again—Ireland positively will be ruined!"

Ormond, looking to Lady Annaly and Miss Annaly for explanation, was somewhat re-assured in this imminent danger, by seeing that Lady Annaly's countenance was perfectly tranquil, and that a slight smile played on the lips of Florence.

"Mr. Ormond," said Lady Annaly, "I am sorry to hear that Ireland is in danger of being ruined by your means."

"By my means!" said Ormond, in great surprise; "I beg your ladyship's pardon for repeating your words, but I really cannot understand them."

"Nor I neither; but by the time you have lived as long as I have in the world," said Lady Annaly, "you will not be so much surprised as you now seem, my good sir, at hearing people say what you do not understand. I am told that Ireland will be undone by means of a *protégé* of yours, of the name of Tommy Dun—not Dun Scotus."

"Dunshaughlin, perhaps," said Ormond, laughing, "Tommy Dunshaughlin! *that* little urchin! What harm can little Tommy do to Ireland, or to any mortal?"

Without condescending to turn her eyes upon Ormond, whose propensity to laughter had of old been offensive to her nature, Mrs. M'Crule continued to Lady Annaly, "It is not of this insignificant child as an individual that I am speaking, Lady Annaly; but your ladyship, who has lived so long in the world, must know that there is no person or thing, however insignificant, that cannot, in the hands of a certain description of people, be made an engine of mischief."

"Very true, indeed," said Lady Annaly.

"And there is no telling or conceiving," pursued Mrs. M'Crule, "how in the hands of a certain party, you know, ma'am, any thing now, even the least and the most innocent child (not that I take upon me to say that this child is so very innocent, though, to be sure, he is very little)—but innocent or not, there is positively nothing, Lady Annaly, ma'am, which a certain party, certain evil-disposed persons, cannot turn to their purposes."

"I cannot contradict that—I wish I could," said Lady Annaly.

"But I see your ladyship and Miss Annaly do not consider this matter as seriously as I could wish. 'Tis an infatuation," said Mrs. M'Crule, uttering a sigh, almost a groan, for her ladyship's and her daughter's infatuation. "But if people, ladies especially, knew but half as much as I have learnt, since I married Mr. M'Crule, of the real state of Ireland; or if they had but half a quarter as many means as I have of obtaining information, Mr. M'Crule being one of his majesty's very active justices of the peace, riding about, and up and down, ma'am, scouring the country, sir, you know, and having informers, high and low, bringing us every sort of intelligence; I say, my dear Lady Annaly, ma'am, you would, if you only heard a hundredth part of what I hear daily, tremble—your ladyship would tremble from morning till night."

"Then I am heartily glad I do not hear it; for I should dislike very much to tremble from morning till night, especially as my trembling could do nobody any good."

"But, Lady Annaly, ma'am, you *can* do good by exerting yourself to prevent the danger in this emergency; you *can* do good, and it becomes your station and your character; you *can* do good, my dear Lady Annaly, ma'am, to thousands in existence, and thousands yet unborn."

"My benevolence having but a limited appetite for thousands," said Lady Annaly, "I should rather, if it be equal to you, Mrs. M'Crule, begin with the thousands already in existence; and of those thousands, why not begin with little Tommy?"

"It is no use!" cried Mrs. M'Crule, rising from her seat in the indignation of disappointed zeal: "Jenny, pull the bell for the car—Mrs. M'Greggor, if you've no objection, I'm at your service, for 'tis no use I see for me to speak here—nor should I have done so, but that I positively thought it my duty; and also a becoming attention to your ladyship and Miss Annaly, as lady patronesses, to let you know beforehand *our* sentiments, as I have collected the opinions of so many of the leading ladies, and apprehended your ladyship might, before it came to a public push, like to have an inkling or inuendo of how matters are likely to be carried at the general meeting of the patronesses on Saturday next, when we are determined to put it to the vote and poll. Jenny, do you see Jack, and the car? Good morning to your ladyship; good day, Miss Annaly."

Ormond put in a detainer: "I am here in obedience to your summons, Mrs. M'Crule—you sent to inform me that you had a few words of consequence to say to me."

"True, sir, I did wrap myself up this winter morning, and came out, as Mrs. M'Greggor can testify, in spite of my poor face, in hopes of doing some little good, and giving a friendly hint, before an explosion should publicly take place. But you will excuse me, since I find I gain so little credit, and so waste my breath; I can only leave gentlemen and ladies in this emergency, if they will be blind to the danger at this crisis, to follow their own opinions."

Ormond still remonstrating on the cruelty of leaving him in utter darkness, and calling it blindness, and assuring Mrs. M'Crule that he had not the slightest conception of what the danger or the emergency to which she alluded might be, or what little Tommy could have to do with it, the lady condescended, in compliance with Mrs. M'Greggor's twitch behind, to stay and recommence her statement. He could not forbear smiling, even more than Lady Annaly had done, when he was made to understand that the *emergency* and *crisis* meant nothing but this child's being admitted or not admitted into a charity school. While Ormond was incapable of speaking in reply with becoming seriousness, Florence, who saw his condition, had the kindness to draw off Mrs. M'Crule's attention, by asking her to partake of some excellent goose-pie, which just then made its entrance. This promised, for a time, to suspend the discussion, and to unite all parties in one common sympathy. When Florence saw that the *consommé*, to which she delicately helped her, was not thrown away upon Mrs. M'Crule, and that the union of goose and turkey in this Christmas dainty was much admired by this good lady, she attempted playfully to pass to a reflection on the happy effect that might to some tastes result from unions in party matters.

But no—"too serious matters these to be jested with," even with a glass of Barsac at the lips. Mrs. M'Crule stopped to say so, and to sigh. Per favour of the Barsac, however, Florence ventured to try what a little raillery might do. It was possible, that, if Mrs. M'Greggor and the chorus of young ladies could be made to laugh, Mrs. M'Crule might be brought to see the whole thing in a less gloomy point of view; and might perhaps be, just in time, made sensible of the ridicule to which she would expose herself, by persisting in sounding so pompously a false alarm.

"But can there really be so much danger," said Florence, "in letting little children, protestant and catholic, come together to the same school—sit on the same bench—learn the same alphabet from the same hornbook?"

"Oh, my dear Miss Annaly," cried Mrs. M'Crule, "I do wonder to hear you treat this matter so lightly—you, from whom I confess I did expect better principles: 'sit on the same bench!' easily said; but, my dear young lady, you do not consider that some errors of popery,—since there is no catholic in the room, I suppose I may say it,—the errors of popery are wonderfully infectious."

"I remember," said Lady Annaly, "when I was a child, being present once, when an *honest man*, that is, a protestant (for in those days no man but a protestant could be called an *honest man*), came to my uncle in a great passion to complain of the priest: 'My lord,' said he, 'what do you think the priest is going to do? he is going to bury a catholic corpse, not only in the churchyard, but, my lord, near to the grave of my father, who died a stanch dissenter.' 'My dear sir,' said my uncle, to the angry *honest man*, 'the clergyman of the parish is using me worse still, for he is going to bury a man, who died last Wednesday of the small-pox, near to my grandmother, who never had the small-pox in her life.'"

Mrs. M'Crule pursed up her mouth very close at this story. She thought Lady Annaly and her uncle were equally wicked, but she did not choose exactly to say so, as her ladyship's uncle was a person of rank, and of character too solidly established for Mrs. M'Crule to shake. She therefore only gave one of her sighs for the sins of the whole generation, and after a recording look at Mrs. M'Greggor, she returned to the charge about the schools and the children.

"It can do no possible good," she said, "to admit catholic children to *our* schools, because, do what you will, you can never make them good protestants."

"Well," said Lady Annaly, "as my friend, the excellent Bishop of —— said in parliament, 'if you cannot make them good protestants, make them good catholics, make them good any-things.'"

Giving up Lady Annaly all together, Mrs. M'Crule now desired to have Mr. Ormond's ultimatum—she wished to know whether he had made up his mind as to the affair in question; but she begged leave to observe, "that since the child had, to use the gentlest expression, the *misfortune* to be born and bred a catholic, it would be most prudent and gentlemanlike in Mr. Ormond not to make him a bone of contention, but to withdraw the poor child from the contest altogether, and strike his name out of the list of candidates, till the general question of admittance to those of his persuasion should have been decided by the lady patronesses."

Ormond declared, with or without submission to Mrs. M'Crule, that he could not think it becoming or gentlemanlike to desert a child whom he had undertaken to befriend—that, whatever the child had the misfortune to be born, he would abide by him; and would not add to his misfortunes by depriving him of the reward of his own industry and application, and of the only chance he had of continuing his good education, and of getting forward in life.

Mrs. M'Crule sighed and groaned.

But Ormond persisted: "The child," he said, "should have fair play—the lady patronesses would decide as they thought proper."

It had been said that the boy had Dr. Cambray's certificate, which Ormond was certain would not have been given undeservedly; he had also the certificate of his own priest.

"Oh! what signifies the certificate of his priest," interrupted Mrs. M'Crule; "and as for Dr. Cambray's, though he is a most respectable man (too liberal, perhaps), yet without meaning to insinuate any thing derogatory—but we all know how things are managed, and Dr. Cambray's great regard for Mr. Ormond might naturally influence him a little in favour of this little protégé."

Florence was very busy in replenishing Mrs. M'Greggor's plate, and Ormond haughtily told Mrs. M'Crule, "that as to Dr. Cambray's character for impartiality, he should leave that securely to speak for itself; and that as to the rest, she was at liberty to say or hint whatever she pleased, as far as he was concerned; but that, for her own sake, he would recommend it to her to be sure of her facts—for that slander was apt to hurt in the recoil."

Alarmed by the tone of confident innocence and determination with which Ormond spoke, Mrs. M'Crule, who like all other bullies was a coward, lowered her voice, and protested she meant nothing—"certainly no offence to Mr. Ormond; and as to slander there was nothing she detested so much—she was quite glad to be set right—for people did talk —and she had endeavoured to silence them, and now could from the best authority."

Ormond looked as if he wished that any authority could silence her—but no hopes of that. "She was sorry to find, however, that Mr. Ormond was positively determined to encourage the boy, whoever he was, to persist as candidate on this occasion, because she should be concerned to do any thing that looked like opposing him; yet she must, and she knew others were determined, and in short, he would be mortified to no purpose."

"Well," Ormond said, "he could only do his best, and bear to be mortified, if necessary, or when necessary."

A smile of approbation from Florence made his heart beat, and for some moments Mrs. M'Crule spoke without his knowing one syllable she said.

Mrs. M'Crule saw the smile, and perceived the effect. As she rose to depart, she turned to Miss Annaly, and whispered, but loud enough for all to hear, "Miss Annaly must excuse me if I warn her, that if she takes the part I am inclined to fear she will on Saturday, people I know *will* draw inferences."

Florence coloured, but with calm dignity and spirit, which Mrs. M'Crule did not expect from her usual gentleness and softness of manners, she replied, that "no inference which might be drawn from her conduct by any persons should prevent her from acting as she thought right, and taking that part which she believed to be just."

So ended the visit, or the visitation. The next day Lady Annaly, Miss Annaly, Sir Herbert, and Ormond, went to Vicar's Dale, and thence with the good doctor to the village school, on purpose that they might see and form an impartial judgment of the little boy. On one day in the week, the parents and friends of the children were admitted if they chose it, to the school-room, to hear the lessons, and to witness the adjudging of the week's premiums. This was *prize day* as they called it, and Sheelah and Moriarty were among the spectators. Their presence, and the presence of Mr. Ormond, so excited—so over-excited Tommy, that when he first stood up to read, his face flushed, his voice faltered, his little hands trembled so much that he could hardly hold the book; he could by no means turn over the leaf, and he was upon the point of disgracing himself by bursting into tears.

"Oh! ho!" cried an ill-natured voice of triumph from one of the spectators. Ormond and the Annalys turned, and saw behind them Mrs. M'Crule.

"Murder!" whispered Sheelah to Moriarty, "if she fixes him with that *evil eye*, and he gets the stroke of it, Moriarty, 'tis all over with him for life."

"Tut, woman, dear—what can hurt him? is not the good doctor in person standing betwixt him and harm? and see! he is recovering upon it fast—quite come to!—Hark!—he is himself again—Tommy, voice and all!—success to him!"

He had success, and he deserved it—the prizes were his; and when they were given to him, the congratulating smiles of his companions showed that Dr. Cambray's justice was unimpeached by those whom it most concerned; that notwithstanding all that had been said and done directly and indirectly, to counteract his benevolent efforts, he had succeeded in preventing envy and party-spirit from spreading discord among these innocent children.

Mrs. M'Crule withdrew, and nobody saw when or how.

"It is clear," said Lady Annaly, "that this boy is no favourite, for he has friends."

"Or, if he be a favourite, and have friends, it is a proof that he has extraordinary merit," said Sir Herbert.

"He is coming to us," said Florence, who had been excessively interested for the child, and whose eyes had followed him wherever he went: "Brother," whispered she, "will you let him pass you? he wants to say something to Mr. Ormond."

The boy brought to Ormond all the prizes which he had won since the time he first came to school: his grandame, Sheelah, had kept them safe in a little basket, which he now put into Ormond's hands, with honest pride and pleasure.

"I got 'em, and Granny said you'd like to see them, so she did—and here's what will please you—see my certificates—see, signed by the doctor himself's own hand, and Father M'Cormuck, that's his name, with his blessing by the same token he gave me."

Ormond looked with great satisfaction on Tommy's treasures, and Miss Annaly looked at them too with no small delight.

"Well, my boy, have you any thing more to say?" said Ormond to the child, who looked as if he was anxious to say something more.

"I have, sir; it's what I'd be glad to speak a word with you, Mr. Harry."

"Speak it then—you are not afraid of this lady?" "Oh, no—that I am not," said the boy, with a very expressive smile and emphasis.

But as the child seemed to wish that no one else should hear, Ormond retired a step or two with him behind the crowd. Tommy would not let go Miss Annaly's hand, so she heard all that passed.

"I am afeard I am too troublesome to you, sir," said the boy.

"To me—not the least," said Ormond: "speak on—say all you have in your mind."

"Why, then," said the child, "I *have* something greatly on my mind, because I heard Granny talking to Moriarty about it last night, over the fire, and I in the bed. Then I know all about Mrs. M'Crule, and how, if I don't give out, and wouldn't give up about the grand school, on Saturday, I should, may be, be bringing you, Mr. Harry, into great trouble: so that being the case, I'll give up entirely—and I'll go back to the Black Islands to-morrow," said Tommy, stoutly; yet swelling so in the chest that he could not say another word. He turned away.

As they were walking home together from the school, Moriarty said to Sheelah, "I'll engage, Sheelah, you did not see all that passed the day."

"I'll engage I did, though," said Sheelah.

"Why, then, Sheelah, you've quick eyes still."

"Oh! I'm not so blind but what I could see *that* with half an eye—ay, and saw how it was with them before you did, Moriarty. From the first minute they comed into the room together, said I to myself, 'there's a pair of angels well matched, if ever there was a pair on earth.' These things is all laid out above, unknownst to us, from the first minute we are born, *who* we are to have in marriage," added Sheelah.

"No; not *fixed* from the first minute we are born, Sheelah: it is *not*," said Moriarty.

"And how should you know, Moriarty," said Sheelah, "whether or not?"

"And why not as well as you, Sheelah, dear," replied Moriarty, "if you go to that?"

"Well, in the name of fortune, have it your own way," said Sheelah; "and how do you think it is then?"

"Why it is partly fixed for us," said Moriarty; "but the choice is still in us, always—"

"Oh! burn me if I understand that," said Sheelah.

"Then you are mighty hard of understanding this morning, Sheelah. See, now, with regard to Master Harry and Peggy Sheridan: it's my opinion, 'twas laid out from the first, that in case he did not do *that* wrong about Peggy—*then* see, Heaven had this lady, this angel, from that time forward in view for him, by way of *compensation* for not doing the wrong he might have chose to do. Now, don't you think, Sheelah, that's the way it was?—be a rasonable woman."

The rasonable woman was puzzled and silent, Sheelah and Moriarty having got, without knowing it, to the dark depths of metaphysics. There was some danger of their knocking their heads against each other there, as wiser heads have done on similar occasions.

It was an auspicious circumstance for Ormond's love that Florence had now a daily object of thought and feeling in common with him. Mrs.

M'Crule's having piqued Florence was in Ormond's favour: it awakened her pride, and conquered her timidity; she ventured to trust her own motives. To be sure, the interest she felt for this child was uncommonly vivid; but she might safely avow this interest—it was in the cause of one who was innocent, and who had been oppressed.

As Mrs. M'Crule was so vindictively busy, going about, daily, among the lady patronesses, preparing for the great battle that was to be decided on the famous Saturday, it was necessary that Lady and Miss Annaly should exert themselves at least to make the truth known to their friends, to take them to see Dr. Cambray's school, and to judge of the little candidate impartially. The day for decision came, and Florence felt an anxiety, an eagerness, which made her infinitely more amiable, and more interesting in Ormond's eyes. The election was decided in favour of humanity and justice. Florence was deputed to tell the decision to the successful little candidate, who was waiting, with his companions, to hear his fate. Radiant with benevolent pleasure, she went to announce the glad tidings.

"Oh! if she is not beautiful!" cried Sheelah, clasping her hands.

Ormond felt it so warmly, and his looks expressed his feelings so strongly, that Florence, suddenly abashed, could scarcely finish her speech.

If Mrs. M'Crule had been present, she might again have cried "Oh! ho!" but she had retreated, too much discomfited, by the disappointments of hatred, to stay even to embarrass the progress of love. Love had made of late rapid progress. Joining in the cause of justice and humanity, mixing with all the virtues, he had taken possession of the heart happily, safely —unconsciously at first, yet triumphantly at last. Where was Colonel Albemarle all this time? Ormond neither knew nor cared; he thought but little of him at this moment. However, said he to himself, Colonel Albemarle will be here in a few days—it is better for me to see how things are there, before I speak—I am sure Florence could not give me a decisive answer, till her brother has disentangled that business for her. Lady Annaly said as much to me the other day, if I understood her rightly—and I am sure this is the state of the case, from the pains Florence takes now to avoid giving me an opportunity of speaking to her alone, which I have been watching for so anxiously. So reasoned Ormond; but his reasonings, whether wise or foolish, were set at nought by unforeseen events.

CHAPTER XXV.

One evening Ormond walked with Sir Herbert Annaly to the sea-shore, to look at the lighthouse which was building. He was struck with all that had been done here in the course of a few months, and especially with the alteration in the appearance of the people. Their countenances had changed from the look of desponding idleness and cunning, to the air of busy, hopeful independence. He could not help congratulating Sir Herbert, and warmly expressing a wish that he might himself, in the whole course of his life, do half as much good as Sir Herbert had already effected. "You will do a great deal more," said Sir Herbert: "you will have a great deal more time. I must make the best of the little—probably the very little time I shall have: while I yet live, let me not live in vain."

"*Yet* live," said Ormond; "I hope—I trust—you will live many years to be happy, and to make others so: your strength seems quite re-established —you have all the appearance of health."

Sir Herbert smiled, but shook his head.

"My dear Ormond, do not trust to outward appearances too much. Do not let my friends entirely deceive themselves. I *know* that my life cannot be long—I wish, before I die, to do as much good as I can."

The manner in which these words were said, and the look with which they were accompanied, impressed Ormond at once with a conviction of the danger, fortitude, and magnanimity of the person who spoke to him. The hectic colour, the brilliant eye, the vividness of fancy, the superiority of intellectual powers, the warmth of the affections, and the amiable gentleness of the disposition of this young man, were, alas! but so many fatal indications of his disease. The energy with which, with decreasing bodily and increasing mental strength, he pursued his daily occupations, and performed more than every duty of his station, the never-failing temper and spirits with which he sustained the hopes of many of his friends, were but so many additional causes of alarm to the too experienced mother. Florence, with less experience, and with a temper happily prone to hope, was more easily deceived. She could not believe that a being, whom she saw so full of life, could be immediately in danger of dying. Her brother had now but a very slight cough—he had, to all appearance, recovered from the accident by which they had been so much alarmed when they were in England. The physicians had pronounced, that with care to avoid cold, and all violent exertion, he might do well and last long.

To fulfil the conditions was difficult; especially that which required him to refrain from any great exertion. Whenever he could be of service to his friends, or could do any good to his fellow-creatures, he spared neither mental nor bodily exertion. Under the influence of benevolent enthusiasm, he continually forgot the precarious tenure by which he held his life.

It was now the middle of winter, and one stormy night a vessel was wrecked on the coast near Annaly. The house was at such a distance from that part of the shore where the vessel struck, that Sir Herbert knew nothing of it till the next morning, when it was all over. No lives were lost. It was a small trading vessel, richly laden. Knowing the vile habits of some of the people who lived on the coast, Sir Herbert, the moment he heard that there was a wreck, went down to see that the property of the sufferers was protected from those depredators, who on such occasions were astonishingly alert. Ormond accompanied him, and by their joint exertions much of the property was placed in safety under a military guard. Some had been seized and carried off before their arrival, but not by any of Sir Herbert's tenants. It became pretty clear that *the neighbours* on Sir Ulick O'Shane's estate were the offenders. They had grown bold from impunity, and from the belief that no *jantleman* "would choose to interfere with them, on account of their landlord."

Sir Herbert's indignation rose. Ormond pledged himself that Sir Ulick O'Shane would never protect such wretches; and eager to assist public justice, to defend his guardian, and, above all, to calm Sir Herbert and prevent him from over-exerting himself, he insisted upon being allowed to go in his stead with the party of military who were to search the suspected houses. It was with some difficulty that he prevailed. He parted with Sir Herbert; and, struck at the moment with his highly-raised colour, and the violent heat and state of excitation he was in, Ormond again urged him to remember his own health, and his mother and sister.

"I will—I do," said Sir Herbert; "but it is my duty to think of public justice before I think of myself."

The apprehension Ormond felt in quitting Sir Herbert recurred frequently as he rode on in silence; but he was called into action and it was dissipated. Ormond spent nearly three hours searching a number of wretched cabins from which the male inhabitants fled at the approach of the military, leaving the women and children to make what excuses and tell what lies they could. This the women and children executed with great readiness and ability, and in the most pity-moving tones imaginable.

The inside of an Irish cabin appears very different to those who come to claim hospitality and to those who come to detect offenders.

Ormond having never before entered a cabin with a search-warrant, constable, or with the military, he was "not *up* to the thing"—as both the serjeant and constable remarked to each other. While he listened to the piteous story of a woman about a husband who had broken his leg from a ladder, *sarving* the masons at Sir Herbert's lighthouse, and was *lying at* the hospital, *not expected*, [Footnote: *Not expected* to live.] the husband was lying all the time with both his legs safe and sound in a potato furrow within a few yards of the house. And *the child* of another eloquent matron was running off with a pair of silver-mounted pistols taken from the wreck, which he was instructed to hide in a bog-hole, snug—the bog-water never rusting. In one hovel—for the houses of these wretches who lived by pillage, after all their ill-gotten gains, were no better than hovels—in one of them, in which, as the information stated, some valuable plunder was concealed, they found nothing but a poor woman groaning in bed, and two little children; one crying as if its heart would break, and the other sitting up behind the mother's bolster supporting her. After the soldiers had searched every place in vain, even the thatch of the house, the woman showing no concern all the while, but groaning on, seeming scarce able to answer Mr. Ormond's questions— the constable, an old hand, roughly bid her get up, that they might search the bed; this Ormond would not permit:—she lay still, thanking his honour faintly, and they quitted the house. The goods which had been carried off were valuable, and were hid in the straw of the very bed on which the woman was lying.

As they were returning homewards after their fruitless search, when they had passed the boundary of Sir Ulick's and had reached Sir Herbert's territory, they were overtaken by a man, who whispered something to the serjeant which made him halt, and burst out a laughing; the laugh ran through the whole serjeant's guard, and reached Ormond's ears; who, asking the cause of it, was told how the woman had cheated them, and how she was now risen from her bed, and was dividing the prize among the *lawful owners*, "share and share alike." These lawful owners, all risen out of the potato furrows, and returning from the bogs, were now assembled, holding their bed of justice. At the moment the serjeant's information came off, their captain, with a bottle of whiskey in his hand, was drinking, "To the health of Sir Ulick O'Shane, our worthy landlord —seldom comes a better. The same to his ward, Harry Ormond, Esq., and may his eyesight never be better nor worse."

Harry Ormond instantly turned his horse's head, much provoked at having been duped, and resolved that the plunderers should not now escape. By the advice of serjeants and constables, he dismounted, that no sound of horses' hoofs might give notice from a distance; though, indeed, on the sands of the sea-shore, no horses' tread, he thought, could be heard. He looked round for some one with whom he could leave his horse, but not a creature, except the men who were with him, was in sight.

"What can have become of all the people?" said Ormond: "it is not the workmen's dinner-hour, and they are gone from the work at the lighthouse; and the horses and cars are left without any one with them." He went on a few paces, and saw a boy who seemed to be left to watch the horses, and who looked very melancholy. The boy did not speak as Ormond came up. "What is the matter?" said Ormond: "something dreadful has happened—speak!"

"Did not you hear it, sir?" said the boy: "I'd be loth to tell it you."

"Has any thing happened to—"

"Sir Herbert—ay—the worst that could. Running to stop one of them villains that was making off with something from the wreck, he dropped sudden as if he was shot, and—when they went to lift him up—But you'll drop yourself, sir," said the boy.

"Give him some of the water out of the bucket, can't ye?"

"Here's my cap," said the serjeant. Ormond was made to swallow the water, and, recovering his senses, heard one of the soldiers near him say, "'Twas only a faint Sir Herbert took, I'll engage."

The thought was new life to Ormond: he started up, mounted his horse, and galloped off—saw no creature on the road—found a crowd at the gate of the avenue—the crowd opened to let him pass, many voices calling as he passed to beg him to *send out word*. This gave him fresh hopes, since nothing certain was known: he spurred on his horse; but when he reached the house, as he was going to Sir Herbert's room he was met by Sir Herbert's own man, O'Reilly. The moment he saw O'Reilly's face, he knew there was no hope—he asked no question: the surgeon came out, and told him that in consequence of having broke a blood-vessel, which bled internally, Sir Herbert had just expired—his mother and sister were with him. Ormond retired—he begged the servants would write to him at Dr. Cambray's—and he immediately went away.

Two days after he had a note from O'Reilly, written in haste, at a very early hour in the morning, to say that he was just setting out with the hearse to the family burial-place at Herbert—it having been thought best that the funeral should not be in this neighbourhood, on account of the poor people at Annaly being so exasperated against those who were thought to be the immediate occasion of his death. Sir Herbert's last orders to O'Reilly were to this effect—"to *take care*, and to have every thing done as privately as possible."

No pomp of funeral was, indeed, necessary for such a person. The great may need it—the good need it not: they are mourned in the heart, and they are remembered without vain pageantry. If public sorrow can soothe private grief—and surely in some measure it must—the family and friends of this young man had this consolation; but they had another and a better.

It is the triumph of religion and of its ministers to be able to support the human heart, when all other resources are of little avail. Time, it is true, at length effaces the recollection of misfortune, and age deadens the sense of sorrow. But that power to console is surely far superior in its effect, more worthy of a rational and a social being, which operates—not by contracting or benumbing our feelings and faculties, but by expanding and ennobling them—inspiring us, not with stoic indifference to the pains and pleasures of humanity, but with pious submission to the will of Heaven—to the order and orderer of the universe.

CHAPTER XXVI.

Though Sir Ulick O'Shane contrived to laugh on most occasions where other people would have wept, and though he had pretty well *case-hardened* his heart, yet he was shocked by the first news of the death of Sir Herbert Annaly. He knew the man must die, he said—so must we all, sooner or later—but for the manner of his death, Sir Ulick could not help feeling a secret pang. He felt conscious of having encouraged, or at least connived at, the practices of those wretches who had roused the generous and just indignation of Sir Herbert, and in pursuit of whom this fine young man had fallen a sacrifice.

Not only the "still small voice," but the cry of the country, was against Sir Ulick on this occasion. He saw that he must give up the offenders, and show decidedly that he desired to have them punished. Decidedly, then, and easily, as ever prince abandoned secretary or chancellor to save his own popularity, quickly as ever grand seignior gave up grand vizier or chief baker to appease the people, Sir Ulick gave up his *"honest rascals*," his *"rare rapparees*," and even his *"wrecker royal."* Sir Ulick set his magistrate, Mr. M'Crule, at work for once on the side both of justice and law; warrants, committals, and constables, cleared the land. Many fled—a few were seized, escorted ostentatiously by *a serjeant and twelve* of Sir Ulick's corps, and lodged in the county jail to stand their trial, bereft of all *favour and purtection*, bonâ fide delivered up to justice.

A considerable tract of Sir Ulick's coast estate, in consequence of this, remained untenanted. Some person in whom he could confide must be selected to inhabit the fishing-lodge, and to take care of the cabins and land till they should be relet. Sir Ulick pitched upon Moriarty Carroll for this purpose, and promised him such liberal reward, that all Moriarty's friends congratulated him upon his "great luck in getting the appointment, against the man, too, that Mr. Marcus had proposed and favoured."

Marcus, who was jealous in the extreme of power, and who made every trifle a matter of party competition, was vexed at the preference given against *an honest man* and a *friend* of his own, in favour of Moriarty, a catholic; a fellow he had always disliked, and a protege of Mr. Ormond. Ormond, though obliged to Sir Ulick for this kindness to Moriarty, was too intent on other things to think much about the matter. *When* he should see Florence Annaly again, seemed to him the only question in the universe of great importance.

Just at this time arrived letters for Mr. Ormond, from Paris, from M. and Mad. de Connal; very kind letters, with pressing invitations to him to pay them a visit. M. de Connal informed him, "that the five hundred pounds, King Corny's legacy, was ready waiting his orders. M. de Connal hoped to put it into Mr. Ormond's hands in Paris in his own hotel, where he trusted that Mr. Ormond would do him the pleasure of soon occupying the apartments which were preparing for him." It did not clearly appear whether they had or had not heard of his accession of fortune. Dora's letter was not from *Dora*—it was from *Mad. de Connal*. It was on green paper, with a border of Cupids and roses, and store of sentimental devices in the corners. The turn of every phrase, the style, as far as Ormond could judge, was quite French—aiming evidently at being perfectly Parisian. Yet it was a letter so flattering to the vanity of man as might well incline him to excuse the vanity of woman. "Besides," as Sir Ulick O'Shane observed, "after making due deductions for French sentiment, there remains enough to satisfy an honest English heart that the lady really desires to see you, Ormond; and that now, in the midst of her Parisian prosperity, she has the grace to wish to show kindness to her father's adopted son, and to the companion and friend of her childhood." Sir Ulick was of opinion that Ormond could not do better than accept the invitation. Ormond was surprised, for he well recollected the manner in which his guardian had formerly, and not many months ago, written and spoken of Connal as a coxcomb and something worse.

"That is true," said Sir Ulick; "but that was when I was angry about your legacy, which was of great consequence to us then, though of none now —I certainly did suspect the man of a design to cheat you; but it is clear that I was wrong—I am ready candidly to acknowledge that I did him injustice. Your money is at your order—and I have nothing to say, but to beg M. de Connal ten thousand French pardons. Observe, I do not beg pardon for calling him a coxcomb, for a coxcomb he certainly is."

"An insufferable coxcomb!" cried Ormond.

"But a coxcomb *in fashion*," said Sir Ulick; "and a coxcomb in fashion is a useful connexion. He did not fable about Versailles—I have made particular inquiries from our ambassador at Paris, and he writes me word that Connal is often at court—*en bonne odeur* at Versailles. The ambassador says he meets the Connals every where in the first circles— how they came there I don't know."

"I am glad to hear that, for Dora's sake," said Ormond.

"I always thought her a sweet, pretty little creature," said Sir Ulick, "and no doubt she has been polished up; and dress and fashion make such a difference in a woman—I suppose she is now ten times better—that is, prettier: she will introduce you at Paris, and your own *merit*—that is, manners, and figure, and fortune—will make your way every where. By-the-bye, I do not see a word about poor Mademoiselle—Oh, yes! here is a Line squeezed in at the edge—'Mille tendres souvenirs de la part de Mdlle. O'Faley.'"

"Poor Mademoiselle!"

"Poor Mademoiselle!" repeated Sir Ulick.

"Do you mean *that thing half Irish, half French, half mud, half tinsel?*" said Ormond.

"Very good memory! very sly, Harry! But still in the Irish half of her I dare say there is a heart; and we must allow her the tinsel, in pure gratitude, for having taught you to speak French so well—that will be a real advantage to you in Paris."

"Whenever I go there, sir," said Ormond, coldly.

Sir Ulick was very much disappointed at perceiving that Ormond had no mind to go to Paris; but dropping the subject, he turned the conversation upon the Annalys: he praised Florence to the skies, hoped that Ormond would be more fortunate than Marcus had been, for somehow or other, he should never live or die in peace till Florence Annaly was more nearly connected with him. He regretted, however, that poor Sir Herbert was carried off before he had completed the levying of those fines, which would have cut off the entail, and barred the heir-at-law from the Herbert estates. Florence was not now the great heiress it was once expected she should be; indeed she had but a moderate gentlewoman's fortune—not even what at Smithfield a man of Ormond's fortune might expect; but Sir Ulick knew, he said, that this would make no difference to his ward, unless to make him in greater impatience to propose for her.

It was impossible to be in greater impatience to propose for her than Ormond was. Sir Ulick did not wonder at it; but he thought that Miss Annaly would not, *could* not, listen to him yet. *Time, the comforter*, must come first; and while time was doing this business, love could not decently be admitted.

"That was the reason," said Ulick, returning by another road to the charge, "why I advised a trip to Paris; but you know best."

"I cannot bear this suspense—I must and will know my fate—I will write instantly, and obtain an answer."

"Do so; and to save time, I can tell what your fate and your answer will be: from Florence Annaly, assurance of perfect esteem and regard, as far as friendship, perhaps; but she will tell you that she cannot think of love at present. Lady Annaly, prudent Lady Annaly, will say that she hopes Mr. Ormond will not think of settling for life till he has seen something more of the world. Well, you don't believe me," said Sir Ulick, interrupting himself just at the moment when he saw that Ormond began to think there was some sense in what he was saying.

"If you don't believe me, Harry," continued he, "consult your oracle, Dr. Cambray: he has just returned from Annaly, and he can tell you how the land lies."

Dr. Cambray agreed with Sir Ulick that both Lady Annaly and her daughter would desire that Ormond should see more of the world before he settled for life; but as to going off to Paris, without waiting to see or write to them, Dr. Cambray agreed with Ormond that it would be the worst thing he could do—that so far from appearing a proof of his respect to their grief, it would only seem a proof of indifference, or a sign of impatience: they would conclude that he was in haste to leave his friends in adversity, to go to those in prosperity, and to enjoy the gaiety and dissipation of Paris. Dr. Cambray advised that he should remain quietly where he was, and wait till Miss Annaly should be disposed to see him. This was most prudent, Ormond allowed. "But then the delay!" To conquer by delay we must begin by conquering our impatience: now that was what our hero could not possibly do—therefore he jumped hastily to this conclusion, that "in love affairs no man should follow any mortal's opinion but his own."

Accordingly he sat down and wrote to Miss Annaly a most passionate letter, enclosed in a most dutiful one to Lady Annaly, as full of respectful attachment and entire obedience, as a son-in-law expectant could devise —beginning very properly and very sincerely, with anxiety and hopes about her ladyship's health, and ending, as properly, and as sincerely, with hopes that her ladyship would permit him, as soon as possible, to take from her the greatest, the only remaining source of happiness she had in life—her daughter.

Having worded this very plausibly—for he had now learned how to write a letter—our hero despatched a servant of Sir Ulick's with his epistle; ordering him to wait certainly for an answer, but above all things to make haste back. Accordingly the man took a cross road—a short cut, and coming to a bridge, which he did not know was broken down till he was *close upon it*, he was obliged to return and to go round, and did not get home till long after dark—and the only answer he brought was, that there was no answer—only Lady Annaly's compliments.

Ormond could scarcely believe that no answer had been sent; but the man took all the saints in heaven, or in the calendar, to witness, that he would not tell his honour, or any *jantleman*, a lie.

Upon a cross-examination, the man gave proof that he had actually seen both the ladies. They were sitting so and so, and dressed so and so, in mourning. Farther, he gave undeniable proof that he had delivered the letters, and that they had been opened and read; for—*by the same token* —he was summoned up to my lady on account of one of Mr. Ormond's letters, he did not know *which*, or to *who*, being dated Monday, whereas it was Wednesday; and he had to clear himself of having been three days on the road.

Ormond, inordinately impatient, could not rest a moment. The next morning he set off at full speed for Annaly, determined to find out what was the matter.

Arrived there, a new footman came to the door with *"Not at home, sir."* Ormond could have knocked him down, but he contented himself with striking his own forehead—however, in a genteel proper voice, he desired to see Sir Herbert's own man, O'Reilly.

"Mr. O'Reilly is not here, sir—absent on business."

Every thing was adverse. Ormond had one hope, that this new fellow, not knowing him, might by mistake have included him in a general order against morning visitors.

"My name is Ormond, sir."

"Yes, sir."

"And I beg you will let Lady Annaly and Miss Annaly know that Mr. Ormond is come to pay his respects to them."

The man seemed very unwilling to carry any message to his ladies. "He was sure," he said, "that the ladies would not see anybody."

"Was Lady Annaly ill?"

"Her ladyship had been but poorly, but was better within the last two days."

"And Miss Annaly?"

"Wonderful better, too, sir; has got up her spirits greatly to-day."

"I am very glad to hear it," said Ormond. "Pray, sir, can you tell me whether a servant from Mr. Ormond brought a letter here yesterday?"

"He did, sir."

"And was there any answer sent?"

"I really can't say, sir."

"Be so good to take my name to your lady," repeated Ormond.

"Indeed, sir, I don't like to go in, for I know my lady—both my ladies is engaged, very particularly engaged—however, if you very positively desire it, sir—"

Ormond did very positively desire it, and the footman obeyed. While Ormond was waiting impatiently for the answer, his horse, as impatient as himself, would not stand still. A groom, who was sauntering about, saw the uneasiness of the horse, and observing that it was occasioned by a peacock, who, with spread tail, was strutting in the sunshine, he ran and chased the bird away. Ormond thanked the groom, and threw him a *luck token*; but not recollecting his face, asked how long he had been at Annaly. "I think you were not here when I was here last?" said Ormond.

"No, sir." said the man, looking a little puzzled; "I never was here till the day before yesterday in my born days. We *bees* from England."

"We!"

"That is, I and master—that is, master and I." Ormond grew pale; but the groom saw nothing of it—his eyes had fixed upon Ormond's horse.

"A very fine horse this of yours, sir, for sartain, if he could but *stand*, sir; he's main restless at a door. My master's horse is just his match for that."

"And pray who is your master, sir?" said Ormond, in a voice which he forced to be calm.

"My master, sir, is one Colonel Albemarle, son of the famous General Albemarle, as lost his arm, sir, you might have heard talk of, time back," said the groom.

At this moment a window-blind was flapped aside, and before the wind blew it back to its place again, Ormond saw Florence Annaly sitting on a sofa, and a gentleman, in regimentals, kneeling at her feet.

"Bless my eyes!" cried the groom, "what made you let go his bridle, sir? Only you sat him well, sir, he would ha' thrown you that minute—Curse the blind! that flapped in his eyes."

The footman re-appeared on the steps. "Sir, it is just as I said—I could not be let in. Mrs. Spencer, my lady's woman, says the ladies is engaged —you can't see them."

Ormond had seen enough.

"Very well, sir," said he—"Mr. Ormond's compliments—he called, that's all."

Ormond put spurs to his horse, and galloped off; and, fast as he went, he urged his horse still faster.

In the agony of disappointed love and jealousy, he railed bitterly against the whole sex, and against Florence Annaly in particular. Many were the rash vows he made that he would never think of her more—that he would tear her from his heart—that he would show her that he was no whining lover, no easy dupe, to be whiffled off and on, the sport of a coquette.

"A coquette!—is it possible, Florence Annaly?—*You*—and after all!"

Certain tender recollections obtruded; but he repelled them—he would not allow one of them to mitigate his rage. His naturally violent passion of anger, now that it broke again from the control of his reason, seemed the more ungovernable from the sense of past and the dread of future restraint.

So, when a horse naturally violent, and half trained to the curb, takes fright, or takes offence, and, starting, throws his master, away he gallops; enraged the more by the falling bridle, he rears, plunges, curvets, and lashes out behind at broken girth or imaginary pursuer.

"Good Heavens! what is the matter with you, my dear boy?—what has happened?" cried Sir Ulick, the moment he saw him; for the disorder of Ormond's mind appeared strongly in his face and gestures—still more strongly in his words.

When he attempted to give an account of what had happened, it was so broken, so exclamatory, that it was wonderful how Sir Ulick made out the plain fact. Sir Ulick, however, well understood the short-hand language of the passions: he listened with eager interest—he sympathized so fully with Ormond's feelings—expressed such astonishment, such indignation, that Harry, feeling him to be his warm friend, loved him as heartily as in the days of his childhood.

Sir Ulick saw and seized the advantage: he had almost despaired of accomplishing his purpose—now was the critical instant.

"Harry Ormond," said he, "would you make Florence Annaly feel to the quick—would you make her repent in sackcloth and ashes—would you make her pine for you, ay! till her very heart is sick?"

"Would I? to be sure—show me how!—only show me how!" cried Ormond.

"Look ye, Harry! to have and to hold a woman—trust me, for I have had and held many—to have and to hold a woman, you must first show her that you can, if you will, fling her from you—ay! and leave her there: set off for Paris to-morrow morning—my life upon it, the moment she hears you are gone, she will wish you back again!"

"I'll set off to-night," said Ormond, ringing the bell to give orders to his servant to prepare immediately for his departure.

Thus Sir Ulick, seizing precisely the moment when Ormond's mind was at the right heat, aiming with dexterity and striking with force, bent and moulded him to his purpose.

While preparations for Ormond's journey were making, Sir Ulick said that there was one thing he must insist upon his doing before he quitted Castle Hermitage—he must look over and settle his guardianship accounts.

Ormond, whose head was far from business at this moment, was very reluctant: he said that the accounts could wait till he should return from France; but Sir Ulick observed that if he, or if Ormond were to die, leaving the thing unsettled, it would be loss of property to the one, and loss of credit to the other. Ormond then begged that the accounts might be sent after him to Paris; he would look over them there at leisure, and sign them. No, Sir Ulick said, they ought to be signed by some forthcoming witness in this country. He urged it so much, and put it upon the footing of his own credit and honour in such a manner, that Ormond could not refuse. He seized the papers, and took a pen to sign them; but Sir Ulick snatched the pen from his hand, and absolutely insisted upon his first knowing what he was going to sign.

"The whole account could have been looked over while we have been talking about it," said Sir Ulick.

Ormond sat down and looked it over, examined all the vouchers, saw that every thing was perfectly right and fair, signed the accounts, and esteemed Sir Ulick the more for having insisted upon showing, and proving that all was exact.

Sir Ulick offered to manage his affairs for him while he was away, particularly a large sum which Ormond had in the English funds. Sir Ulick had a banker and a broker in London, on whom he could depend, and he had, from his place and connexions, means of obtaining good information in public affairs; he had made a great deal himself by speculations in the funds, and he could buy in and sell out to great advantage, he said, for Ormond. But for this purpose a *power of attorney* was necessary to be given by Ormond to Sir Ulick.

There was scarcely time to draw one up, nor was Sir Ulick sure that there was a printed form in the house. Luckily, however, a proper *power* was found, and filled up, and Ormond had just time to sign it before he stepped into the carriage: he embraced his guardian, and thanked him heartily for his care of the interests of his purse, and still more for the sympathy he had shown in the interests of his heart. Sir Ulick was moved at parting with him, and this struck Harry the more, because he certainly struggled to suppress his feelings. Ormond stopped at Vicar's Dale to tell Dr. Cambray all that had happened, to thank him and his family for their kindness, and to take leave of them.

They were indeed astonished when he entered, saying, "Any commands, my good friends, for London or Paris? I am on my way there—carriage at the door."

At first they could not believe him to be serious; but when they heard his story, and saw by the agitation of his manner that he was in earnest, they were still more surprised at the suddenness of his determination. They all believed and represented to him that there must be some mistake, and that he was not cool enough to judge sanely at this moment.

Dr. Cambray observed that Miss Annaly could not prevent any man from kneeling to her. Ormond haughtily said, "He did not know what she could prevent, he only knew what she did. She had not vouchsafed an answer to his letter—she had not admitted him. These he thought were sufficient indications that the person at her feet was accepted. Whether he were or not, Ormond would inquire no further. She might now accept or refuse, as she pleased—he would go to Paris."

His friends had nothing more to say or to do, but to sigh, and to wish him a good journey, and much pleasure at Paris.

Ormond now requested that Dr. Cambray would have the goodness to write to him from time to time, to inform him of whatever he might wish to know during his absence. He was much mortified to hear from the doctor that he was obliged to proceed, with his family, for some months, to a distant part of the north of England; and that, as to the Annalys, they were immediately removing to the sea-coast of Devonshire, for the benefit of a mild climate and of sea-bathing. Ormond, therefore, had no resource but in his guardian. Sir Ulick's affairs, however, were to take him over to London, from whence Ormond could not expect much satisfactory intelligence with respect to Ireland.

Ormond flew to Dublin, crossed the channel in an express boat, travelled night and day in the mail to London, from thence to Dover—crossed the water in a storm, and travelled with the utmost expedition to Paris, though there was no one reason why he should be in haste; and for so much, his travelling was as little profitable or amusing as possible. He saw, heard, and understood nothing, till he reached Paris.

It has been said that the traveller without sensibility may travel from Dan to Beersheba, without finding any thing worth seeing. The traveller who has too much sensibility often observes as little—of this all persons must be sensible, who have ever travelled when their minds were engrossed with painful feelings, or possessed by any strong passion.

CHAPTER XXVII.

Ormond had written to M. and Madame de Connal to announce his intentions of spending some time in Paris, and to thank them for the invitation to their house; an invitation which, however, he declined accepting; but he requested M. de Connal to secure apartments for him in some hotel near them.

Upon his arrival he found every thing prepared for a Milord Anglois: handsome apartments, fashionable carriage, well-powdered laquais, and a valet-de-chambre, waited the orders of monsieur.

Connal was with him a few minutes after his arrival—welcomed him to Paris with cordial gaiety—was more glad, and more sorry, and said more in five minutes, and above all made more protestations of regard, than an Englishman would make in a year.

He was rejoiced—delighted—enchanted to see Mr. Ormond. Madame de Connal was absolutely transported with joy when she heard he was on his road to Paris. Madame was now at Versailles; but she would return in a few days: she would be in despair at Mr. Ormond's not accepting the apartments in the Hotel de Connal, which were actually prepared for him; but in fact it was nearly the same thing, within two doors of them. He hoped Mr. Ormond liked his apartments—but in truth that was of little consequence, for he would never be in them, except when he was asleep or dressing.

Ormond thought the apartments quite superb, and was going to have thanked M. de Connal for the trouble he had taken; but at the word *superbe*, Connal ran on again with French vivacity of imagination.

"Certainly, Mr. Ormond ought," he said, "to have every thing now in the first style." He congratulated our hero on his accession of fortune, "of which Madame de Connal and he had heard with inexpressible joy. And

Mdlle. O'Faley, too, she who had always prophesied that they should meet in happiness at Paris, was now absolutely in ecstasy."

"You have no idea, in short, my dear Ormond, of what a strong impression you left on all our minds—no conception of the lively interest you always inspired."

It was a lively interest which had slumbered quietly for a considerable time, but now it wakened with perfectly good grace. Ormond set little value on these sudden protestations, and his pride felt a sort of fear that it should be supposed he was deceived by them; yet, altogether, the manner was agreeable, and Connal was essentially useful at this moment: as Sir Ulick had justly observed, a coxcomb in fashion may, in certain circumstances, be a useful friend.

"But, my dear fellow," cried Connal, "what savage cut your hair last?—It is a sin to trust your fine head to the barbarians—my hairdresser shall be with you in the twinkling of an eye: I will send my tailor—allow me to choose your embroidery, and see your lace, before you decide—I am said to have a tolerable taste—the ladies say so, and they are always the best judges. The French dress will become you prodigiously, I foresee—but, just Heaven!—what buckles!—those must have been made before the flood: no disparagement to your taste, but what could you do better in the Black Islands? Paris is the only place for *bijouterie*—except in steel, Paris surpasses the universe—your eyes will be dazzled by the Palais Royal. But this hat!—you know it can't appear—it would destroy you: my *chapelier* shall be with you instantly. It will all be done in five minutes—you have no idea of the celerity with which you may command every thing at Paris. But I am so sorry that madame is at Versailles, and that I am under a necessity of being there myself to-morrow for the rest of this week; but I have a friend, a little *Abbé*, who will be delighted in the mean time to show you Paris."

From the moment of his arrival at Paris, Ormond resolved to put Florence Annaly completely out of his thoughts, and to drown in gaiety and dissipation the too painful recollection of her duplicity towards him.

He was glad to have a few days to look about him, and to see something of Paris.

He should like, as he told M. de Connal, to go to the play, to accustom himself to the language. He must wear off his English or Irish awkwardness a little, before he should be presented to Madame de Connal, or appear in French society. A profusion of compliments followed from M. de Connal; but Ormond persisting, it was settled that he should go incog. this night to the Théâtre François.

Connal called upon him in the evening, and took him to the theatre.

They were in *une petite loge*, where they could see without being seen. In the box with them was the young Abbé, and a pretty little French actress, Mdlle. Adrienne. At the first coup-d'oeil, the French ladies did not strike him as handsome; they looked, as he said, like dolls, all eyes and rouge; and rouge, as he thought, very unbecomingly put on, in one frightful red patch or plaster, high upon the cheek, without any pretence to the imitation of natural colour.

"Eh fi donc!" said the Abbé, "what you call the natural colour, that would be *rouge coquette*, which no woman of quality can permit herself."

"No, Dieu merci," said the actress, "that is for us: 'tis very fair we should have some advantages in the competition, they have so many—by birth —if not by nature."

M. de Connal explained to Ormond that the frightful red patch which offended his eye, was the mark of a woman of quality: "women only of a certain rank have the privilege of wearing their rouge in that manner— your eye will soon grow accustomed to it, and you will like it as a sign of rank and fashion."

The actress shrugged her shoulders, said something about "*la belle nature*," and the good taste of Monsieur l'Anglois. The moment the curtain drew up, she told him the names of all the actors and actresses as they appeared—noting the value and celebrity of each. The play was, unfortunately for Ormond, a tragedy; and Le Kain was at Versailles. Ormond thought he understood French pretty well, but he did not comprehend what was going on. The French tone of tragic declamation, so unnatural to his ear, distracted his attention so much, that he could not make out the sense of what any of the actors said.

"'Tis like the quality rouge," said Connal; "your taste must be formed to it. But your eye and your ear will accommodate themselves to both. You will like it in a month."

M. de Connal said this was always the first feeling of foreigners. "But have patience," said he; "go on listening, and in a night or two, perhaps in an hour or two, the sense will break in upon you all at once. You will never find yourself at a loss in society. Talk, at all events, whether you speak ill or well, talk: don't aim at correctness—we don't expect it. Besides, as they will tell you, we like to see how a stranger 'play with our language.'"

M. de Connal's manner was infinitely more agreeable toward Ormond now than in former days.

There was perhaps still at the bottom of his mind the same fund of self-conceit, but he did not take the same arrogant tone. It was the tone not of a superior to an inferior, but of a friend, in a new society, and a country to which he is a stranger. There was as little of the protector in his manner as possible, considering his natural presumption and acquired habits: considering that he had made his own way in Paris, and that he thought that to be the first man in a certain circle there, was to be nearly the first man in the universe. The next morning, the little Abbé called to pay his compliments, and to offer his services.

M. de Connal being obliged to go to Versailles, in his absence the Abbé would be very happy, he said, to attend Mr. Ormond, and to show him Paris: he believed, he humbly said, that he had the means of showing him every thing that was worth his attention.

Away they drove.

"Gare! gare!" cried the coachman, chasing away the droves of walkers before him. There being no footpaths in the streets of Paris, they were continually driven up close to the walls.

Ormond at first shrunk at the sight of their peril and narrow escapes.

"Monsieur apparemment is nervous after his *voyage?*" said the Abbé.

"No, but I am afraid the people will be run over. I will make the coachman drive more quietly."

"Du tout!—not at all," said the little Abbé, who was of a noble family, and had all the airs of it. "Leave him to settle it with the people—they are used to it. And, after all, what have they to think of, but to take care of themselves—*la canaille?*"

"*La canaille,*" synonymous with the *swinish multitude,* an expression of contempt for which the Parisian nobility have since paid terribly dear.

Ormond, who was not used to it, found it difficult to abstract his sympathy from his fellow-creatures, by whatever name they were called; and he could not exclusively command his attention, to admire the houses and churches, which his Abbé continually pointed out to his notice.

He admired, however, the fine façade of the Louvre, the Place de Louis XV., the astonishingly brilliant spectacle of the Palais Royal, Notre Dame, a few handsome bridges, and the drives on the Boulevards.

But in fact there was at that time much more to be heard, and less to be seen, than at present in Paris. Paris was not then as fine a city as it now is. Ormond, in his secret soul, preferred the bay of Dublin to all he then saw on the banks of the Seine.

The little Abbé was not satisfied with the paucity of his exclamations, and would have given him up, as *un froid Anglois,* but that, fortunately, our young hero had each night an opportunity of redeeming his credit. They went to the play—he saw French comedy!—he saw and heard

Molet, and Madame de la Ruette: the Abbé was charmed with his delight, his enthusiasm, his genuine enjoyment of high comedy, and his quick feeling of dramatic excellence. It was indeed perfection—beyond any thing of which Ormond could have formed an idea. Every part well performed—nothing to break the illusion!

This first fit of dramatic enthusiasm was the third day at its height, when Connal returned from Versailles; and it was so strong upon him, and he was so full of Molet and Madame de la Ruette, that he could scarcely listen to what Connal said of Versailles, the king's supper, and Madame la Dauphine.

"No doubt—he should like to see all that—but at all events he was positively determined to see Molet, and Madame de la Ruette, every night they acted."

Connal smiled, and only answered, "Of course he would do as he pleased." But in the mean time, it was now Madame de Connal's *night* for seeing company, and he was to make his debut in a French assembly. Connal called for him early, that they might have a few minutes to themselves before the company should arrive.

Ormond felt some curiosity, a little anxiety, a slight flutter at the heart, at the thought of seeing Dora again.

The arrival of her husband interrupted these thoughts.

Connal took the light from the hands of Crepin, the valet, and reviewed Ormond from head to foot.

"Very well, Crepin: you have done your part, and Nature has done hers, for Monsieur."

"Yes, truly," said Crepin, "Nature has done wonders for Monsieur; and Monsieur, now he is dressed, has really all the air of a Frenchman."

"Quite l'air comme il faut! l'air noble!" added Connal; and he agreed with Crepin in opinion that French dress made an astonishing difference in Mr. Ormond.

"Madame de Connal, I am sure, will think so," continued Connal, "will see it with admiration—for she really has good taste. I will pledge myself for your success. With that figure, with that air, you will turn many heads in Paris—if you will but talk enough. Say every thing that comes into your head—don't be like an Englishman, always thinking about the sense—the more nonsense the better—trust me—*livrez-vous*—let yourself out—follow me, and fear nothing," cried he, running down stairs, delighted with Ormond and with himself.

He foresaw that he should gain credit by *producing* such a man. He really wished that Ormond should *succeed* in French society, and that he should pass his time agreeably in Paris.

No man could feel better disposed towards another. Even if he should take a fancy to Madame, it was to the polite French husband a matter of indifference, except so far as the *arrangement* might, or might not, interfere with his own views.

And these views—what were they?—Only to win all the young man's fortune at play. A cela près—excepting this, he was sincerely Ormond's friend, ready to do every thing possible—de faire l'impossible—to oblige and entertain him.

Connal enjoyed Ormond's surprise at the magnificence of his hotel. After ascending a spacious staircase, and passing through antechamber after antechamber, they reached the splendid salon, blazing with lights, reflected on all sides in mirrors, that reached from the painted ceiling to the inlaid floor.

"Not a creature here yet—happily." "Madame begs," said the servant, "that Monsieur will pass on into the boudoir."

"Any body with Madame?"

"No one but Madame de Clairville."

"Only *l'amie intime*," said Connal, "the bosom friend."

"How will Dora feel?—How will it be with us both?" thought Ormond, as he followed the light step of the husband.

"Entrez!—Entrez toujours."

Ormond stopped at the threshold, absolutely dazzled by the brilliancy of Dora's beauty, her face, her figure, her air, so infinitely improved, so fashioned!

"Dora!—Ah! Madame de Connal," cried Ormond.

No French actor could have done it better than nature did it for him.

Dora gave one glance at Ormond—pleasure, joy, sparkled in her eyes; then leaning on the lady who stood beside her, almost sinking, Dora sighed, and exclaimed, "Ah! Harry Ormond!"

The husband vanished.

"Ah ciel!" said l'amie intime, looking towards Ormond.

"Help me to support her, Monsieur—while I seek de l'eau de Cologne."

Ormond, seized with sudden tremor, could scarcely advance.

Dora sunk on the sofa, clasping her beautiful hands, and exclaiming, "The companion of my earliest days!"

Then Ormond, excused to himself, sprang forward,—"Friend of my childhood!" cried he: "yes, my sister: your father promised me this friendship—this happiness," said he supporting her, as she raised herself from the sofa.

"Où est-il? où est-il?—Where is he, Monsieur Ormond?" cried Mademoiselle, throwing open the door. "Ah ciel, comme il est beau! A perfect Frenchman already! And how much embellished by dress!—Ah! Paris for that. Did I not prophesy?—Dora, my darling, do me the justice. —But—comme vous voilà saisie!—here's l'amie with l'eau de Cologne. Ah! my child, recover yourself, for here is some one—the Comte de Jarillac it is entering the salon."

The promptitude of Dora's recovery was a new surprise to our hero. "Follow me," said she to him, and with Parisian ease and grace she glided into the salon to receive M. de Jarillac—presented Ormond to M. le Comte—"Anglois—Irlandois—an English, an Irish gentleman—the companion of her childhood," with the slightest, lightest tone of sentiment imaginable; and another count and another came, and a baron, and a marquis, and a duke, and Madame la Comtesse de ——, and Madame la Duchesse ——; and all were received with ease, respect, vivacity, or sentiment as the occasion required—now advancing a step or two to mark *empressement* where requisite;—regaining always, imperceptibly, the most advantageous situation and attitude for herself; —presenting Ormond to every one—quite intent upon him, yet appearing entirely occupied with every body else; and, in short, never forgetting them, him, or herself for an instant.

"Can this be Dora?" thought Ormond in admiration, yet in astonishment that divided his feelings. It was indeed wonderful to see how quickly, how completely, the Irish country girl had been metamorphosed into a French woman of fashion.

And now surrounded by admirers, by adorers in embroidery and blazing with crosses and stars, she received *les hommages*—enjoyed *le succès*— accepted the incense without bending too low or holding herself too high —not too sober, nor too obviously intoxicated. Vanity in all her heart, yet vanity not quite turning her head, not more than was agreeable and becoming—extending her smiles to all, and hoping all the time that Harry Ormond envied each. Charmed with him—for her early passion for him had revived in an instant—the first sight of his figure and air, the first glance in the boudoir, had been sufficient. She knew, too, how well he would *succeed* at Paris—how many rivals she would have in a week: these perceptions, sensations, and conclusions, requiring so much time in slow words to express, had darted through Dora's head in one instant, had exalted her imagination, and touched her heart—as much as that heart could be touched.

Ormond meantime breathed more freely, and recovered from his tremors. Madame de Connal, surrounded by adorers, and shining in the salon, was not so dangerous as Dora, half fainting in the boudoir; nor had any words that wit or sentiment could devise power to please or touch him so much as the "*Harry Ormond!*" which had burst naturally from Dora's lips. Now he began almost to doubt whether nature or art prevailed. Now he felt himself safe at least, since he saw that it was only the coquette of the Black Islands transformed into the coquette of the Hotel de Connal. The transformation was curious, was admirable; Ormond thought he could admire without danger, and, in due time, perhaps gallant, with the best of them, without feeling—without scruple.

The tables were now arranging for play. The conversation he heard every where round him related to the good or bad fortune of the preceding nights. Ormond perceived that it was the custom of the house to play every evening, and the expressions that reached him about bets and debts confirmed the hint which his guardian had given him, that Connal played high.

At present, however, he did not seem to have any design upon Ormond— he was engaged at the further end of the room. He left him quite to himself, and to Madame, and never once even asked him to play.

There seemed more danger of his being *left out*, than of his being *taken in*.

"Donnez-moi le bras—Come with me, Monsieur Ormond," said Mademoiselle, "and you shall lose nothing—while they are settling about their parties, we can get one little moment's chat."

She took him back to the boudoir.

"I want to make you know our Paris," said she: "here we can see the whole world pass in review, and I shall tell you every thing most necessary for you to know; for example—who is who—and still more it imports you to know who and who are together."

"Look at that lady, beautiful as the day, in diamonds."

"Madame de Connal, do you mean?" said Ormond.

"Ah! no; not her always," said Mademoiselle: "though she has the apple here, without contradiction," continued Mademoiselle, still speaking in English, which it was always her pride to speak to whomsoever could understand her. "Absolutely, without vanity, though my niece, I may say it, she is a perfect creature—and mise à ravir!—Did you ever see such a change for the best in one season? Ah! Paris!—Did I not tell you well?— And you felt it well yourself—you lost your head, I saw that, at first sight of her *à la Françoise*—the best proof of your taste and sensibilité—she has infinite sensibility too!—interesting, and at the height, what you English call the tip-top, of the fashion here."

"So it appears, indeed," said Ormond, "by the crowd of admirers I see round Madame de Connal."

"Admirers! yes, adorers, you may say—encore, if you added lovers, you would not be much wrong; dying for love—éperdument épris! See, there, he who is bowing now—Monsieur le Marquis de Beaulieu—homme de cour—plein d'esprit—homme marquant—very remarkable man. But— Ah! voilà que entre—of the court. Did you ever see finer entrée made by man into a room, so full of grace? Ah! le Comte de Belle Chasse—How many women already he has *lost!*—It is a real triumph to Madame de Connal to have him in her chains. What a smile!—C'est lui qui est aimable pour nous autres—d'une soumission pour les femmes—d'une fierté pour les hommes. As the lamb gentle for the pretty woman; as the lion terrible for the man. It is that Comte de Belle Chasse who is absolutely irresistible."

"*Absolutely* irresistible," Ormond repeated, smiling; "not absolutely, I hope."

"Oh! that is understood—you do not doubt la sagesse de Madame?—Besides, *heureusement*, there is an infinite safety for her in the number, as you see, of her adorers. Wait till I name them to you—I shall give you a catalogue raisonnée."

With rapid enunciation Mademoiselle went through the names and rank of the circle of adorers, noting with complacency the number of ladies to whom each man of gallantry was supposed to have paid his addresses—next to being of the blood royal, this appearing to be of the highest distinction.

"And à propos, Monsieur d'Ormond, you, yourself, when do you count to go to Versailles?—Ah!—when you shall see the king and the king's supper, and Madame la Dauphine! Ah!"

Mademoiselle was recalled from the ecstasy in which she had thrown up her eyes to Heaven, by some gentleman speaking to her as he passed the open door of the boudoir arm in arm with a lady—Mademoiselle answered, with a profound inclination of the head, whispering to Ormond after they had passed, "M. le Due de C—— with Madame de la Tour. Why he is constant always to that woman, Heaven knows better than me! Stand, if you are so good, Monsieur, a little more this way, and give your attention—they don't want you yet at play."

Then designating every person at the different card-tables, she said, "That lady is the wife of M.——, and there is M. le Baron de L—— her lover, the gentleman who looks over her cards—and that other lady with the joli pompon, she is intimate with M. de la Tour, the husband of the lady who passed with M. le Duc." Mademoiselle explained all these arrangements with the most perfect sang froid, as things of course, that every body knew and spoke of, except just before the husbands; but there was no mystery, no concealment: "What use?—To what good?"

Ormond asked whether there were *any* ladies in the room who were supposed to be faithful to their husbands.

"Eh!—Ma nièce, par exemple, Madame de Connal, I may cite as a woman of la plus belle réputation, sans tâche—what you call unblemish."

"Assuredly," said Ormond, "you could not, I hope, think me so indiscreet —I believe I said *ladies* in the plural number."

"Ah! oui, assuredly, and I can name you twenty. To begin, there, do you see that woman standing up, who has the air as if she think of nothing at all, and nobody thinking of her, with only her husband near her, *cet grand homme blême?*—There is Madame de la Rousse—*d'une réputation intacte!*—frightfully dressed, as she is always. But, hold, you see that pretty little Comtesse de la Brie, all in white?—Charmante! I give her to you as a reputation against which slander cannot breathe— Nouvelle mariée—bride—in what you call de honey-moon; but we don't know that in French—no matter! Again, since you are curious in these things, there is another reputation without spot, Madame de St. Ange, I warrant her to you—bien froide, celle-là, cold as any English—married a full year, and still her choice to make; allons,—there is three I give you already, without counting my niece; and, wait, I will find you yet another," said Mademoiselle, looking carefully through the crowd.

She was relieved from her difficulty by the entrance of the little Abbé, who came to summon Monsieur to Madame de Connal, who did him the honour to invite him to the table. Ormond played, and fortune smiled upon him, as she usually does upon a new votary; and beauty smiled upon him perhaps on the same principle. Connal never came near him till supper was announced; then only to desire him to give his arm to a charming little Countess—la nouvelle mariée—Madame de Connal, belonging, by right of rank, to Monsieur le Comte de Belle Chasse. The supper was one of the delightful *petit soupers* for which Paris was famous at that day, and which she will never see again.

The moralist, who considers the essential interests of morality, more than the immediate pleasures of society, will think this rather a matter of rejoicing than regret. How far such society and correct female conduct be compatible, is a question which it might take too long a time to decide.

Therefore, be it sufficient here to say, that Ormond, without staying to examine it, was charmed with the present effect; with the gaiety, the wit, the politeness, the ease, and altogether with that indescribable thing, that untranslatable esprit de société. He could not afterwards remember any thing very striking or very solid that had been said, but all was agreeable at the moment, and there was great variety. Ormond's self-love was, he knew not how, flattered. Without effort, it seemed to be the object of every body to make Paris agreeable to him; and they convinced him that he would find it the most charming place in the world—without any disparagement to his own country, to which all solid honours and advantages were left undisputed. The ladies, whom he had thought so little captivating at first view, at the theatre, were all charming on *farther acquaintance*: so full of vivacity, and something so flattering in their manner, that it put a stranger at once at his ease. Towards the end of the supper he found himself talking to two very pretty women at once, with good effect, and thinking at the same time of Dora and the Comte de Belle Chasse. Moreover, he thought he saw that Dora was doing the same between the irresistible Comte, and the Marquis, plein d'esprit, from whom, while she was listening and talking without intermission, her eyes occasionally strayed, and once or twice met those of Ormond.

"Is it indiscreet to ask you whether you passed your evening agreeably?" said M. de Connal, when the company had retired.

"Delightfully!" said Ormond: "the most agreeable evening I ever passed in my life!"

Then fearing that he had spoken with too much enthusiasm, and that the husband might observe that his eyes, as he spoke, involuntarily turned towards Madame de Connal, he moderated (he might have saved himself the trouble), he moderated his expression by adding, that as far as he could yet judge, he thought French society very agreeable.

"You have seen nothing yet—you are right not to judge hastily," said Connal; "but so far, I am glad you are tolerably well satisfied."

"Ah! oui, Monsieur Ormond," cried Mademoiselle, joining them, "we shall fix you at Paris, I expect."

"You hope, I suppose you mean, my dear aunt," said Dora, with such flattering hope in her voice, and in the expression of her countenance, that Ormond decided that he "certainly intended to spend the winter at Paris."

Connal, satisfied with this certainty, would have let Ormond go. But Mademoiselle had many compliments to make him and herself upon his pronunciation, and his fluency in speaking the French language—really like a Frenchman himself—the Marquis de Beaulieu had said to her: she was sure M. d'Ormond could not fail to *succeed* in Paris with that perfection added to all his other advantages. It was the greatest of all the advantages in the world—the greatest advantage in the *universe*, she was going on to say, but M. de Connal finished the flattery better.

"You would pity us, Ormond," cried he, interrupting Mademoiselle, "if you could see and hear the Vandals they send to us from England with letters of introduction—barbarians, who can neither sit, stand, nor speak —nor even articulate the language. How many of these *butors*, rich, of good family, I have been sometimes called upon to introduce into society, and to present at court! Upon my honour it has happened to me to wish they might hang themselves out of my way, or be found dead in their beds the day I was to take them to Versailles."

"It is really too great a tax upon the good-breeding of the lady of the house," said Madame de Connal, "deplorable, when she has nothing better to say of an English guest than that 'Ce monsieur là a un grand talent pour le silence.'"

Ormond, conscious that he had talked away at a great rate, was pleased by this indirect compliment.

"But such personnages muëts never really see French society. They never obtain more than a supper—not a *petit souper*—no, no, an invitation to a great assembly, where they see nothing. Milord Anglois is lost in the crowd, or stuck across a door-way by his own sword. Now, what could any letter of recommendation do for such a fellow as that?"

"The letters of recommendation which are of most advantage," said Madame de Connal, "are those which are written in the countenance."

Ormond had presence of mind enough not to bow, though the compliment was directed distinctly to him—a look of thanks he knew was sufficient. As he retired, Mademoiselle, pursuing him to the door, begged that he would come as early as he could next morning, that she might introduce him to her apartments, and explain to him all the superior conveniences of a French house. M. de Connal representing, however, that the next day Mr. Ormond was to go to Versailles, Mademoiselle acknowledged *that* was an affair to which all others must yield.

Well flattered by all the trio, and still more perhaps by his own vanity, our young hero was at last suffered to depart.

The first appearance at Versailles was a matter of great consequence. Court-dress was then an affair of as much importance at Paris as it seems to be now in London, if we may judge by the columns of birthday dresses, and the *honourable notice* of gentlemen's coats and waistcoats. It was then at Paris, however, as it is now and ever will be all over the world, essential to the appearance of a gentleman, that whatever time, pains, or expense, it might have cost, he should, from the moment he is dressed, *be*, or at least *seem* to be, above his dress. In this as in most cases, the shortest and safest way to *seem* is to *be*. Our young hero being free from personal conceit, or overweening anxiety about his appearance, looked at ease. He called at the Hotel de Connal the day he was to go to Versailles, and Mademoiselle was in ecstasy at the sight of his dress, exclaiming, "superbe!—magnifique!"

M. de Connal seemed more struck with his air than his dress, and Dora, perhaps, was more pleased with his figure; she was silent, but it was a silence that spoke; her husband heeded not what it said, but, pursuing his own course, observed, that, to borrow the expression of Crepin, the valet-de-chambre, no contemptible judge in these cases, M. Ormond looked not only as if he was *né coiffé*, but as if he had been born with a sword by his side. "Really, my dear friend," continued M. de Connal, "you look as if you had come at once full dressed into the world, which in our days is better than coming ready armed out of the head of Jupiter."

Mdlle. O'Faley, now seizing upon Ormond, whom she called her pupil, carried him off, to show him her apartments and the whole house; which she did with many useful notes—pointing out the convenience and entire liberty that result from the complete separation of the apartments of the husband and wife in French houses.

"You see, Monsieur et Madame with their own staircases, their own passages, their own doors in and out, and all separate for the people of Monsieur, and the women of Madame, and here through this little door you go into the apartments of Madame."

Ormond's English foot stopped respectfully.

"Eh, entrez toujours," said Mademoiselle, as the husband had said before at the door of the boudoir.

"But Madame de Connal is dressing, perhaps," said Ormond.

"Et puis?—and what then? you must get rid as fast as you can of your English préjugés—and she is not here neither," said Mademoiselle, opening the door.

Madame de Connal was in an inner apartment; and Ormond, the instant after he entered this room with Mademoiselle, heard a quick step, which he knew was Dora's, running to bolt the door of the inner room—he was glad that she had not quite got rid of her English prejudices.

Mdlle. O'Faley pointed out to him all the accommodations of a French apartment: she had not at this moment the slightest *malice* or bad intention in any thing she was saying—she simply spoke in all the innocence of a Frenchwoman—if that term be intelligible. If she had any secret motive, it was merely the vanity of showing that she was quite Parisienne; and there again she was mistaken; for having lived half her life out of Paris, she had forgotten, if she ever had it, the tone of good society, and upon her return had overdone the matter, exaggerated French manners, to prove to her niece that she knew les usages, les convenances, les nuances—enfin, la mode de Paris! A more dangerous guide in Paris for a young married woman in every respect could scarcely be found.

M. de Connal's valet now came to let Mr. Ormond know that Monsieur waited his orders. But for this interruption, he was in a fair way to hear all the private history of the family, all the secrets that Mademoiselle knew.

Of the amazing communicativeness of Frenchwomen on all subjects, our young hero had as yet no conception.

CHAPTER XXVIII.

It was during the latter years of the life of Louis the Fifteenth, and during the reign of Madame du Barry, that Ormond was at Paris. The court of Versailles was at this time in all its splendour, if not in all its glory. At the souper du roi, Ormond beheld, in all the magnificence of dress and jewels, the nobility, wealth, fashion, and beauty of France. Well might the brilliancy dazzle the eyes of a youth fresh from Ireland, when it amazed even old ambassadors, accustomed to the ordinary grandeur of courts. When he recovered from his first astonishment, when his eyes were a little better used to the light, and he looked round and considered all these magnificently decorated personages, assembled for the purpose of standing at a certain distance to see one man eat his supper, it did appear to him an extraordinary spectacle; and the very great solemnity and devotion of the assistants, so unsuited to the French countenance, inclined him to smile. It was well for him, however, that he kept his Irish risible muscles in order, and that no courtier could guess his thoughts—a smile would have lost him his reputation. Nothing in the world appeared to Frenchmen, formerly, of more importance than their court etiquette, though there were some who began about this time to suspect that the court order of things might not be co-existent with the order of nature—though there were some philosophers and statesmen who began to be aware, that the daily routine of the courtier's etiquette was not as necessary as the motions of the sun, moon, and planets. Nor could it have been possible to convince half at least of the crowd, who assisted at the king's supper this night, that all the French national eagerness about the health, the looks, the words, of *le roi*, all the attachment, *le dévouement*, professed habitually—perhaps felt habitually—for the reigning monarch, whoever or whatever he might be, by whatever name—notre bon roi, or simply notre roi de France—should in a few years pass away, and be no more seen.

Ormond had no concern with the affairs of the nation, nor with the future fate of any thing he beheld: he was only a spectator, a foreigner; and his business was, according to Mademoiselle's maxim, to enjoy to-day and to reflect to-morrow. His enjoyment of this day was complete: he not only admired, but was admired. In the vast crowd he was distinguished: some nobleman of note asked who he was—another observed *l'air noble*—another exclaimed, " *Le bel Anglois!*" and his fortune was made at Paris; especially as a friend of Madame du Barry's asked where he bought his embroidery.

He went afterwards, at least in Connal's society, by the name of "*Le bel Anglois.*" Half in a tone of raillery, yet with a look that showed she felt it to be just, Madame de Connal first adopted the appellation, and then changed the term to "*mon bel Irlandois.*" Invitations upon invitations poured upon Ormond—all were eager to have him at their parties—he was every where—attending Madame de Connal—and she, how proud to be attended by Ormond! He dreaded lest his principles should not withstand the strong temptation. He could not leave her, but he determined to see her only in crowds; accordingly, he avoided every select party: l'amie intime could never for the first three weeks get him to one *petit comité*, though Madame de Connal assured him that her friend's *petit soupers* "were charming, worth all the crowded assemblies in Paris." Still he pursued his plan, and sought for safety in a course of dissipation.

"I give you joy," said Connal to him one day, "you are fairly launched! you are no distressed vessel to be *taken in tow*, nor a petty bark to sail in any man's *wake*. You have a gale, and are likely to have a triumph of your own." Connal was, upon all occasions, careful to impress upon Ormond's mind, that he left him wholly to himself, for he was aware, that in former days, he had offended his independent spirit by airs of protection. He managed better now—he never even invited him to play, though it was his main object to draw him to his faro-table. He made use of some of his friends or confederates, who played for him: Connal occasionally coming to the table as an unconcerned spectator. Ormond played with so much freedom, and seemed to have so gentlemanlike an indifference whether he lost or won, that he was considered as an easy dupe. Time only was necessary, M. de Connal thought, to lead him on gradually and without alarm, to let him warm to the passion for play. Meanwhile Madame de Connal felt as fully persuaded that Ormond's passion for her would increase. It was her object to *fix* him at Paris; but she should be content, perfectly happy with his friendship, his society, his sentiments: her own *sentiment* for him, as she confessed to Madame de Clairville, was absolutely invincible; but it should never lead her beyond the bounds of virtue. It was involuntary, but it should never be a crime.

Madame de Clairville, who understood her business, and spoke with all the fashionable *cant* of sensibility, asked how it was possible that an involuntary sentiment could ever be a crime?

As certainly as the novice among a band of sharpers is taught, by the technical language of the gang, to conquer his horror of crime, so certainly does the *cant of sentiment* operate upon the female novice, and vanquish her fear of shame and moral horror of vice.

The allusion is coarse—so much the better: strength, not elegance, is necessary on some occasions to make an impression. The truth will strike the good sense and good feelings of our countrywomen, and unadorned, they will prefer it to German or French sophistry. By such sophistry, however, was Dora insensibly led on.

But Ormond did not yet advance in learning the language of sentiment— he was amusing himself in the world—and Dora imagined that the dissipation in which he lived prevented him from having time to think of his passion: she began to hate the dissipation.

Connal one day, when Dora was present, observed that Ormond seemed to be quite in his natural element in this sea of pleasure.

"Who would have thought it?" said Dora: "I thought Mr. Ormond's taste was more for domestic happiness and retirement."

"Retirement at Paris!" said Ormond.

"Domestic happiness at Paris!" said Connal.

Madame de Connal sighed—No, it was Dora that sighed.

"Where do you go to-night?" said her husband.

"Nowhere—I shall stay at home. And you?" said she, looking up at Harry Ormond.

"To Madame de la Tour's."

"That's the affair of half an hour—only to appear—"

"Afterwards to the opera," said Ormond.

"And after the opera—can't you sup here?" said Madame de Connal.

"With the utmost pleasure—but that I am engaged to Madame de la Brie's ball."

"That's true," cried Madame de Connal, starting up—"I had forgot it—so am I this fortnight—I may as well go to the opera, too, and I can carry you to Madame de la Tour's—I owe her a five minutes' sitting—though she is un peu precieuse. And what can you find in that little cold Madame de la Brie—do you like ice?"

"He like to break de ice, I suppose," said Mademoiselle. "Ma foi, you must then take a hatchet there!"

"No occasion; I had rather slide upon the ice than break it. My business at Paris is merely, you know, to amuse myself," said he, looking at Connal—"Glissez, mortels, n'appuyez pas."

"But if de ice should melt of itself," said Mademoiselle, "what would you do den? What would become of him, den, do you think, my dear niece?"

It was a case which she did not like to consider—Dora blushed—no creature was so blind as Mademoiselle, with all her boasted quickness and penetration.

From this time forward no more was heard of Madame de Connal's taste for domestic life and retirement—she seemed quite convinced, either by her husband, or by Mr. Ormond, or both, that no such thing was practicable at Paris. She had always liked le grand monde—she liked it better now than ever, when she found Ormond in every crowded assembly, every place of public amusement—a continual round of breakfasts, dinners, balls—court balls—bal masqué—bal de l'opera—plays—grand entertainments—petits soupers—fêtes at Versailles—pleasure in every possible form and variety of luxury and extravagance succeeded day after day, and night after night—and Ormond, le bel Irlandois, once in fashion, was every where, and every where admired; flattered by the women, who wished to draw him in to be their partners at play—still more flattered by those who wished to engage him as a lover—most of all flattered by Dora. He felt his danger. Improved in coquetry by Parisian practice and power, Dora tried her utmost skill—she played off with great dexterity her various admirers to excite his jealousy: the

Marquis de Beaulieu, the witty marquis, and the Count de Belle Chasse, the irresistible count, were dangerous rivals. She succeeded in exciting Ormond's jealousy; but in his noble mind there were strong opposing principles to withstand his selfish gratification. It was surprising with what politeness to each other, with how little love, all the suitors carried on this game of gallantry and competition of vanity.

Till Ormond appeared, it had been the general opinion that before the end of the winter or the spring, the Count de Belle Chasse would be triumphant. Why Ormond did not enter the lists, when there appeared to all the judges such a chance of his winning the prize, seemed incomprehensible to the spectators, and still more to the rival candidates. Some settled it with the exclamation "Inouï!" Others pronounced that it was English bizarrerie. Every thing seemed to smooth the slippery path of temptation—the indifference of her husband—the imprudence of her aunt, and the sophistry of Madame de Clairville—the general customs of French society—the peculiar profligacy of the society into which he happened to be thrown—the opinion which he saw prevailed, that if he withdrew from the competition a rival would immediately profit by his forbearance, conspired to weaken his resolution.

Many accidental circumstances concurred to increase the danger. At these balls, to which he went originally to avoid Dora in smaller parties, Madame de Connal, though she constantly appeared, seldom danced. She did not dance well enough to bear comparison with French dancers; Ormond was in the same situation. The dancing which was very well in England would not do in Paris—no late lessons could, by any art, bring them to an equality with French nature.

"Ah, il ne danse pas!—He dances like an Englishman." At the first ball this comforted the suitors, and most the Comte de Belle Chasse; but this very circumstance drew Ormond and Dora closer together—she pretended headaches, and languor, and lassitude, and, in short, sat still.

But it was not to be expected that the Comte de Belle Chasse could give up dancing: the Comte de Belle Chasse danced like le dieu de la danse, another Vestris; he danced every night, and Ormond sat and talked to

Dora, for it was his duty to attend Madame when the little Abbé was out of the way.

The spring was now appearing, and the spring is delightful in Paris, and the *promenades* in the Champs Elysées, and in the Bois de Boulogne, and the promenade in Long-Champ, commenced. Riding was just coming into high fashion with the French ladies; and, instead of riding in men's clothes, and like a man, it was now the ambition de monter à cheval à l'Angloise: to ride on a side-saddle and in an English riding habit was now the ambition. Now Dora, though she could not dance as well, could ride better than any French woman; and she was ambitious to show herself and her horsemanship in the Bois de Boulogne: but she had no horse that she liked. Le Comte de Belle Chasse offered to get one broke for her at the king's riding-house—this she refused: but fortunately Ormond, as was the custom with the English at that time, had, after his arrival, some English horses brought over to him at Paris. Among these was the horse he had once broke for Dora.

For this an English side-saddle was procured—she was properly equipped and mounted.

And the two friends, le bel Irlandois, as they persisted in calling Ormond, and la belle Irlandoise, and their horses, and their horsemanship, were the admiration of the promenade.

The Comte de Belle Chasse sent to London for an English horse at any price. He was out of humour—and Ormond in the finest humour imaginable. Dora was grateful; her horse was a beautiful, gentle-spirited creature: it was called Harry—it was frequently patted and caressed, and told how much it was valued and loved.

Ormond was now in great danger, because he felt himself secure that he was only a friend—*l'ami de la maison*.

CHAPTER XXIX.

There was a picture of Dagote's which was at this moment an object of fashionable curiosity in Paris. It was a representation of one of the many charitable actions of the unfortunate Marie Antoinette, "then Dauphiness —at that time full of life, and splendour, and joy, adorning and cheering the elevated sphere she just began to move in;" and yet diffusing life, and hope, and joy, in that lower sphere, to which the radiance of the great and happy seldom reaches. The Dauphiness was at that time the pride of France, and the darling of Paris; not only worshipped by the court, but loved by the people. While she was Dauphiness, and during the commencement of her reign, every thing, even disastrous accidents, and the rigour of the season, served to give her fresh opportunity of winning the affection and exciting the enthusiasm of the people. When, during the festivities on her marriage, hundreds were crushed to death by the fall of a temporary building, the sensibility of the Dauphiness, the eagerness with which she sent all her money to the lieutenant de police for the families of those who had perished, conciliated the people, and turned even the evil presage to good. Again, during a severe frost, her munificence to the suffering poor excited such gratitude, that the people erected to her honour a vast pyramid of snow—Frail memorial!—"These marks of respect were almost as transitory as the snowy pyramid."

Ormond went with Mademoiselle O'Faley one morning to see the picture of the Dauphiness; and he had now an opportunity of seeing a display of French sensibility, that eagerness to feel and to excite *a sensation*; that desire to *produce an effect*, to have a scene; that half real, half theatric enthusiasm, by which the French character is peculiarly distinguished from the English. He was perfectly astonished by the quantity of exclamations he heard at the sight of this picture; the lifting up of hands and eyes, the transports, the ecstasies, the tears—the actual tears that he saw streaming in despite of rouge. It was real! and it was not real feeling! Of one thing he was clear—that this superfluity of feeling or exaggeration of expression completely silenced him, and made him cold indeed: like one unskilled or dumb he seemed to stand.

"But are you of marble?" cried Mademoiselle—"where is your sensibilité then?"

"I hope it is safe at the bottom of my heart," said Ormond; "but when it is called for, I cannot always find it—especially on these public occasions."

"Ah! but what good all the sensibilité in the world do at the bottom of your heart, where nobody see it? It is on these public occasions too, you must always contrive and find it quick at Paris, or after all you will seem but an Englishman."

"I must be content to seem and to be what I am," said Ormond, in a tone of playful but determined resignation.

"Bon!" said a voice near him. Mademoiselle went off in impatience to find some better auditor—she did not hear the "*Bon.*"

Ormond turned, and saw near him a gentleman, whom he had often met at some of the first houses in Paris—the Abbé Morellet, then respected as the most *reasonable* of all the wits of France, and who has since, through all the trying scenes of the revolution, through the varieties of unprincipled change, preserved unaltered the integrity and frankness of his character; retaining even to his eighty-seventh year all his characteristic warmth of heart and clearness of understanding—*le doyen de la littérature Françoise*—the love, respect, and admiration, of every honest heart in France. May he live to receive among all the other tributes, which his countrymen pay publicly and privately to his merit, this record of the impression his kindness left on grateful English hearts!

Our young hero had often desired to be acquainted with the Abbé; but the Abbé had really hitherto passed him over as a mere young man of fashion, a mere Milord Anglois, one of the ephemeral race, who appear in Parisian society, vanish, and leave no trace behind. But now he did him the honour to enter into conversation with him. The Abbé peculiarly disliked all affectation of sentiment and exaggeration: they were revolting to his good sense, good taste, and feeling. Ormond won directly his good opinion and good-will, by having insisted upon it to Mademoiselle, that he would not for the sake of fashion or effect pretend to feel more than he really did.

"Bah!" said the Abbé, "hear all those women now and all those men—they do not know what they are saying—they make me sick. And, besides, I am afraid these flattering courtiers will do no good to our young Dauphiness, on whom so much of the future happiness or misery of France will depend. Her heart is excellent, and they tell me she announces a strong character; but what head of a young beauty and a young Queen will be able to withstand perpetual flattery? They will lead her wrong, and then will be the first to desert her—trust me, I know Paris. All this might change as quickly as the turn of a weathercock; but I will not trouble you with forebodings perhaps never to be realized. You see Paris, Monsieur, at a fortunate time," continued he; "society is now more agreeable, has more freedom, more life and variety, than at any other period that I can remember."

Ormond replied by a just compliment to the men of letters, who at this period added so much to the brilliancy and pleasure of Parisian society.

"But you have seen nothing of our men of literature, have you?" said the Abbé.

"Much less than I wish. I meet them frequently in society, but as, unluckily, I have no pretensions to their notice, I can only catch a little of their conversation, when I am fortunate enough to be near them."

"Yes," said the Abbé, with his peculiar look and tone of good-natured irony, "between the pretty things you are saying and hearing from—Fear nothing, I am not going to name any *one*, but—every pretty woman in company. I grant you it must be difficult to hear reason in such a situation—as difficult almost as in the midst of the din of all the passions at the faro-table. I observe, however, that you play with astonishing coolness—there is something still—wanting. Excuse me—but you interest me, monsieur; the determination not to play at all—

"Beyond a certain sum I have resolved never to play," said Ormond.

"Ah! but the appetite grows—l'appetit vient en mangeant—the danger is in acquiring the taste—excuse me if I speak too freely."

"Not at all—you cannot oblige me more. But there is no danger of my acquiring a taste for play, because I am determined to lose."

"Bon!" said the Abbé; "that is the most singular determination I ever heard: explain that to me, then, Monsieur."

"I have determined to lose a certain sum—suppose five hundred guineas. I have won and lost backwards and forwards, and have been longer about it than you would conceive to be probable; but it is not lost yet. The moment it is, I shall stop short. By this means I have acquired all the advantages of yielding to the fashionable madness, without risking my future happiness."

The Abbé was pleased with the idea, and with the frankness and firmness of our young hero.

"Really, Monsieur," said he, "you must have a strong head—you, le bel Irlandois—to have prevented it from being turned with all the flattery you have received in Paris. There is nothing which gets into the head— worse still, into the heart,—so soon, so dangerously, as the flattery of pretty women. And yet I declare you seem wonderfully sober, considering."

"Ne jurez pas," said Ormond; "but at least in one respect I have not quite lost my senses; I know the value and feel the want of a safe, good guide in Paris: if I dared to ask such a favour, I should, since he has expressed some interest for me, beg to be permitted to cultivate the acquaintance of M. l'Abbé Morellet."

"Ah ça—now my head will turn, for no head can stand the dose of flattery that happens to suit the taste. I am particularly flattered by the idea of being a safe, good friend; and frankly, if I can be of any service to you, I will. Is there any thing I can do for you?"

Ormond thanked him, and told him that it was his great ambition to become acquainted with the celebrated men of literature in Paris—he said he should feel extremely obliged if M. Morellet would take occasion to introduce him to any of them they might meet in society.

"We must do better for you," said the abbé—"we must show you our men of letters." He concluded by begging Ormond to name a day when he could do him the honour to breakfast with him. "I will promise you Marmontel, at least; for he is just going to be married to my niece, and of him we shall be secure: as to the rest I will promise nothing, but do as much as I can."

The men of letters about this period in Paris, as the Abbé explained to Ormond, began to feel their own power and consequence, and had assumed a tone of independence, as yet tempered with due respect for rank. Many of them lived or were connected with men of rank, by places about the court, by secretaryships and pensions, obtained through court influence. Some were attached by early friendship to certain great families; had apartments to themselves in their hotels, where they received what friends they pleased; and, in short, lived as if they were at home. Their company was much sought for by the great; and they enjoyed good houses, good tables, carriages, all the conveniences of life, and all the luxuries of the rich, without the trouble of an establishment. Their mornings were their own, usually employed in study; and the rest of the day they gave themselves to society. The most agreeable period of French literary society was, perhaps, while this state of things lasted.

The Abbé Morellet's breakfast was very agreeable; and Ormond saw at his house what had been promised him, many of the literary men at Paris. Voltaire was not then in France; and Rousseau, who was always quarrelling with somebody, and generally with every body, could not be prevailed upon to go to this breakfast. Ormond was assured that he lost nothing by not seeing him, or by not hearing his conversation, for that it was by no means equal to his writings; his temper was so susceptible and wayward,, that he was not fit for society—neither capable of enjoying, nor of adding to its pleasures. Ormond heard, perhaps, more of Rousseau and Voltaire, and learnt more of their characters, by the anecdotes that were related, and the bon-mots that were repeated, than he could have done if they had been present. There was great variety of different characters and talents at this breakfast; and the Abbé amused himself by making his young friend guess who the people were, before he told their names. It was happy for Ormond that he was acquainted with some of their writings (this he owed to Lady Annaly's well-chosen present of French books). He was fortunate in his first guess—Marivaux's conversation was so like the style of his writings, so full of hair-breadth distinctions, subtle exceptions, and metaphysical refinement and digressions, that Ormond soon guessed him, and was applauded for his quickness. Marmontel he discovered, by his being the only man in the room who had not mentioned to him any of "Les Contes Moraux." But there was one person who set all his skill at defiance: he pronounced that he was no author—that he was l'ami de la maison: he was so indeed wherever he went—but he was both a man of literature, and a man of deep science—no less a person than the great D'Alembert. Ormond thought D'Alembert and Marmontel were the two most agreeable men in company. D'Alembert was simple, open-hearted, unpresuming, and cheerful in society. Far from being subject to that absence of mind with which profound mathematicians are sometimes reproached, D'Alembert was present to every thing that was going forward—every trifle he enjoyed with the zest of youth, and the playfulness of childhood. Ormond confessed that he should never have guessed that he was a great mathematician and profound calculator.

Marmontel was distinguished for combining in his conversation, as in his character, two qualities for which there are no precise English words, *naïveté* and *finesse*. Whoever is acquainted with Marmontel's writings must have a perfect knowledge of what is meant by both.

It was fortunate for our young hero that Marmontel was, at this time, no longer the dissipated man he had been during too great a period of his life. He had now returned to his early tastes for simple pleasures and domestic virtues—had formed that attachment which afterwards made the happiness of his life: he was just going to be married to the amiable Mdlle. Montigny, a niece of the Abbé Morellet. She and her excellent mother lived with him; and Ormond was most agreeably surprised and touched at the unexpected sight of an amiable, united, happy family, when he had expected only a meeting of literati.

The sight of this domestic happiness reminded him of the Annalys— brought the image of Florence to his mind. If she had been but sincere, how he should have preferred her to all he had seen!

It came upon him just at the right moment. It contrasted with all the dissipation he had seen, and it struck him the more strongly, because it could not possibly have been prepared as a moral lesson to make an impression. He saw the real, natural course of things—he heard in a few hours the result of the experience of a man of great vivacity, great talents, who had led a life of pleasure, and who had had opportunities of seeing and feeling all that it could possibly afford, at the period of the greatest luxury and dissipation ever known in France. No evidence could be stronger than Marmontel's in favour of virtue and of domestic life, nor could any one express it with more grace and persuasive eloquence.

It did Ormond infinite good. He required such a lesson at this juncture, and he was capable of taking it—it recalled him to his better self.

The good Abbé seemed to see something of what in Ormond's mind, and became still more interested about him.

"Ah, ça," said he to Marmontel, as soon as Ormond was gone, "that young man is worth something: I thought he was only *le bel Irlandois*, but I find he is much more. We must do what we can for him, and not let him leave Paris, as so many do, having seen only the worst part of our society."

Marmontel, who had also been pleased with him, was willing, he said, to do any thing in his power; but he could scarcely hope that they had the means of withdrawing from the double attraction of the faro-table and coquetry, a young man of that age and figure.

"Fear nothing, or rather hope every thing," said the Abbé: "his head and his heart are more in our favour, trust me, than his age and his figure are against us. To begin, my good Marmontel, did not you see how much he was struck and *edified* by your reformation?"

"Ah! if there was another Mdlle. de Montigny for him, I should fear nothing, or rather hope every thing," said Marmontel "but where shall he find such another in all Paris?"

"In his own country, perhaps, all in good time," said the Abbé.

"In his own country?—True," cried Marmontel, "now you recall it to my mind, how eager he grew in disputing with Marivaux upon the distinction between *aimable* and *amiable*. His description of an *amiable woman*, according to the English taste, was, I recollect, made *con amore*; and there was a sigh at the close which came from the heart, and which showed the heart was in England or Ireland."

"Wherever his heart is, *c'est bien placé*," said the Abbé. "I like him—we must get him into good company—he is worthy to be acquainted with your amiable and *aimable*Madame de Beauveau and Madame de Seran."

"True," said Marmontel; "and for the honour of Paris, we must convince him that he has taken up false notions, and that there is such a thing as conjugal fidelity and domestic happiness here."

"Bon. That is peculiarly incumbent on the author of *Les Contes Moraux*," said the Abbé.

It happened, fortunately for our hero, that Madame de Connal was, about this time, engaged to pass a fortnight at the country house of Madame de Clairville. During her absence, the good Abbé had time to put in execution all his benevolent intentions, and introduced his young friend to some of the really good company of Paris. He pointed out to him at Madame Geoffrin's, Madame de Tencin's, Madame du Detfand's, and Madame Trudaine's, the difference between the society at the house of a rich farmer general—or at the house of one connected with the court, and with people in place and political power—and the society of mixed rank and literature. The mere passing pictures of these things, to one who was not to live in Paris, might not, perhaps, except as a matter of curiosity, be of much value; but his judicious friend led Ormond from these to make comparisons and deductions which were of use to him all his life afterwards.

CHAPTER XXX.

One morning when Ormond awoke, the first thing he heard was, that a *person* from Ireland was below, who was very impatient to see him. It was Patrickson, Sir Ulick O'Shane's confidential man of business.

"What news from Castle Hermitage?" cried Ormond, starting up in his bed, surprised at the sight of Patrickson.

"The best that can be—never saw Sir Ulick in such heart—he has a share of the loan, and—"

"And what news of the Annalys?" interrupted Ormond.

"I know nothing about them at all, sir," said Patrickson, who was a methodical man of business, and whose head was always intent upon what he called the main chance. "I have been in Dublin, and heard no country news."

"But have you no letter for me? and what brings you over so suddenly to Paris?"

"I have a letter for you somewhere here, sir—only I have so many 'tis hard to find," said Patrickson, looking carefully over a parcel of letters in his pocket-book, but with such a drawling slowness of manner as put Ormond quite out of patience. Patrickson laid the letters on the bed one by one. "That's not it—and that's not it; that's for Monsieur un tel, marchand, rue ——; that packet's from the Hamburgh merchants—What brings me over?—Why, sir, I have business enough, Heaven knows!"

Patrickson was employed not only by Sir Ulick O'Shane, but by many Dublin merchants and bankers, to settle business for them with different houses on the continent. Ormond, without listening to the various digressions he made concerning the persons of mercantile consequence to whom the letters were addressed, or from whom they were answers, pounced upon the letter in Sir Ulick's handwriting directed to himself, and tore it open eagerly, to see if there was any news of the Annalys. None—they were in Devonshire. The letter was merely a few lines on business—Sir Ulick had now the opportunity he had foreseen of laying out Ormond's money in the loan most advantageously for him; but there had been an omission in the drawing up of his power of attorney, which had been done in such a hurry on Ormond's leaving home. It gave power only to sell out of the Three per Cents.; whereas much of Ormond's money was in the Four per Cents. Another power, Patrickson said, was necessary, and he had brought one for him to sign. Patrickson in his slow manner descanted upon the folly of signing papers in a hurry, just when people were getting into carriages, which was always the way with young gentlemen, he said. He took care that Ormond should do nothing in a hurry now; for he put on his spectacles, and read the power, sparing him not a syllable of the law forms and repetitions. Ormond wrote a few kind lines to Sir Ulick, and earnestly besought him to find out something more about the Annalys. If Miss Annaly were married, it must have appeared in the papers. What delayed the marriage? Was Colonel Albemarle dismissed or accepted?—Where was he?—Ormond said he would be content if Sir Ulick could obtain an answer to that single plain question.

All the time Ormond was writing, Patrickson never stirred his forefinger from the spot where the signature was to be written at the bottom of the power of attorney.

"Pray," said Ormond, looking up from the paper he going to sign, "pray, Patrickson, are you really and truly an Irishman?"

"By the father's side, I apprehend, sir—but my mother was English. Stay, sir, if you please—I must witness it."

"Witness away," said Ormond; and after having signed this paper, empowering Sir Ulick to sell 30,000*l*. out of the Four per cents., Ormond lay down, and wishing him a good journey, settled himself to sleep; while Patrickson, packing up his papers, deliberately said, "He hoped to be in London *in short*; but that he should go by Havre de Grace, and that he should be happy to execute any commands for Mr. Ormond there or in Dublin." More he would have said, but finding Ormond by this time past reply, he left the room on tiptoe. The next morning Madame de Connal returned from the country, and sent Ormond word that she should expect him at her assembly that night.

Every body complimented Madame de Connal upon the improvement which the country air had made in her beauty—even her husband was struck with it, and paid her his compliments on the occasion; but she stood conversing so long with Ormond, that the faro-players grew impatient: she led him to the table, but evidently had little interest herself in the game. He played at first with more than his usual success, but late at night his fortune suddenly changed; he lost—lost—till at last he stopped, and rising from table, said he had no more money, and he could play no longer. Connal, who was not one of the players, but merely looking on, offered to lend him any sum he pleased. "Here's a rouleau— here are two rouleaus—what will you have?" said Connal.

Ormond declined playing any more: he said that he had lost the sum he had resolved to lose, and there he would stop. Connal did not urge him, but laughing said, that a resolution to *lose* at play was the most extraordinary he had ever heard.

"And yet you see I have kept it," said Ormond.

"Then I hope you will next make a resolution to win," said Connal, "and no doubt you will keep that as well—I prophesy that you will; and you will give fortune fair play to-morrow night." Ormond simply repeated that he should play no more. Madame de Connal soon afterwards rose from the table, and went to talk to Mr. Ormond. She said she was concerned for his loss at play this night. He answered, as he felt, that it was a matter of no consequence to him—that he had done exactly what he had determined; that in the course of the whole time he had been losing this money he had had a great deal of amusement in society, had seen a vast deal of human nature and manners, which he could not otherwise have seen, and that he thought his money exceedingly well employed.

"But you shall not lose your money," said Dora; "when next you play it shall be on my account as well as your own—you know this is not only a compliment, but a solid advantage. The bank has certain advantages—and it is fair that you should share them. I must explain to you," continued Madame de Connal—"they are all busy about their own affairs, and we may speak in English at our ease—I must explain to you, that a good portion of my fortune has been settled, so as to be at my own disposal—my aunt, you know, has also a good fortune—we are partners, and put a considerable sum into the faro bank. We find it answers well. You see how handsomely we live. M. de Connal has his own share. We have nothing to do with *that*. If you would take my advice," continued she, speaking in a very persuasive tone, "instead of forswearing play, as you seem inclined to do at the first reverse of fortune, you would join forces with us; you cannot imagine that *I* would advise you to any thing which I was not persuaded would be advantageous to you—you little know how much I am interested." She checked herself, blushed, hesitated, and hurried on—"you have no ties in Ireland—you seem to like Paris—where can you spend your time more agreeably?"

"More agreeably—nowhere upon earth!" cried Ormond. Her manner, tone, and look, at this moment were so flattering, so bewitching, that he was scarcely master of himself. They went to the boudoir—the company had risen from the faro-table, and, one after another, had most of them departed. Connal was gone—only a few remained in a distant apartment, listening to some music. It was late. Ormond had never till this evening stayed later than the generality of the company, but he had now an excuse to himself, something that he had long wished to have an opportunity of saying to Dora, when she should be quite alone; it was a word of advice about le Comte de Belle Chasse—her intimacy with him was beginning to be talked of. She had been invited to a bal paré at the Spanish ambassador's for the ensuing night—but she had more inclination to go to a bal masqué, as Ormond had heard her declare. Now certain persons had whispered that it was to meet the Comte de Belle Chasse that she intended to go to this ball; and Ormond feared that such whispers might be injurious to her reputation. It was difficult to him to speak, because the counsels of the friend might be mistaken for the jealous fears of a lover. With some embarrassment he delicately, timidly, hinted his apprehensions.

Dora, though naturally of a temper apt to take alarm at the touch of blame, and offence at the tone of advice, now in the most graceful manner thanked her friend for his counsel; said she was flattered, gratified, by the interest it showed in her happiness—and she immediately yielded her will, her *fantaisie*, to his better judgment. This compliance, and the look with which it was accompanied, convinced him of the absolute power he possessed over her heart. He was enchanted with Dora—she never looked so beautiful; never before, not even in the first days of his early youth, had he felt her beauty so attractive.

"Dear Madame de Connal, dear Dora!" he exclaimed.

"Call me Dora," said she: "I wish ever to be Dora to Harry Ormond. Oh! Harry, my first, my best, my only friend, I have enjoyed but little real happiness since we parted."

Tears filled her fine eyes—no longer knowing where he was, Harry Ormond found himself at her feet. But while he held and kissed in transport the beautiful hand, which was but feebly withdrawn, he seemed to be suddenly shocked by the sight of one of the rings on her finger.

"My wedding-ring," said Dora, with a sigh. "Unfortunate marriage!"

That was not the ring on which Ormond's eyes were fixed.

"Dora, whose gray hair is this?"

"My father's," said Dora, in a tremulous voice.

"Your father!" cried Ormond, starting up. The full recollection of that fond father, that generous benefactor, that confiding friend, rushed upon his heart.

"And is this the return I make!—Oh, if he could see us at this instant!"

"And if he could," cried Dora, "oh! how he would admire and love you, Ormond, and how he would—"

Her voice failed, and with a sudden motion she hid her face with both her hands.

"He would see you, Dora, without a guide, protector, or friend; surrounded with admirers, among profligate men, and women still more profligate, yet he would see that you have preserved a reputation of which your father would be proud."

"My father! oh, my poor father!" cried Dora: "Oh! generous, dear, ever generous Ormond!"

Bursting into tears—alternate passions seizing her—at one moment the thoughts of her father, the next of her lover, possessed her imagination.

At this instant the noise of some one approaching recalled them both to their senses. They were found in earnest conversation about a party of pleasure that was to be arranged for the next day. Madame de Connal made Ormond promise that he would come the next morning, and settle every thing with M. de Connal for their intended expedition into the country.

The next day, as Ormond was returning to Madame de Connal's, with the firm intention of adhering to the honourable line of conduct he had traced out for himself, just as he was crossing the Pont Neuf, some one ran full against him. Surprised at what happens so seldom in the streets of Paris, where all meet, pass, or cross, in crowds with magical celerity and address, he looked back, and at the same instant the person who had passed looked back also. An apparition in broad daylight could not have surprised Ormond more than the sight of this person. "Could it be— could it possibly be Moriarty Carroll, on the Pont Neuf in Paris?"

"By the blessing, then, it's the man himself—Master Harry!—though I didn't know him through the French disguise. Oh! master, then, I've been tried and cast, and all but hanged—sentenced to Botany— transported any way—for a robbery I didn't commit—since I saw you last. But your honour's uneasy, and it's not proper, I know, to be stopping a jantleman in the street; but I have a word to say that will bear no delay, not a minute."

Ormond's surprise and curiosity increased—he desired Moriarty to follow him.

"And now, Moriarty, what is it you have to say?"

"It is a long story, then, please your honour. I was transported to Botany, though innocent. But first and foremost for what consarns your honour first."

"First," said Ormond, "if you were transported, how came you here?"

"Because I was not transported, plase your honour—only sentenced—for I escaped from Kilmainham, where I was sent to be put on board the tender; but I got on board of an American ship, by the help of a friend— and this ship being knocked against the rocks, I came safe ashore in this country on one of the *sticks* of the vessel: so when I knowed it was France I was in, and recollected Miss Dora that was married in Paris, I thought if I could just make my way any hows to Paris, she'd befriend me in case of need.

"But, dear master," said Moriarty, interrupting, "it's a folly to talk—I'll not tell you a word more of myself till you hear the news I have for you. The worst news I have to tell you is, there is great fear of the breaking of Sir Ulick's bank!"

"The breaking of Sir Ulick's bank? I heard from him the day before yesterday."

"May be you did; but the captain of the American ship in which I came was complaining of his having been kept two hours at that bank, where they were paying large sums in small notes, and where there was the greatest run upon the house that ever was seen."

Ormond instantly saw his danger—he recollected the power of attorney he had signed two days before. But Patrickson was to go by Havre de Grace—that would delay him. It was possible that Ormond by setting out instantly might get to London time enough to save his property. He went directly and ordered post horses. He had no debts in Paris, nothing to pay, but for his stables and lodging. He had a faithful servant, whom he could leave behind, to make all necessary arrangements.

"You are right, jewel, to be in a hurry," said Carroll. "But sure you won't leave poor Moriarty behind ye here in distress, when he has no friend in the wide world but yourself?"

"Tell me, in the first place, Moriarty, are you innocent?"

"Upon my conscience, master, I am perfectly innocent as the child unborn, both of the murder and the robbery. If your honour will give me leave, I'll tell you the whole story."

"That will be a long affair, Moriarty, *if you talk out of the face*, as you used to do. I will, however, find an opportunity to hear it all. But, in the meantime, stay where you are till I return."

Ormond went instantly to Connal's, to inform him of what had happened. His astonishment was obviously mixed with disappointment. But to do him justice, besides the interest which he really had in the preservation of the fortune, he felt some personal regard for Ormond himself.

"What shall we do without you?" said he. "I assure you, Madame and I have never been so happy together since the first month after our marriage as we have been since you came to Paris."

Connal was somewhat consoled by hearing Ormond say, that if he were time enough in London to save his fortune, he proposed returning immediately to Paris, intending to make the tour of Switzerland and Italy.

Connal had no doubt that they should yet be able to fix him at Paris.

Madame de Connal and Mademoiselle were out—Connal did not know where they were gone. Ormond was glad to tear himself away with as few adieus as possible. He got into his travelling carriage, put his servant on the box, and took Moriarty with him in the carriage, that he might relate his history at leisure.

"Plase your honour," said Moriarty, "Mr. Marcus never missed any opportunity of showing me ill-will. The supercargo of the ship that was cast away, when you were with Sir Herbert Annaly, God rest his soul! came down to the sea-side to look for some of the things that he had lost: the day after he came, early in the morning, his horse, and bridle, and saddle, and a surtout coat, was found in a lane, near the place where we lived, and the supercargo was never heard any more of. Suspicion fell upon many—the country rung with the noise that was made about this murder—and at last I was taken up for it, because people had seen me buy cattle at the fair, and the people would not believe it was with money your honour sent me by the good parson—for the parson was gone out of the country, and I had nobody to stand my friend; for Mr. Marcus was on the grand jury, and the sheriff was his friend, and Sir Ulick was in Dublin, at the bank. Howsomdever, after a long trial, which lasted the whole day, a 'cute lawyer on my side found out that there was no proof that any body had been murdered, and that a man might lose his horse, his saddle, and his bridle, and his big coat, without being kilt: so that the judge ordered the jury to let me off for the murder. They then tried me for the robbery; and sure enough that went again me: for a pair of silver-mounted pistols, with the man's name engraved upon them, was found in my house. They knew the man's name by the letters in the big coat. The judge asked me what I had to say for myself: 'My lard,' says I, 'those pistols were brought into my house about a fortnight ago, by a little boy, one little Tommy Dunshaughlin, who found them in a punk-horn, at the edge of a bog-hole.'

"The jidge favoured me more than the jury—for he asked how old the boy was, and whether I could produce him? The little fellow was brought into court, and it was surprising how clear he told his story. The jidge listened to the child, young as he was. But M'Crule was on the jury, and said that he knew the child to be as cunning as any in Ireland, and that he would not believe a word that came out of his mouth. So the short and the long of it was, I was condemned to be transported.

"It would have done you good, if you'd heard the cry in the court when sentence was given, for I was loved in the country. Poor Peggy and Sheelah!—But I'll not be troubling your honour's tender heart with our parting. I was transmuted to Dublin, to be put on board the tender, and lodged in Kilmainham, waiting for the ship that was to go to Botany. I had not been long there, when another prisoner was brought to the same room with me. He was a handsome-looking man, about thirty years of age, of the most penetrating eye and determined countenance that I ever saw. He appeared to be worn down with ill-health, and his limbs much swelled: notwithstanding which, he had strong handcuffs on his wrists, and he seemed to be guarded with uncommon care. He begged the turnkey to lay him down upon the miserable iron bed that was in the cell; and he begged him, for God's sake, to let him have a jug of water by his bedside, and to leave him to his fate.

"I could not help pitying this poor cratur; I went to him, and offered him any assistance in my power. He answered me shortly, 'What are you here for?'—I told him. 'Well,' says he, 'whether you are guilty or not, is your affair, not mine; but answer me at once—are you a *good man*?—Can you go through with a thing?—and are you steel to the back-bone?'—'I am,' said I. 'Then,' said he, 'you are a lucky man—for he that is talking to you is Michael Dunne, who knows how to make his way out of any jail in Ireland.' Saying this, he sprung with great activity from the bed. 'It is my cue,' said he, 'to be sick and weak, whenever the turnkey comes in, to put him off his guard—for they have all orders to watch me strictly; because as how, do you see, I broke out of the jail of Trim; and when they catched me, they took me before his honour the police magistrate, who did all he could to get out of me the way which I made my escape.' 'Well,' says the magistrate, 'I'll put you in a place where you can't get out—till you're sent to 'Botany.' 'Plase your worship,' says I, 'if there's no offence in saying it, there's no such place in Ireland.'—'No such place as what?' 'No such place as will hold Michael Dunne.'—'What do you think of Kilmainbam?' says he. 'I think it's a fine jail—and it will be no asy matter to get out of it—but it is not impossible.'—'Well, Mr. Dunne,' said the magistrate, 'I have heard of your fame, and that you have secrets of your own for getting out. Now, if you'll tell me how you got out of the jail of Trim, I'll make your confinement at Kilmainham as asy as may be, so as to keep you safe; and if you do not, you must be ironed, and I will have sentinels from an English regiment, who shall be continually changed: so that you can't get any of them to help you.'—'Plase your worship,' said Dunne, 'that's very hard usage; but I know as how that you are going to build new jails all over Ireland, and that you'd be glad to know the best way to make them secure. If your worship will promise me that if I get out of Kilmainham, and if I tell you how I do it, then you'll get me a free pardon, I'll try hard but what before three months are over I'll be a prisoner at large.'—'That's more than I can promise you,' said the magistrate; 'but if you will disclose to me the best means of keeping other people in, I will endeavour to keep you from Botany Bay.'—'Now, sir,' says Dunne, 'I know your worship to be a man of honour, and that your own honour regards yourself, and not me; so that if I was ten times as bad as I am, you'd keep your promise with me, as well as if I was the best gentleman in Ireland. So that now, Mr. Moriarty,' said Dunne, 'do you see, if I get out, I shall be safe; and if you get out along with me, you have nothing to do but to go over to America. And if you are a married man, and tired of your wife, you'll get rid of her. If you are not tired of her, and you have any substance, she may sell it and follow you.'

"There was something, Master Harry, about the man that made me have great confidence in him—and I was ready to follow his advice.

Whenever the turnkey was coming he was groaning and moaning on the bed. At other times he made me keep bathing his wrists with cold water, so that in three or four days they were not half the size they were at first. This change he kept carefully from the jailor. I observed that he frequently asked what day of the month it was, but that he never made any attempt to speak to the sentinels; nor did he seem to make any preparation, or to lay any scheme for getting out. I held my tongue, and waited qui'tely. At last, he took out of his pocket a little flageolet, and began to play upon it. He asked me if I could play: I said I could a little, but very badly. 'I don't care how bad it is, if you can play at all.' He got off the bed where he was lying, and with the utmost ease pulled his hands out of his handcuffs. Besides the swelling of his wrists having gone down, he had some method of getting rid of his thumb that I never could understand. Says I, 'Mr. Dunne, the jailor will miss the fetters,'—'No,' said he, 'for I will put them on again;' and so he did, with great ease. 'Now,' said he, 'it is time to begin our work.'

"He took off one of his shoes, and taking out the in-sole, he showed me a hole, that was cut where the heel was, in which there was a little small flat bottle, which he told me was the most precious thing in life. And under the rest of the sole there were a number of saws, made of watch spring, that lay quite flat and snug under his foot. The next time the turnkey came in, he begged, for the love of God, to have a pipe and some tobacco, which was accordingly granted to him. What the pipes and tobacco were for, I could not then guess, but they were found to be useful. He now made a paste of some of the bread of his allowance, with which he made a cup round the bottom of one of the bars of the window; into this cup he poured some of the contents of the little bottle, which was, I believe, oil of vitriol: in a little time, this made a bad smell, and it was then I found the use of the pipe and tobacco, for the smell of the tobacco quite bothered the smell of the vitriol. When he thought he had softened the iron bar sufficiently, he began to work away with the saws, and he soon taught me how to use them; so that we kept working on continually, no matter how little we did at a time; but as we were constantly at it, what I thought never could be done was finished in three or four days. The use of the flageolet was to drown the noise of the filing; for when one filed, the other piped.

"When the bar was cut through, he fitted the parts nicely together, and covered them over with rust. He proceeded in the same manner to cut out another bar; so that we had a free opening out of the window. Our cell was at the very top of the jail, so that even to look down to the ground was terrible.

"Under various pretences, we had got an unusual quantity of blankets on our beds; these he examined with the utmost care, as upon their strength our lives were to depend. We calculated with great coolness the breadth of the strips into which he might cut the blankets, so as to reach from the window to the ground; allowing for the knots by which they were to be joined, and for other knots that were to hinder the hands and feet from slipping.

"'Now,' said he, 'Mr. Moriarty, all this is quite asy, and requires nothing but a determined heart and a sound head: but the difficulty is to baffle the sentinel that is below, and who is walking backward and forward continually, day and night, under the window; and there is another, you see, in a sentry-box, at the door of the yard: and, for all I know, there may be another sentinel at the other side of the wall. Now these men are never twice on the same duty: I have friends enough out of doors, who have money enough, and would have talked reason to them; but as these sentinels are changed every day, no good can be got of *them*: but stay till to-morrow night, and we'll try what we can do.'

"I was determined to follow him. The next night, the moment that we were locked in for the night, we set to work to cut the blankets into slips, and tied them together with great care. We put this rope round one of the fixed bars of the window; and, pulling at each knot, we satisfied ourselves that every part was sufficiently strong. Dunne looked frequently out of the window with the utmost anxiety—it was a moonlight night.

"'The moon,' said he, 'will be down in an hour and a half.'

"In a little while we heard the noise of several girls singing at a distance from the windows, and we could see, as they approached, that they were dancing, and making free with the sentinels: I saw that they were provided with bottles of spirits, with which they pledged the deluded soldiers. By degrees the sentinels forgot their duty; and, by the assistance of some laudanum contained in some of the spirits, they were left senseless on the ground. The whole of this plan, and the very night and hour, had been arranged by Dunne with his associates, before he was put into Kilmainham. The success of this scheme, which was totally unexpected by me, gave me, I suppose, plase your honour, fresh courage. He, very honourably, gave me the choice to go down first or to follow him. I was ashamed not to go first: after I had got out of the window, and had fairly hold of the rope, my fear diminished, and I went cautiously down to the bottom. Here I waited for Dunne, and we both of us silently stole along in the dark, for the moon had gone in, and we did not meet with the least obstruction. Our out of door's assistants had the prudence to get entirely out of sight. Dunne led me to a hiding-place in a safe part of the town, and committed me to the care of a seafaring man, who promised to get me on board an American ship.

"'As for my part,' said Dunne, 'I will go in the morning, boldly, to the magistrate, and claim his promise.'

"He did so—and the magistrate with good sense, and good faith, kept his promise, and obtained a pardon for Dunne.

"I wrote to Peggy, to get aboard an American ship. I was cast away on the coast of France—made my way to the first religious house that I could hear of, where I luckily found an Irishman, who saved me from starvation, and who sent me on from convent to convent, till I got to Paris, where your honour met me on that bridge, just when I was looking for Miss Dora's house. And that's all I've got to tell," concluded Moriarty, "and all true."

No adventures of any sort happened to our hero in the course of his journey. The wind was fair for England when he reached Calais: he had a good passage; and with all the expedition that good horses, good roads, good money, and civil words, ensure in England, he pursued his way; and arrived in the shortest time possible in London.

He reached town in the morning, before the usual hour when the banks are open. Leaving orders with his servant, on whose punctuality he could depend, to awaken him at the proper hour, he lay down, overcome with fatigue, and slept—yes—slept soundly.

CHAPTER XXXI.

Ormond was wakened at the proper hour—went immediately to ——'s bank. It was but just open, and beginning to do business. He had never been there before—his person was not known to any of the firm. He entered a long narrow room, so dark at the entrance from the street that he could at first scarcely see what was on either side of him—a clerk from some obscure nook, and from a desk higher than himself, put out his head, with a long pen behind his ear, and looked at Ormond as he came in. "Pray, sir, am I right?—Is this Mr. ——'s bank?"

"Yes, sir."

With mercantile economy of words, and a motion of his head, the clerk pointed out to Ormond the way he should go—and continued casting up his books. Ormond walked down the narrow aisle, and it became light as he advanced towards a large window at the farther end, before which three clerks sat at a table opposite to him. A person stood with his back to Ormond, and was speaking earnestly to one of the clerks, who leaned over the table listening. Just as Ormond came up he heard his own name mentioned—he recollected the voice—he recollected the back of the figure—the very bottle-green coat—it was Patrickson—Ormond stood still behind him, and waited to hear what was going on.

"Sir," said the clerk, "it is a very sudden order for a very large sum."

"True, sir—but you see my power—you know Mr. Ormond's handwriting, and you know Sir Ulick O'Shane's—"

"Mr. James," said the principal clerk, turning to one of the others, "be so good to hand me the letters we have of Mr. Ormond. As we have never seen the gentleman sign his name, sir, it is necessary that we should be more particular in comparing."

"Oh! sir, no doubt—compare as much as you please—no doubt people cannot be too exact and deliberate in doing business."

"It certainly is his signature," said the clerk.

"I witnessed the paper," said Patrickson.

"Sir, I don't dispute it," replied the clerk; "but you cannot blame us for being cautious when such a *very* large sum is in question, and when we have no letter of advice from the gentleman."

"But I tell you I come straight from Mr. Ormond; I saw him last Tuesday at Paris—"

"And you see him now, sir," said Ormond, advancing.

Patrickson's countenance changed beyond all power of control.

"Mr. Ormond!—I thought you were at Paris."

"Mr. Patrickson!—I thought you were at Havre de Grace—what brought you here so suddenly?"

"I acted for another," hesitated Patrickson: "I therefore made no delay."

"And, thank Heaven!" said Ormond, "I have acted for myself!—but just in time!—Sir," continued he, addressing himself to the principal clerk, "Gentlemen, I have to return you my thanks for your caution—it has actually saved me from ruin—for I understand—"

Ormond suddenly stopped, recollecting that he might injure Sir Ulick O'Shane essentially by a premature disclosure, or by repeating a report which might be ill-founded.

He turned again to speak to Patrickson, but Patrickson had disappeared.

Then continuing to address himself to the clerks. "Gentlemen," said Ormond, speaking carefully, "have you heard any thing of or from Sir Ulick O'Shane lately, except what you may have heard from this Mr. Patrickson?"

"Not *from* but *of* Sir Ulick O'Shane we heard from our Dublin correspondent—in due course we have heard," replied the head clerk. "Too true, I am afraid, sir, that his bank had come to paying in sixpences on Saturday."

The second clerk seeing great concern in Ormond's countenance, added, "But Sunday, you know, is in their favour, sir; and Monday and Tuesday are holidays: so they may stand the run, and recover yet."

With the help of this gentleman's thirty thousand, they might have recovered, perhaps—but Mr. Ormond would scarcely have recovered it.

As to the ten thousand pounds in the Three per Cents., of which Sir Ulick had obtained possession a month ago, that was irrecoverable, *if* his bank should break—"*If.*"—The clerks all spoke with due caution; but their opinion was sufficiently plain. They were honestly indignant against the guardian who had thus attempted to ruin his ward.

Though almost stunned and breathless with the sense of the danger he had so narrowly escaped, yet Ormond's instinct of generosity, if we may use the expression, and his gratitude for early kindness, operated; he *would* not believe that Sir Ulick had been guilty of a deliberate desire to injure him. At all events, he determined that, instead of returning to France, as he had intended, he would go immediately to Ireland, and try if it were possible to assist Sir Ulick, without materially injuring himself.

Having ordered horses, he made inquiry wherever he thought he might obtain information with respect to the Annalys. All that he could learn was, that they were at some sea-bathing place in the south of England, and that Miss Annaly was still unmarried. A ray of hope darted into the mind of our hero—and he began his journey to Ireland with feelings which every good and generous mind will know how to appreciate.

He had escaped at Paris from a temptation which it was scarcely possible to resist. He had by decision and activity preserved his fortune from ruin —he had under his protection an humble friend, whom he had saved from banishment and disgrace, and whom he hoped to restore to his wretched wife and family. Forgetful of the designs that had been meditated against him by his guardian, to whose necessities he attributed his late conduct, he hastened to his immediate assistance; determined to do every thing in his power to save Sir Ulick from ruin, *if* his difficulties arose from misfortune, and not from criminality: if, on the contrary, he should find that Sir Ulick was fraudulently a bankrupt, he determined to quit Ireland immediately, and to resume his scheme of foreign travel.

The system of posting had at this time been carried to the highest perfection in England. It was the amusement and the fashion of the time, to squander large sums in hurrying from place to place, without any immediate motive for arriving at the end of a journey, but that of having the satisfaction of boasting in what a short time it had been performed; or, as it is expressed in one of our comedies, "to enter London like a meteor, with a prodigious tail of dust."

Moriarty Carroll, who was perched upon the box with Ormond's servant, made excellent observations wherever he went. His English companion could not comprehend how a man of common sense could be ignorant of various things, which excited the wonder and curiosity of Moriarty. Afterwards, however, when they travelled in Ireland, Moriarty had as much reason to be surprised at the impression which Irish manners and customs made upon his companion. After a rapid journey to Holyhead, our hero found to his mortification that the packet had sailed with a fair wind about half an hour before his arrival.

Notwithstanding his impatience, he learned that it was impossible to overtake the vessel in a boat, and that he must wait for the sailing of the next day's packet.

Fortunately, however, the Lord-Lieutenant's secretary arrived from London at Holyhead time enough for the tide; and as he had an order from the post-office for a packet to sail whenever he should require it, the intelligent landlord of the inn suggested to Ormond that he might probably obtain permission from the secretary to have a berth in this packet.

Ormond's manner and address were such as to obtain from the good-natured secretary the permission he required; and, in a short time, he found himself out of sight of the coast of Wales. During the beginning of their voyage the motion of the vessel was so steady, and the weather so fine, that every body remained on deck; but on the wind shifting and becoming more violent, the landsmen soon retired below decks, and poor Moriarty and his English companion slunk down into the steerage, submitting to their fate. Ormond was never sea-sick; he walked the deck, and enjoyed the admirable manoeuvring of the vessel. Two or three naval officers, and some other passengers, who were used to the sea, and who had quietly gone to bed during the beginning of the voyage, now came from below, to avoid the miseries of the cabin. As one of these gentlemen walked backwards and forwards upon deck, he eyed our hero from time to time with looks of anxious curiosity—Ormond perceiving this, addressed the stranger, and inquired from him whether he had mistaken his looks, or whether he had any wish to speak to him. "Sir," said the stranger, "I do think that I have seen you before, and I believe that I am under considerable obligations to you—I was supercargo to that vessel that was wrecked on the coast of Ireland, when you and your young friend exerted yourselves to save the vessel from plunder. After the shipwreck, the moment I found myself on land, I hastened to the neighbouring town to obtain protection and assistance. In the mean time, your exertions had saved a great deal of our property, which was lodged in safety in the neighbourhood. I had procured a horse in the town to which I had gone, and had ridden back to the shore with the utmost expedition. Along with the vessel which had been shipwrecked there had sailed another American sloop. We were both bound from New York to Bourdeaux. In the morning after the shipwreck, our consort hove in sight of the wreck, and sent a boat on shore, to inquire what had become of the crew, and of the cargo, but they found not a human creature on the shore, except myself. The plunderers had escaped to their hiding-places, and all the rest of the inhabitants had accompanied the poor young gentleman, who had fallen a sacrifice to his exertions in our favour.

"It was of the utmost consequence to my employers, that I should arrive as soon as possible at Bourdeaux, to give an account of what had happened. I therefore, without hesitation, abandoned my horse, with its bridle and saddle, and I got on board the American vessel without delay. In my hurry I forgot my great coat on the shore, a loss which proved extremely inconvenient to me—as there were papers in the pockets which might be necessary to produce before my employers.

"I arrived safely at Bourdeaux, settled with my principals to their satisfaction, and I am now on my way to Ireland, to reclaim such part of my property, and that of my employers, as was saved from the savages who pillaged us in our distress."—This detail, which was given with great simplicity and precision, excited considerable interest among the persons upon the deck of the packet. Moriarty, who was pretty well recovered from his sickness, was now summoned upon deck. Ormond confronted him with the American supercargo, but neither of them had the least recollection of each other. "And yet," said Ormond to the American, "though you do not know this man, he is at this moment under sentence of transportation for having robbed you, and he very narrowly escaped being hanged for your murder. A fate from which he was saved by the patience and sagacity of the judge who tried him."

Moriarty's surprise was expressed with such strange contortions of delight, and with a tone, and in a phraseology, so peculiarly his own, as to astonish and entertain the spectators. Among these was the Irish secretary, who, without any application being made to him, promised Moriarty to procure for him a free pardon.

On Ormond's landing in Dublin, the first news he heard, and it was repeated a hundred times in a quarter of an hour, was that "Sir Ulick O'Shane was bankrupt—that his bank shut up yesterday." It was a public calamity, a source of private distress, that reached lower and farther than any bankruptcy had ever done in Ireland. Ormond heard of it from every tongue, it was written in every face—in every house it was the subject of lamentation, of invective. In every street, poor men, with ragged notes in their hands, were stopping to pore over the names at the back of the notes, or hurrying to and fro, looking up at the shop-windows for "*half price given here for O'Shane's notes.*" Groups of people, of all ranks, gathered—stopped—dispersed, talking of Sir Ulick O'Shane's bankruptcy—their hopes—their fears—their losses—their ruin—their despair—their rage. Some said it was all owing to Sir Ulick's shameful extravagance: "His house in Dublin, fit for a duke!—Castle Hermitage full of company to the last week—balls—dinners—the most expensive luxuries—scandalous!"

Others accused Sir Ulick's absurd speculations. Many pronounced the bankruptcy to be fraudulent, and asserted that an estate had been made over to Marcus, who would live in affluence on the ruin of the creditors.

At Sir Ulick's house in town every window-shutter was closed. Ormond rang and knocked in vain—not that he wished to see Sir Ulick—no, he would not have intruded on his misery for the world; but Ormond longed to inquire from the servants how things were with him. No servant could be seen. Ormond went to Sir Ulick's bank. Such crowds of people filled the street that it was with the utmost difficulty and after a great working of elbows, that in an hour or two he made his way to one of the barred windows. There was a place where notes were handed in and *accepted*, as they called it, by the clerks, who thus for the hour soothed and pacified the sufferers, with the hopes that this *acceptance* would be good, and would *stand in stead* at some future day. They were told that when things should come to a settlement, all would be paid. There was property enough to satisfy the creditors, when the *commissioners* should look into it. Sir Ulick would pay all honourably—as far as possible— fifteen shillings in the pound, or certainly ten shillings— the *accepted* notes would pass for that any where. The crowd pressed closer and closer, arms crossing over each other to get notes in at the window, the clerks' heads appearing and disappearing. It was said they were laughing while they thus deluded the people.

All the intelligence that Ormond, after being nearly suffocated, could obtain from any of the clerks, was, that Sir Ulick was in the country. "They believed at Castle Hermitage—could not be certain—had no letters for him to-day—he was ill when they heard last—so ill he could do no business—confined to his bed."

The people in the street hearing these answers replied, "Confined in his bed, is he?—In the jail, it should be, as many will be along of him. Ill, is he, Sir Ulick?—Sham sickness, may be—all his life a *sham*." All these and innumerable other taunts and imprecations, with which the poor people vented their rage, Ormond heard as he made his way out of the crowd.

Of all who had suffered, he who had probably lost the most, and who certainly had been on the brink of losing the greatest part of what he possessed, was the only individual who uttered no reproach.

He was impatient to get down to Castle Hermitage, and if he found that Sir Ulick had acted fairly, to be some comfort to him, to be with him at least when deserted by all the rest of the world.

At all the inns upon the road, as he went from Dublin to Castle Hermitage, even at the villages where he stopped to water the horses, every creature, down to the hostlers, were talking of the bankruptcy— and abusing Sir Ulick O'Shane and his son. The curses that were deep, not loud, were the worst—and the faces of distress worse than all. Gathering round his carriage, wherever it stopped, the people questioned him and his servants about the news, and then turned away, saying they were ruined. The men stood in unutterable despair. The women crying, loudly bewailed "their husbands, their sons, that must waste in the jail or fly the country; for what should they do for the rents that had been made up in Sir Ulick's notes, and *no good* now?"

Ormond felt the more on hearing these complaints, from his sense of the absolute impossibility of relieving the universal distress.

He pursued his melancholy journey, and took Moriarty into the carriage with him, that he might not be recognized on the road.

When he came within sight of Castle Hermitage, he stopped at the top of the hill at a cottage, where many a time in his boyish days he had rested with Sir Ulick out hunting. The mistress of the house, now an old woman, came to the door.

"Master Harry dear!" cried she, when she saw who it was. But the sudden flash of joy in her old face was over in an instant.

"But did you hear it?" cried she, "and the great change it caused him—poor Sir Ulick O'Shane? I went up with eggs on purpose to see him, but could only hear—he was in his bed—wasting with trouble—nobody knows any thing more—all is kept hush and close. Mr. Marcus took off all he could rap, and ran, even to—"

"Well, well, I don't want to hear of Marcus—can you tell me whether Dr. Cambray is come home?"

"Not expected to come till Monday."

"Are you sure?"

"Oh! not a morning but I'm there the first thing, asking, and longing for them."

"Lie back, Moriarty, in the carriage, and pull your hat over your face," whispered Ormond: "postilions, drive on to that little cabin, with the trees about it, at the foot of the hill." This was Moriarty's cabin. When they stopped, poor Peggy was called out. Alas! how altered from the dancing, sprightly, blooming girl, whom Ormond had known so few years since in the Black Islands! How different from the happy wife, whom he had left, comfortably settled in a cottage suited to her station and her wishes! She was thin, pale, and haggard—her dress was neglected—an ill-nursed child, that she had in her arms she gave to a young girl near her. Approaching the carriage, and seeing Harry Ormond, she seemed ready to sink into the earth: however, after having drank some water, she recovered sufficiently to be able to answer Ormond's inquiries.

"What do you intend to do, Peggy?"

"Do, sir!—go to America, to join my husband sure; every thing was to have been sold, Monday last—but nobody has any money—and I am tould it will cost a great deal to get across the sea."

At this she burst into tears and cried most bitterly; and at this moment the carriage door flew open—Moriarty's impatience could be no longer restrained—he flung himself into the arms of his wife.

Leaving this happy and innocent couple to enjoy their felicity we proceed to Castle Hermitage.

Ormond directed the postilions to go the back way to the house. They drove down the old avenue.

Presently they saw a boy, who seemed to be standing on the watch, run back towards the castle, leaping over hedge and ditch with desperate haste. Then came running from the house three men, calling to one another to shut the gates for the love of God!

They all ran towards the gateway through which the postilions were going to drive, reached it just as the foremost horses turned, and flung the gate full against the horses' heads. The men, without looking or caring, went on locking the gate. Ormond jumped out of the carriage—at the sight of him, the padlock fell from the hand of the man who held it.

"Master Harry himself!—and is it you?—We ask your pardon, your honour."

The men were three of Sir Ulick's workmen—Ormond forbad the carriage to follow. "For perhaps you are afraid of the noise disturbing Sir Ulick?" said be.

"No, plase your honour," said the foremost man, "it will not disturb him —as well let the carriage come on—only," whispered he, "best to send the hack postilions with their horses always to the inn, afore they'd learn any thing."

Ormond walked on quickly, and as soon as he was out of hearing of the postilions again asked the men, "What news?—how is Sir Ulick?"

"Poor gentleman! he has had a deal of trouble—and no help for him," said the man.

"Better tell him plain," whispered the next. "Master Harry, Sir Ulick O'Shane's trouble is over in this world, sir."

"Is he—"

"Dead, he is, and cold, and in his coffin—this minute—and thanks be to God, if he is safe there even from them that are on the watch to seize on his body!—In the dread of them creditors, orders were given to keep the gates locked. He is dead since Tuesday, sir,—but hardly one knows it out of the castle—except us."

Ormond walked on silently, while they followed, talking at intervals.

"There is a very great cry against him, sir, I hear, in Dublin,—and here in the country, too," said one.

"The distress, they say, is very great, he caused; but they might let his body rest any way—what good can that do them?"

"Bad or good, they sha'n't touch it," said the other: "by the blessing, we shall have him buried safe in the morning, afore they are stirring. We shall carry the coffin through the under ground passage, that goes to the stables, and out by the lane to the churchyard asy—and the gentleman, the clergyman, has notice all will be ready, and the housekeeper only attending."

"Oh! the pitiful funeral," said the eldest of the men, "the pitiful funeral for Sir Ulick O'Shane, that was born to better."

"Well, we can only do the best we can," said the other, "let what will happen to ourselves; for Sir Marcus said he wouldn't take one of his father's notes from any of us."

Ormond involuntarily felt for his purse.

"Oh! don't be bothering the gentleman, don't be talking," said the old man.

"This way, Master Harry, if you please, sir, the underground way to the back yard. We keep all close till after the burying, for fear—that was the housekeeper's order. Sent all off to Dublin when Sir Ulick took to his bed, and Lady Norton went off."

Ormond refrained from asking any questions about his illness, fearing to inquire into the manner of his death. He walked on more quickly and silently. When they were going through the dark passage, one of the men, in a low voice, observed to Mr. Ormond that the housekeeper would tell him all about it.

When they got to the house, the housekeeper and Sir Ulick's man appeared, seeming much surprised at the sight of Mr. Ormond. They said a great deal about the *unfortunate event*, and their own sorrow and *distress*; but Ormond saw that theirs were only the long faces, dismal tones, and outward show of grief. They were just a common housekeeper and gentleman's gentleman, neither worse nor better than ordinary servants in a great house. Sir Ulick had only treated them as such.

The housekeeper, without Ormond's asking a single question, went on to tell him that "Castle Hermitage was as full of company, even to the last week, as ever it could hold, and all as grand as ever; the first people in Ireland—champagne and burgundy, and ices, and all as usual—and a ball that very week. Sir Ulick was very considerate, and sent Lady Norton off to her other friends; he took ill suddenly that night with a great pain in his head: he had been writing hard, and in great trouble, and he took to his bed, and never rose from it—he was found by Mr. Dempsey, his own man, dead in his bed in the morning—of a broken heart, to be sure!— Poor gentleman!—Some people in the neighbourhood was mighty busy talking how the coroner ought to be sent for; but that blew over, sir. But then we were in dread of the seizure of the body for debt, so the gates was kept locked; and now you know all we know about it, sir."

Ormond said he would attend the funeral. There was no attempt to seize upon the body; only the three workmen, the servants, a very few of the cottagers, and Harry Ormond, attended to the grave the body of the once popular Sir Ulick O'Shane. This was considered by the country people as the greatest of all the misfortunes that had befallen him; the lowest degradation to which an O'Shane could be reduced. They compared him with King Corny, and "see the difference!" said they; "the one was *the true thing*, and never *changed*—and after all, where is the great friends now?—the quality that used to be entertained at the castle above? Where is all the favour promised him now? What is it come to? See, with all his wit, and the schemes upon schemes, broke and gone, and forsook and forgot, and buried without a funeral, or a tear, but from Master Harry." Ormond was surprised to hear, in the midst of many of their popular superstitions and prejudices, how justly they estimated Sir Ulick's abilities and character.

As the men filled up his grave, one of them said, "There lies the making of an excellent gentleman—but the cunning of his head spoiled the goodness of his heart."

The day after the funeral an agent came from Dublin to settle Sir Ulick O'Shane's affairs in the country.

On opening his desk, the first thing that appeared was a bundle of accounts, and a letter, directed to H. Ormond, Esq. He took it to his own room and read—

"ORMOND,

"I intended to *employ* your money to re-establish my falling credit, but I never intended to *defraud* you.

"ULICK O'SHANE."

CHAPTER XXXII.

Both from a sense of justice to the poor people concerned, and from a desire to save Sir Ulick O'Shane's memory as far as it was in his power from reproach, Ormond determined to pay whatever small debts were due to his servants, workmen, and immediate dependents. For this purpose, when the funeral was over, he had them all assembled at Castle Hermitage. Every just demand of this sort was paid, all were satisfied; even the bare-footed kitchen-maid, the drudge of this great house, who, in despair, had looked at her poor one guinea note of Sir Ulick's, had that note paid in gold, and went away blessing Master Harry. Happy for all that he is come home to us, was the general feeling. But there was one man, a groom of Sir Ulick's, who did not join in any of these blessings or praises: he stood silent and motionless, with his eyes on the money which Mr. Ormond had put into his hand.

"Is your money right?" said Ormond.

"It is, sir; but I had something to tell you."

When all the other servants had left the room, the man said, "I am the groom, sir, that was sent, just before you went to France, with a letter to Annaly: there was an answer to that letter, sir, though you never got it."

"There was an answer!" cried Ormond, anger flashing, but an instant afterwards joy sparkling in his eyes. "There was a letter!—From whom? —I'll forgive you all, if you will tell me the whole truth."

"I will—and not a word of lie, and I beg your honour's pardon, if—"

"Go on—straight to the fact, this instant, or you shall never have my pardon."

"Why then I stopped to take a glass coming home; and, not knowing how it was, I had the misfortune to lose the bit of a note, and I thought no more about it till, plase your honour, after you was gone, it was found."

"Found!" cried Ormond, stepping hastily up to him—"where is it?"

"I have it safe here," said the man, opening a sort of pocket-book "here I have kept it safe till your honour came back."

Ormond saw and seized upon a letter in Lady Armaly's hand, directed to him. Tore it open—two notes—one from Florence.

"I forgive you!" said he to the man, and made a sign to him to leave the room.

When Ormond had read, or without reading had taken in, by one glance of the eye, the sense of the letters—he rang the bell instantly.

"Inquire at the post-office," said he to his servant, "whether Lady Annaly is in England or Ireland?—If in England, where?—if in Ireland, whether at Annaly or at Herbert's Town? Quick—an answer."

An answer was quickly brought, "In England—in Devonshire, sir: here is the exact direction to the place, sir. I shall pack up, I suppose, sir?"

"Certainly—directly."

Leaving a few lines of explanation and affection for Dr. Cambray, our young hero was *off again*, to the surprise and regret of all who saw him driving away as fast as horses could carry him. His servant, from the box, however, spread as he went, for the comfort of the deploring village, the assurance that "Master and he would soon be back again, please Heaven! —and happier than ever."

And now that he is safe in the carriage, what was in that note of Miss Annaly's which has produced such a *sensation*? No talismanic charm ever operated with more magical celerity than this note. What were the words of the charm?

That is a secret which shall never be known to the world.

The only point which it much imports the public to know is probably already guessed—that the letter did not contain a refusal, nor any absolute discouragement of Ormond's hopes. But Lady Annaly and Florence had both distinctly told him that they could not receive him at Annaly till after a certain day, on which they said that they should be particularly engaged. They told him that Colonel Albemarle was at Annaly—that he would leave it at such a time—and they requested that Mr. Ormond would postpone his visit till after that time.

Not receiving this notice, Ormond had unfortunately gone upon the day that was specially prohibited.

Now that the kneeling figure appeared to him as a rival in despair, not in triumph, Ormond asked himself how he could ever have been such an idiot as to doubt Florence Annaly.

"Why did I set off in such haste for Paris?—Could not I have waited a day?—Could not I have written again?—Could I not have cross-questioned the drunken servant when he was sober?—Could not I have done any thing, in short, but what I did?"

Clearly as a man, when his anger is dissipated, sees what he ought to have done or to have left undone while the fury lasted; vividly as a man in a different kind of passion sees the folly of all he did, said, or thought, when he was possessed by the past madness; so clearly, so vividly, did Ormond now see and feel—and vehemently execrate, his jealous folly and mad precipitation; and then he came to the question, could his folly be repaired?—would his madness ever be forgiven? Ormond, in love affairs, never had any presumption—any tinge of the Connal coxcombry in his nature: he was not apt to flatter himself that he had made a deep impression; and now he was, perhaps from his sense of the superior value of the object, more than usually diffident. Though Miss Annaly was still unmarried, she might have resolved irrevocably against him. Though she was not a girl to act in the high-flown heroine style, and, in a fit of pride or revenge, to punish the man she liked, by marrying his rival, whom she did not like; yet Florence Annaly, as Ormond well knew, inherited some of her mother's strength of character; and, in circumstances that deeply touched her heart, might be capable of all her mother's warmth of indignation. It was in her character decidedly to refuse to connect herself with any man, however her heart might incline towards him, if he had any essential defect of temper; or if she thought that his attachment to her was not steady and strong, such as she deserved it should be, and such as her sensibility and all her hopes of domestic happiness required in a husband. And then there was Lady Annaly to be considered—how indignant she would be at his conduct!

While Ormond was travelling alone, he had full leisure to torment himself with these thoughts. Pressed forward alternately by hope and fear, each urging expedition, he hastened on—reached Dublin—crossed the water—and travelling day and night, lost not a moment till he was at the feet of his fair mistress.

To those who like to know the how, the when, and the where, it should be told that it was evening when he arrived. Florence Annaly was walking with her mother by the seaside, in one of the most beautiful and retired parts of the coasts of Devonshire, when they were told by a servant that a gentleman from Ireland had just arrived at their house, and wished to see them. A minute afterwards they saw—"Could it be?" Lady Annaly said, turning in doubt to her daughter; but the cheek of Florence instantly convinced the mother that it could be none but Mr. Ormond himself.

"Mr. Ormond!" said Lady Annaly, advancing kindly, yet with dignified reserve—"Mr. Ormond, after his long absence, is welcome to his old friend."

There was in Ormond's look and manner, as he approached, something that much inclined the daughter to hope that he might prove not utterly unworthy of her mother's forgiveness; and when he spoke to the daughter, there was in his voice and look something that softened the mother's heart, and irresistibly inclined her to wish that he might be able to give a satisfactory explanation of his strange conduct. Where the parties are thus happily disposed both to hear reason, to excuse passion, and to pardon the errors to which passion, even in the most reasonable minds, is liable, explanations are seldom tedious, or difficult to be comprehended. The moment Ormond produced the cover, the soiled cover of the letters, a glimpse of the truth struck Florence Annaly; and before he had got farther in his sentence than these words, "I did not receive your ladyship's letter till within these few days," all the reserve of Lady Annaly's manner was dispelled: her smiles relieved his apprehensions, and encouraged him to proceed in his story with happy fluency. The carelessness of the drunken servant, who had occasioned so much mischief, was talked of for a few minutes with great satisfaction.

Ormond took his own share of the blame so frankly and with so good a grace, and described with such truth the agony he had been thrown into by the sight of the kneeling figure in regimentals, that Lady Annaly could not help comforting him by the assurance that Florence had, at the same moment, been *sufficiently* alarmed by the rearing of his horse at the sight of the flapping window-blind.

"The kneeling gentleman," said Lady Annaly, "whom you thought at the height of joy and glory, was at that moment in the depths of despair. So ill do the passions see what is even before their eyes!"

If Lady Annaly had had a mind to moralize, she might have done so to any length, without fear of interruption from either of her auditors, and with the most perfect certainty of unqualified submission and dignified humility on the part of our hero, who was too happy at this moment not to be ready to acknowledge himself to have been wrong and absurd, and worthy of any quantity of reprehension or indignation that could have been bestowed upon him.

Her ladyship went, however, as far from morality as possible—to Paris. She spoke of the success Mr. Ormond had had in Parisian society—she spoke of M. and Madame de Connal, and various persons with whom he had been intimate, among others of the Abbé Morellet.

Ormond rejoiced to find that Lady Annaly knew he had been in the Abbé Morellet's distinguished society. The happiest hopes for the future rose in his mind, from perceiving that her ladyship, by whatever means, knew all that he had been doing in Paris. It seems that they had had accounts of him from several English travellers, who had met him at Paris, and had heard him spoken of in different companies.

Ormond took care—give him credit for it all who have ever been in love —even in these first moments, with the object of his present affection, Ormond took care to do justice to the absent Dora, whom he now never expected to see again. He seized, dexterously, an opportunity, in reply to something Lady Annaly said about the Connals, to observe that Madame de Connal was not only much admired for her beauty at Paris, but that she did honour to Ireland by having preserved her reputation; young, and without a guide, as she was, in dissipated French society, with few examples of conjugal virtues to preserve in her mind the precepts and habits of her British education.

He was glad of this opportunity to give, as he now did with all the energy of truth, the result of his feelings and reflections on what he had seen of the modes of living among the French; their superior pleasures of society, and their want of our domestic happiness.

While Ormond was speaking, both the mother and daughter could not help admiring, in the midst of his moralizing, the great improvement which had been made in his appearance and manners.

With all his own characteristic frankness, he acknowledged the impression which French gaiety and the brilliancy of Parisian society had at first made upon him: he was glad, however, that he had now seen all that the imagination often paints as far more delightful than it really is. He had, thank Heaven, passed through this course of dissipation without losing his taste for better and happier modes of life. The last few months, though they might seem but a splendid or feverish dream in his existence, had in reality been, he believed, of essential service in confirming his principles, settling his character, and deciding for ever his taste and judgment, after full opportunity of comparison, in favour of his own country—and especially of his own countrywomen.

Lady Annaly smiled benignantly, and after observing that this seemingly unlucky excursion, which had begun in anger, had ended advantageously to Mr. Ormond; and after having congratulated him upon having saved his fortune, and established his character solidly, she left him to plead his own cause with her daughter—in her heart cordially wishing him success.

What he said, or what Florence answered, we do not know; but we are perfectly sure that if we did, the repetition of it would tire the reader. Lady Annaly and tea waited for them with great patience to an unusually late, which they conceived to be an unusually early, hour. The result of this conversation was, that Ormond remained with them in this beautiful retirement in Devonshire the next day, and the next, and—how many days are not precisely recorded; a blank was left for the number, which the editor of these memoirs does not dare to fill up at random, lest some Mrs. M'Crule should exclaim, "Scandalously too long to keep the young man there!"—or, "Scandalously too short a courtship, after all!"

It is humbly requested that every young lady of delicacy and feeling will put herself in the place of Florence Annaly—then, imagining the man she most approves of to be in the place of Mr. Ormond, she will be pleased to fill up the blank with what number of days she may think proper.

When the happy day was named, it was agreed that they should return to Ireland, to Annaly; and that their kind friend, Dr. Cambray, should be the person to complete that union which he had so long foreseen and so anxiously desired.

Those who wish to hear something of estates, as well as of weddings, should be told that about the same time Ormond received letters from Marcus O'Shane, and from M. de Connal; Marcus informing him that the estate of Castle Hermitage was to be sold by the commissioners of bankrupts, and beseeching him to bid for it, that it might not be sold under value. M. de Connal also besought his dear friend, Mr. Ormond to take the Black Islands off his hands, for they encumbered him terribly. No wonder, living, as he did, at Paris, with his head at Versailles, and his heart in a faro bank. Ormond could not oblige both the gentlemen, though they had each pressing reasons for getting rid speedily of their property, and were assured that he would be the most agreeable purchaser. Castle Hermitage was the finest estate, and by far the best bargain. But other considerations weighed with our hero. While Sir Ulick O'Shane's son and natural representative was living, banished by debts from his native country, Ormond could not bear to take possession of Castle Hermitage. For the Black Islands he had a fondness—they were associated with all the tender recollections of his generous benefactor. He should hurt no one's feelings by this purchase—and he might do a great deal of good, by carrying on his old friend's improvements, and by farther civilizing the people of the Islands, all of whom were warmly attached to him. They considered Prince Harry as the lawful representative of their dear King Corny, and actually offered up prayers for his coming again to *reign* over them.

To those who think that the mind is a kingdom of yet more consequence than even that of the Black Islands, it may be agreeable to hear that Ormond continued to enjoy the empire which he had gained over himself; and to maintain that high character, which in spite of his neglected education, and of all the adverse circumstances to which he was early exposed, he had formed for himself by resolute energy.

Lady Annaly with the pride of affection, gloried in the full accomplishment of her prophecies; and was rewarded in the best manner for that benevolent interest which she had early taken in our hero's improvement, by seeing the perfect felicity that subsisted between her daughter and Ormond.

The End.

Made in the USA
Lexington, KY
15 January 2019